Volumes previously published by the University of California Press, Berkeley, Los Angeles, London, for the Center for Chinese Studies of The University of Michigan:

MICHIGAN STUDIES ON CHINA

Communications and National Integration in Communist China, by Alan P. L. Liu

Mao's Revolution and the Chinese Political Culture, by Richard Solomon

Capital Formation in Mainland China, 1952–1965, by Kang Chao

Small Groups and Political Rituals in China, by Martin King Whyte

Backward Toward Revolution: The Chinese Revolutionary Party, by Edward Friedman

Peking Politics, 1918–1923: Factionalism and the Failure of Constitutionalism, by Andrew Nathan

Reform and Revolution in China: The 1911 Revolution in Hunan and Hubei, by Joseph W. Esherick

THE CONCEPT OF MAN IN CONTEMPORARY CHINA

Michigan Studies on China
Published for the Center for Chinese Studies
of The University of Michigan

The research on which these books are based was supported by the Center for Chinese Studies of The University of Michigan. Research for the present book was also supported by the Center for Chinese Studies of The University of California, Berkeley.

The Concept of Man
in
Contemporary China

DONALD J. MUNRO

Ann Arbor   The University of Michigan Press

Grateful acknowledgment is made to the following publishers for permission to reprint copyrighted material:

Contemporary China Institute, for material from "The Malleability of Man in Chinese Marxism," by Donald J. Munro, in *The China Quarterly,* No. 48 (October–December 1971), pp. 609–40. Reprinted by permission of *The China Quarterly.*

Praeger Publishers, Inc., for material from "Belief Control in China: The Psychological and Ethical Foundations," by Donald J. Munro, in *Social Control and Deviance in China,* edited by Richard W. Wilson and Sidney Greenblatt (New York: Praeger Publishers, Inc., 1977), pp. 14–36. Copyright © 1977, Praeger Publishers, Inc. Reprinted by permission of the publisher.

Library of Congress Cataloging in Publication Data

Munro, Donald J
    The concept of man in contemporary China.

    (Michigan studies on China)
    Bibliography: p.
    Includes index.
    1. Man. 2. Philosophy, Chinese—20th
century. I. Title. II. Series.
B5233.M27M86   128   77-7209
ISBN 0-472-08677-4
ISBN 0-472-08678-2 pbk.

For Ann

Preface

Like *The Concept of Man in Early China,* this book deals with theories of
human nature and associated social control principles in a specific time
period. In another sense, its aims are more ambitious than this description
indicates. They are to reveal the existence of a number of enduring assumptions about human behavior and related, equally lasting, beliefs about the
proper function of government that are reflected in Confucian and Chinese
Marxist thought. One consequence of so doing is to suggest that in some
respects, the common distinction between modern and premodern China
implies the existence of a cultural gulf that does not in fact exist.

My experiences in studying and teaching about the political philosophies
of various societies have led me to the conclusion that the best way to discuss
contemporary Chinese philosophy with an audience reared in a liberal
democracy may differ considerably from the best way of presenting it to one
raised in a monarchy or another socialist state. These differing groups often
operate with quite different assumptions and values, which make it necessary to emphasize certain dimensions of the topic rather than others, and to
take account of matters that might need very little attention if the reader came
from another background. When such precautions are not taken, the reader
may become so confused or outraged that he will fail to consider seriously
what he subsequently studies about that foreign philosophy.

I will simply mention two of many examples that have played a role in the
organization and content of the present book. Most people educated in
liberal democracies believe that among the top priorities in any state should
be legal protections against many kinds of government infringement in the
private lives of the people, especially in matters of belief or conscience.
Otherwise stated, people need legal protection from their rulers. Manipula-

tion is often considered a dirty word. When they find that Chinese philosophers do not now and have never had much interest in individual rights, there may be a feeling of revulsion that will cloud any future interest in the philosophies. Yet this concern about protection may not be so significant to a Spanish or a Russian philosopher. Because it is important to readers in America and England, I have examined its content and origins in liberal democratic theories of human nature. This helps to set off the assumptions about man operative in our societies from those in China and hopefully alters somewhat the quality of understanding of the Chinese position by the American or Englishman.

The other example concerns the status of educational affairs and educators. It is common knowledge that in America, schools of education rank close to the bottom of the academic totem pole, the social prestige of public school teaching is low, and many topics are more newsworthy than educational ones. It is difficult to convince an American audience to take seriously the claim that educational policy and professional educators in China past and present have enormous importance and stature, and that changes affecting either one should be treated with unaccustomed weight by American political scientists, journalists, and government analysts. An understanding of the relative absence in China of belief in innate defects of natural endowment may help Americans to comprehend the extraordinary faith and optimism the Chinese place in the educational system for the solution of the most vital social issues of the day: Alter people's conduct with educational means and thereby solve the problem. In another society in which the educational ranks have not suffered so much from insular professionalization and also have had a more valued historical position, it might not be as necessary to dwell at such length on these issues in contemporary Chinese philosophy.

In any case, these kinds of considerations account for the attention given to comparisons and contrasts between liberal democratic theory and practice on the one hand and Chinese on the other. The Soviet material is introduced in order to distinguish the Communist approach from the uniquely Chinese approach.

I recognize that any attempt to explain a position may be confused by some people with advocacy. However, in writing this book I am not engaged in a justification of the Chinese Marxist position. Rather, I am making an appeal to people in one society to try to comprehend why those in another society judge things differently from themselves. Although periodic analyses of specific features of the Chinese, Russian, and liberal democratic (American) doctrines are presented, overall there is no attempt to judge among them. I am willing to grant, however, that in making any doctrinal exposition, a writer may tend to make some kind of advocacy. He has probably decided that at least some of the doctrine is worth spending time elucidating. To this extent, I must admit that I hope that the reader may seriously entertain and consider some of the assumptions behind the Chinese view of man and society. I hope so because I expect that this will make his own reflections on social problems more flexible and rational, because he understands that there are other ways of looking at these things. In a similar manner, a Chinese would gain from thoughtful attention to some of the liberal democratic ideas. A related benefit to readers is that they may place their own commitment to a given way of life on a firmer foundation. When one chooses a way of life, one also chooses assumptions about man that are consistent with that way of life. It is useful to be mindful of what those are.

There is no attempt to claim in this study that Mao Tse-tung was the only interpreter of Marxism in China. Indeed, there are periodic references to divergent thinkers, such as the advocates of a more traditional view of human nature (Pa Jen and Liu Chieh), the spokesmen for the John Dewey-Hu Shih educational line, the economist Lo Keng-mo, and the political leaders Liu Shao-ch'i and Lin Piao. Nevertheless, this is primarily a study of the Maoist concept of man, from the guerrilla period until the Chairman's death in 1976. The period of the People's Republic and its communist antecedents in Yenan has been an era in which Mao's influence has been pervasive. It certainly has been so in all of the books, journals, and newspapers that I have consulted. It is not clear now if the degree to which the predominance of his views in the media fully reflects the thrust of unwritten, possibly opposing views. But in the absence of much competing, systematic evidence to the contrary, when one speaks of "contemporary China" in reference to this period, one cannot but mean China with the great influence of Chairman Mao. And the fact that many strands of thought reflecting his impact also are congruent with preceding strands in Confucian thought makes us wary of assigning to them a merely transitory, controlled existence. Finally, Mao's doctrines in some areas, such as economic policy, changed strikingly over time (the period of Soviet influence, Great Leap Forward, 1960s, 1970s). However, many of the main features of his concept of man have persisted with few modifications. This makes some generalization about them possible.

A word about the perspective from which to view a number of the Chinese values encountered in the analysis that follows. Often one can understand these best as existing in a state of tension with other, often conflicting values with which they seem to form sets. In any set, both values are at different times treated as desirable, in spite of the polarization that may exist between them. Viewing them in this way helps to uncover their complexities. It is also the way in which Mao himself regarded some of them: ''We must bring about a political climate which has both centralism and democracy, discipline and freedom, unity of purpose and ease of mind for the individual.''[1] The existence of tensions within these sets is manifest in periodic policy shifts since 1949 from an emphasis that tilts toward one pole and then to another.

This study is based on an examination of almost all available writings on human nature and personality by Chinese philosophers and psychologists since the 1940s. (The psychological sources terminated in 1966, when that field went under a cloud. Although psychologists are still teaching in institutions of higher learning—there is even one attached to Peking University's Philosophy Department—they have written almost nothing for public consumption since then. Furthermore, they no longer have the political clout they once had through their influence on teaching material preparation at Peking Normal University.) These writings appeared not only in such journals as *Che-hsüeh yen-chiu* (Philosophical investigations) and *Hsin-li hsüeh-pao* (Acta psychologica Sinica), but also in newspapers like *Jen-min jih-pao* (People's daily) and *Kuang-ming jih pao*. Chinese newspapers, unlike our own, regularly carry highly theoretical articles on such subjects to facilitate their widespread distribution. This was supplemented by interviews with Chinese philosophers in the People's Republic of China (PRC) and with those who had some training in psychology courses in the PRC. But I have not restricted my sources exclusively to professional philosophers and psychologists. This is an analysis of the dominant concept of man in a society, not simply of the concept of man in the minds of Peking University professors. Thus I have also used sources that reflect the attempt by individuals faced with specific problems to interpret the often vague principles articulated by such sometime formulators of orthodoxy as Mao, Liu Shao-ch'i, Ch'en Po-ta, and Kuan Feng. These additional sources may be anything from *Chung-kuo ch'ing-nien* (China youth daily) to a provincial educational journal, to a manual on how to be a successful military commander. In the case of the chapter on model emulation, it included interviews with people who had actively been engaged in the selection of models. How especially important this approach is in a society that has made the "unity of theory and practice" a part of its litany. It is the legitimate task of philosophy to study the assumptions underlying component parts of popularly accepted belief systems. These do not have to be belief systems held and articulated only by professional philosophers. After all, Socrates did not talk only to the likes of Heraclitus, Parmenides, and Democritus. He spent most of his time examining the convictions of those in the marketplace.

I had thought of apologizing to the reader for using a few tortuous technical terms (fosterage, legitimacy criterion, and promptings to act). But the more I thought, the more I realized that I actually was unable to find any other terms to express in full the meanings that these terms describe, as I have employed them. The problem is precipitated by the need to discuss in English, Chinese concepts for which there are no commonplace counterparts in the vocabularies of Western philosophy, psychology, or political theory. The analyst then has the undesirable choice of annoying the reader with what seems to be jargon, or with using other, conventional words that simply are inadequate to suggest the richness of the ideas in question.

Portions of this book were delivered in an earlier form in 1970 at Stanford University as the Walter Y. Evans-Wentz Lectures. For permission to quote from copyright material, I wish to thank the following publishers: *The China Quarterly,* for permission to reprint segments of my article, "The Malleability of Man in Chinese Marxism," that appeared in Number 48 (October/December, 1971), pp. 609–40; S. Karger AG, Basel, for permission to reprint segments of my article, "The Chinese View of Modeling," that appeared in *Human Development,* volume 18, number 5 (1975), pp. 333–52; and Praeger Publishers, Inc., for permission to reprint portions of my article, "Belief Control in China: The Psychological and Ethical Foundations," which appeared in *Social Control and Deviance in China,* edited by Richard W. Wilson and Sidney Greenblatt, pp. 14–36; Copyright © 1977, Praeger Publishers, Inc.

I am indebted to the Social Science Research Council for a grant under which part of the present study was carried out. The Council is not to be understood as approving by virtue of its grant any of the statements made or views expressed in this work. I am grateful for additional support from the Center for Chinese Studies at the University of Michigan, and for the continuing friendship and stimulation of so many of its faculty associates. I must also express my gratitude to the associates of the Center for Chinese

Studies at the University of California, Berkeley, for their support and hospitality during a year that I spent in residence there doing research for this book. I acknowledge especially the many courtesies of its director at that time, Chalmers Johnson. I note with thanks the assistance of several people in the course of this study: Cordia Schak, Hsiao-long Young, and Mei-hsia Tseng. Because she is unusually knowledgeable about both Chinese and American psychology, and also about childhood education in the two countries, Ms. Tseng was particularly helpful in connection with several of the chapters in this work. She has been a guide through many sources and a friend as well. I owe a special debt to the many writings on political philosophy of John Plamenatz. I think that I have read almost all of them, and I have learned enormously from him. I am grateful to Stuart Schram, who read and commented helpfully on an earlier, somewhat different manuscript, large parts of which are incorporated in the present work. I have benefited considerably from the constructive advice of other readers, including Albert Feuerwerker, the late Alexander Eckstein, Eleanor Kahn, and Edward Friedman. Chad Hansen, Tu Wei-ming, Philip Grier, and Jack Meiland have been of great help in leading me to formulate more clearly a number of specific points. Robert Eno prepared the index with unusual skill. Sometimes some of us need the pruning knife and pen of a humanely merciless editor. I am fortunate in having found the best, Janet Eckstein.

DONALD J. MUNRO

Contents

Chapter 1

Three Concepts of Man

A concept of man or of human nature is concerned with the nontrivial attributes of all people or of large groups of people. Routine biological features such as eating, drinking, and procreating are often assumed to have some part in the concept, but that part has low priority. The significant attributes purport to explain much of people's regular, predictable behavior. In most societies philosophers occasionally can be found evaluating such concepts because behind these theories lurk the arguments used by leaders to defend their acts. But in China, presenting and defending a concept of man have been taken more seriously and energetically than in most other areas.

Traditionally, theories and philosophical claims have been accepted or rejected in China less because of logically or empirically convincing demonstrations of their truth than because of their behavioral implications.[1] In other words, acceptance or rejection often would be based primarily (though of course not entirely) on answers to such questions as: Can the theory be interpreted to imply that people should act in a certain way? What kind of behavior is likely to occur if people accept it? The Chinese interest in such predictions of behavior is strengthened by their assumption that covert promptings to act are associated with most ideas and feelings. (This assumption is discussed in detail in chapter 2.) There is a special interest in predictions about how people will behave if they accept or reject a particular theory of human nature. It is assumed that once such a theory is understood and accepted, promptings to act associated with that understanding and acceptance will manifest themselves in action. The nature of predicted manifestations is more important to the Chinese than any empirical or logical arguments in favor of or against the theory.[2] One can find as much evidence of this in the attacks on deviant theories of human nature published by contemporary academic philosophers as in classical works along the Mencian vein.

Concepts of man often differ fundamentally from society to society, with resulting implications for political institutions and social control. We will now examine three such concepts—Western liberal, Soviet, and Chinese— concentrating briefly in each case on the status of two elements that lie at the core of the Chinese view. The striking contrast between the Western liberal concept and the Chinese concept will help the Western reader ultimately to appreciate why the Chinese perception of the proper role of the state and the place of man within it varies so completely from his own, and to understand that there are other ways of looking at these matters. Because the Chinese both drew from and rejected parts of the Soviet concept of man and its Marxist antecedents, a consideration of the Soviet view will help us to recognize what in the Chinese view is derivative and what is distinctive. The stage is then set for introducing the two central dimensions of the Chinese idea, detailed analysis of which is the subject of subsequent chapters.

A Western Liberal Concept

Almost all advocates of liberal democratic individualism presume that man's dominant traits exist independently of any social context. As Steven Lukes has written, "According to this conception, individuals are pictured abstractly as given, with given interests, wants, purposes, needs, etc.; while society and the state are pictured as sets of actual or possible social arrangements which respond more or less adequately to those individuals' requirements."[3] Specifically, in the following pages we will be concerned with two general categories of extrasocial human traits. One concerns the supposedly private domain of opinions or beliefs and the ability of man to make free and rational choices concerning them. The other concerns primarily innate traits in the realm of motives and abilities that limit the range of personality change or skill acquisition possible.

There are many views about human nature embedded in the philosophies that have influenced liberal democratic governments. Some of them contain doctrines inimical to as well as consistent with the concepts we are about to describe.[4] At the very least, however, adherents of these concepts will accept some dimensions of the two doctrines of the private self and innate limitations, both conceived in an extrasocial context, even though they differ as to the specific content assigned to either of those doctrines. The idea of man as possessing the ability to make rational, autonomous decisions and requiring the protection of his private self is still vibrant in the works of people like Anthony Downs (*An Economic Theory of Democracy,* 1957) and John Rawls (*A Theory of Justice,* 1972).

The Private Self

There are several facets to the notion of a private realm that must be presented. First, we must distinguish between what factual traits are actually being assigned to people and what conditions of their lives are being advocated as ideal. Second, we need to distinguish between one of the assigned traits, namely the existence of transsocial beliefs, and another, namely our ability to make choices for action involving them (autonomy).

In 1829, Benjamin Constant wrote,

> everything which does not interfere with order; everything which belongs only to the inward nature of man, such as opinion; everything which, in the expression of opinion, does not harm others . . .; everything which, in regard to industry, allows the free exercise of rival industry is individual and cannot legitimately be subjected to the power of society.[5]

His claim was that, as individuals, people possess a realm (that of consciousness, beliefs, or thought) that normally does not affect others and that should remain immune from tampering by external agents. In other words, the human personality was divided into a social and a private realm, and society should have no control over the latter. One component of the private realm is what Mill calls "the inward domain of consciousness, demanding liberty of conscience."[6] Normally, two distinct claims are mixed together in this kind of doctrine, which refers to the first of three traits we will identify. One is the psychological claim that matters of belief usually do not affect other people.[7]

The other contention contained within this first private-public division is the normative claim that beliefs should remain the sole concern of the believer and be immune from manipulation. Positively stated, man's ideal condition is one in which there is no such interference.[8] In its origins, this ideal is inseparable from the view that natural man (apart from society) is born with rights which impose limitations on any societal restrictions to their pursuit. Within these limits the private arena is protected from external agents. This is one of the most common situations in which we say that a person's rights are being safeguarded.

The natural rights about which many European and English philosophers spoke in the sixteenth and seventeenth centuries were not discovered by observations. Rather, it was claimed that pure reason could discover what it is to be human. People have certain needs, interests, and goals because they are the kind of creatures they are. Being rational, people discover that other people have the same needs and interests, and they learn God's rules whereby all can satisfy these interests. Learning God's rules, they are led to an understanding of rights: Each person has the right to require others to observe the rules in interacting with him. These rights exist in the "state of nature" before human beings form societies.

People supposedly enter this world with an interest in life, liberty, and property (John Locke), or, life, liberty, and happiness (Thomas Jefferson) and with the right to enjoy them. Life is but another way of referring to self-preservation. Liberty is more complex, to say the least. It is also the most important right in democratic thought, one with a particularly European historical antecedent. Liberty refers to the absence of restrictions on belief or expressions of them.[9] In its earliest formulation, it referred to matters of religious conscience, a sense of liberty absent in classical Greece and Rome. Religious, political, and philosophical arguments have been offered in defense of liberty of conscience. On the philosophic side, J. S. Mill gave a utilitarian argument for toleration: plurality of belief helps generate truth and thereby promotes progress. The rationalist Descartes argued that there should be general toleration because each person's faculty of understanding by itself discovers truth. As John Plamenatz has shown, some of the origins of the claim to freedom of belief can be found in religious. sects in Protestant countries in the seventeenth century, where various religious minorities, such as the Anabaptists and the Baptists, flourished and none had the possibility of imposing its beliefs on others. They claimed the "right" against the political authorities and the religious orthodoxy they enforced. (In part because of the relative absence in Chinese history of these kinds of ecclesiastical events, the Chinese have not been urgently motivated to construct arguments in favor of natural rights in general.)

In the long run philosophers made the transition to belief in a natural right to freedom of all beliefs, not just concerning religious matters. Thomas Jefferson absorbed the position set forth in Locke's letter on Toleration (1689). The American political thinkers celebrated the rights of man but added no new philosophical dimensions to them. Jefferson, who had "sworn upon the altar of God eternal hostility to every form of tyranny over the mind of man"[10] was a poet about liberty, not an original philosophical thinker. His originality lay in devising the means to protect it.

The second trait often assigned to man that can be discussed under the rubric of the private sphere is what J. S. Mill called the "inner forces."

> Human nature is not a machine to be built after a model and set to do exactly the work prescribed for it, but a tree, which requires to grow and develop itself on all sides, according to the tendency of the inward forces which make it a living thing.[11]

These include the innate capacities and talents unique to each individual that can develop when not interfered with by outsiders. There is reference to an ideal state of man associated with this psychological claim about capacities that are not socially induced. The development of these inner forces is intrinsically desirable and also instrumentally useful as a means of achieving social progress. Therefore, society should not interfere with their realization. They belong to man's individuality. Privacy as a value is closely related to the individual's being left alone by other people to the extent that he can lead a life in a style and with satisfactions that give realization to the inner forces. This is what Mill meant by speaking in the Introduction to *On Liberty* of freedom as requiring "liberty of tastes and pursuits, of framing the plan of our life to suit our own character."

Autonomy is a third trait and value sometimes associated with the first two. The factual assumption is that people are capable of self-direction. They are not immune to social influences, but they are capable of reviewing their beliefs about values and norms that they and others have formed under that influence, critically evaluating them, and as independent individuals selecting or rejecting them, and making choices for action on the basis of the review. Incompatible with determinism, autonomy was central to Kantian morality (to "the idea of freedom there is inseparably attached the concept of *autonomy,* and to this in turn the universal principle of morality").[12] Kant, as well as John Stuart Mill and John Dewey in later years, moved from assuming the existence of the capacity for autonomy (a matter of fact) to advocating it as an ideal. Man's most desirable condition is one in which the formation of his beliefs and the direction of his choice making stems from himself rather than from outside agencies.

At the base of many claims about the sanctity of the private realm is a claim about man that has no exact counterpart in China. This claim is constructed from the concept of the dignity of man that is based on each person's possessing a soul in the likeness of God. State policies that some people regard as violations of autonomy through the manipulation of beliefs and choices are also viewed as violations of human dignity. This is because they seem to treat people as means to state goals rather than as ends in themselves.

Limits on Change

Three additional characteristics have been regularly associated with human nature in the theories of liberal democratic philosophers. Although they do not necessarily appear as a set, they share the quality of seeming to establish prenatal or early childhood limits on the kind or quantity of change possible in personality and learning ability. The first characteristic emerged in the pre-nineteenth-century foundations of American thought and continues to influence our perceptions of people: the belief that people are self-regarding, motivated by self-interest. Some writers spoke of the universal drive by the individual to maximize his pleasure or power. Other characteristics, the existence of psychic tensions in need of resolution (Oedipus complex, aggression), and inherent differences in intelligence, came on the scene in the late nineteenth and early twentieth centuries.

At first, the precursors of a mature American philosophy believed that every human act is motivated by selfish desires; this position is technically known as "psychological egoism." Eventually it fused with another position called "ethical egoism" that sanctions self-interested motivation. Some writers attempted to justify ethical egoism by appeal to a combination of empirical proof and intuitive insight: People can be observed to have an instinct toward self-preservation and the satisfaction of other forms of self-interest, and our intuition tells us that they have a natural right to take all measures necessary to secure them.

Of the two sources of the egotistical portrait—the religious and the philosophical—the former had the deepest roots. They lay in the Calvinism of Puritans like John Winthrop and John Cotton: as a result of the fall from purity to depravity, man will remain selfish until he receives God's grace. Roger Williams described the egotistical soul in these terms: "in the best natural Soul in the World, there is nothing but a Kennil, an Hogstie, a den of Atheisme, Murther, Theft, Fornication, Adultry, and all Kinde of Wickednesse."[13] For the Puritans, the proper path for people was to distinguish between the sinful pursuit of self-interest and the glorious acceptance of one's "calling."

The pre-Revolutionary pamphleteers and the authors of the *Federalist* papers, perpetuated the egoist assumption. Hamilton remarked that "every man ought to be supposed a knave and to have no other end in all his actions, but private interest."[14] The *Federalist* contains constant references to the "ordinary depravity of human nature," and in No. 51 James Madison observed, "But what is government itself, but the greatest of all reflections on human nature? If men were angels, no government would be necessary."[15]

A major symbolic watershed is Thomas Jefferson's acceptance of the legitimacy of man's natural self-interest. The Puritan notion that it was a sign of human depravity nearly fell by the wayside. The roots of this development in the egoist portrait lay with the philosophers as opposed to the religionists. Nearly two centuries before Jefferson, Thomas Hobbes had made the shocking claim that "The Desires, and other Passions of Man, are in themselves no Sin. No more are the Actions that proceed from those Passions, till they know a Law that forbids them."[16] Jefferson believed as strongly as Hamilton that self-interest was the basic human motive. He only wanted to enlighten it and ensure that the interests of all citizens were the concern of their government. The Benthamite doctrine that the only motive for each person's actions is the desire to maximize his own pleasure was taken very seriously by many liberal democratic thinkers. Bentham wanted to explain moral judgments without reference to any special moral sense, and he thought that he had found an answer in the hedonistic calculus. Therein lay another attempt to give ethical legitimacy to the psychological egoist's description of human motivation.

The self-regarding characteristic of human beings constituted the primary limitation on personality change in the Anglo-American conceptions of man from the seventeenth through the nineteenth centuries. This idea has by no means died out. It is very much alive in the low priority given to motivation by nonmaterial incentives by both ordinary managers and union officials and also by professional economists in the United States. But during the first part of the twentieth century the second limitation on malleability was introduced and has since blossomed. Writing in *Psychoanalysis for Teachers and Parents,* Freud said, "burdened with his past, the child is indeed anything but a blank sheet."[17] For Freud, the sexual and aggressive drives are the origins of most problems; they constitute parameters within which statesmen and educators must work, not transitory features that can be altered. This led Freud to the view that there is a basic conflict between the individual and society, with society customarily warping people through sex taboos and religion. The existence of social rules is enduring evidence of the human tendency to break them, according to Freud. Those tendencies cannot be eliminated. The educator can only hope to sublimate them into socially useful ends.[18] A number of scholars have placed Freud in the liberal tradition, along with Locke, Jefferson, and Mill.[19] They share a belief in innate or early childhood limitations on change. But more important, they focus more on removing obstacles than on directing change. Freud took up more space discussing the restrictive aspects of society than he did the positive directional possibilities in it.

Innate intelligence is a third limitation on the educability of persons that is associated with the conceptions of man in the United States. In the intelligence scale developed between 1905 and 1908 by Alfred Binet, the term Intelligence Quotient was used to express the relation between an individual's mental age and his chronological age. The First World War is important to the widespread ramifications of this principle in the United States in terms of limitations on educability. At that time, scales that had their ultimate origin in the results of tests given to schoolchildren were used to measure the mental age of adults. A number of writers thought that they found proof in the data of Robert M. Yerkes, who analyzed the test results, that the average age of most Americans was fourteen. On this basis they concluded that most were uneducable beyond high school. The President of Colgate University, for example, said that only 15 percent of the population could benefit from college.[20] Although some prominent educational philosophers like John Dewey condemned such judgments, the practical consequences of the doctrine of innate intelligence differences were quite clear: there are unalterable limitations on the educability of large numbers of people.

In sum, features in the American conception of human nature conflict directly with the central dimensions of the Chinese idea as presented on pages 15–25. The primacy of natural man, not social man, is clear; and a place in the psyche is made for the private self. At the outset there are limitations on what any improved environmental (especially educational) features can or should try to accomplish in the way of personality and skill transformation.

The Soviet Concept

In contrast to the liberal democratic concept of man, Marxist theory—both in the classical German works themselves and in later Soviet writings—claims that man's essential nature is social and that talk of a natural man apart from social relations is nonsense. In addition, the new Soviet concept of man constituted a rather special evolution within the confines of an established Marxist principle. The idea of malleability reversed the pessimism associated with Western claims about limitations on change and thereby met the emotional demands of those who wished to change decay into utopia.

Marxist Man

Marx made an implicit distinction between man's social and biological natures.[21] The Marxian statements assumed that when one talks about nontrivial aspects of man, one is talking about his social nature. Philosophers in the eighteenth century, such as August Comte and Adam Smith, had commonly referred to man's unique social instincts and moral sense, which lead him alone into altruistic acts on behalf of his fellows. But Charles Darwin took aim at this position when he wrote:

> Besides Love and Sympathy the animals show other qualities connected with the social instincts, which we should call moral in man; and I agree with Agassiz that dogs have something like conscience. Dogs certainly have a power of self control, and this does not appear to be altogether a consequence of fear.[22]

Karl Marx too would repudiate the existence of any innate drive to sympathetic conduct in man. But insisting on the singularity of man's social productive activity he was still departing from the avant garde intellectual stream represented by Darwin that tended to downplay the differences between man and beast. Marx's classic statement concerning the human essence is contained in his "Sixth Thesis on Feuerbach": "the human essence is no abstraction inherent in each single individual. In its reality it is the ensemble of social relations."[23] Generally speaking, social relations are legally defined links in cooperative production (of goods other than those needed for biological survival) that exist between the dominant groups in any historical period: slave-master, serf-lord, employee-employer. In this passage, Marx was repudiating the notion that man's social nature is a static substance. Rather, it is something that changes as the relations change.

Although man is not the only social being (cooperative behavior occurs among ants and bees), he is the only creature for whom social relationships take on a class form. Second, man uniquely fulfills his social essence or becomes a social being through labor—a position that echoes a point of Hegel. Other animals may get goods needed to survive from what is around them, but man, through his productive labor, creates these goods. His singular social and economic activity satisfies his needs and realizes his potentialities. In addition, man's productive labor, when human and not bestial, is conscious, planned activity carried out in order to satisfy his needs.

> But what distinguishes the worst architect from the best of bees is this, that the architect raises his structure in imagination before he erects it in reality. At the end of every labour-process, we get a result that already existed in the imagination of the labourer at its commencement.[24]

Conscious planning is unique to man. Finally, language, which is consciousness manifested at the practical level, is man's special tool that makes cooperative work possible. Differently stated, as a result of man's need for communication with co-workers, laboring gives rise to language and the two together promote the development of the human brain, making possible typically human forms of conscious thought.

The writings of Marx and Engels laid the foundation for a development in Soviet thought on which the Chinese drew in evolving their own particular idea of malleability. Marx wrote in *Poverty of Philosophy,* "All history is nothing but the continuous transformation of human nature."[25] Elsewhere he dismissed the notion that there is any immutable human nature common to all men past and present, akin to an underlying substance that suffers only accidental changes from place to place and time to time.

Marx and Engels maintained that "thought is action" (praxis), and thus the objects of thought will never be static things but always processes. Processes are always in a state of becoming, understood by dialectics. There cannot be fixed concepts patterned after static things—no fixed human nature and no static concept of one.

The Marxist rejection of an unchanging essence or nature of man provides a philosophical basis for attacking the concept of man as self-regarding in the Western tradition. An innate predisposition to calculate pleasure is a good example of an enduring essence that is ruled out, along with that other favorite of philosophers and the clergy, rationality. Marx associated the hedonistic calculus with the money calculations that form part of the capitalist's daily routine. For an individual to select the proper moral course of action on the basis of expected quantities of pleasure that would accrue to himself was like measuring the desirability of an act in terms of financial profit and loss. He referred to Bentham as "the insipid, pedantic, leather-tongued oracle of the commonplace bourgeois intelligence of the nineteenth century" and said that he "assumes that modern petty bourgeois, and above all the modern English petty bourgeois, to be the normal man."[26] To conceive of man as a "selfish pleasure calculator" is characteristic of bourgeois conceptions of human nature. Furthermore, besides eliminating the self-regarding portrait of man, the Marxist critique of enduring essences also suggests that there are no immutable attributes that place theoretical limits on man's educability.

But we still must identify precisely to what kind of change human beings are subject. The Soviet and Chinese concepts of man contain notions of malleability that take the Marx-Engels principle of change as their starting point, but go on radically to depart from it. In the Marx-Engels account, human nature is determined by both what men produce and how they produce it. New developments in technology occur continually, which means that *how* men produce is always evolving. Thus gradual changes in human nature are inevitable. They spoke of long-term change of large groups of people or of the species. The human "essence" which is the "ensemble of social relations" changes over long historical periods as the types of relations into which they enter with other people alter. Marx and Engels also spoke of other kinds of change. A fundamental assumption in their historical materialism is the belief in the perfectibility of the human species. The history of the species as a whole is leading up to the moment when the full range of each individual's inner capacities can be manifested. Engels voices his faith in this "irresistible evolution" when he says:

> To see the glory of human nature, to understand the development of the human species in history and its irresistible evolution, to realize its always certain victory over the unreasonableness of the individual, we do not have to call in the abstractions of a God to whom we attribute all that is beautiful, great, sublime, and truly human.[27]

Note that in this discussion of an "irresistible evolution" to eventual perfection the subject is not individuals or groups, but man the species.

Regardless of the potential philosophical inconsistency and regardless of the fame of his remarks about the "continuous transformation of human nature," Marx *did* also believe that there are static elements in human nature. It contains both static and changing dimensions, which are interrelated and interdependent. It is useful to be mindful of this fact, because in their selective borrowing from Marx, the Soviets and the Chinese draw on the changing and ignore the static.

We may lose something of Marx, but not much, if we simplify by saying that the social nature is personality, and that it is a product of the "ensemble of social relations" that changes. However, there is no necessity to introduce a new term to explain the static elements in human nature, because Marx uses one that is clear—needs. Human beings past and present have certain natural needs. He also assumes that there is a kind of society that is congenial to people with such needs. Personality and needs are interrelated in that prior to communism people develop personalities (or social natures) as a result of the existing social relations that keep them psychological cripples or only partially human. For example, they acquire values (a matter of personality) in the pursuit of which they cannot satisfy their natural needs.[28] Under communism, in contrast, a personality emerges that is appropriate to people's needs; that is, they have goals and interests that, when satisfied, concurrently ensure the realization of the natural needs. Structural changes in the society have permitted this, particularly the abolition of private property and the elimination of the division of labor. The needs described here are what Marx calls human needs (what we might term real needs). They can be distinguished from those other essential needs more directly related to biological survival (for food, drink, etc.), and nonessential or acquired needs.[29]

To state that all people have these human needs is not to claim that they are necessarily aware of them. It is rather to assume they exist and then to claim two things: that men should experience them and that they would be happier if they could express them. Three such needs regularly appear in Marx's discussions. The first is the need to express one's individuality in a manner that most closely resembles the creative act of the artist. This idea was initially suggested in the writings of the young Marx on the alienation of the laborer from his product and from the act of producing it.[30] (This need dovetails with the liberal democratic idea of the individual's right to free and full development of his individual interests.) The second is the need to treat other people as ends, not as means. It is the need to care for others, to help them satisfy their own needs. Finally, people need to be able to exercise all of their capacities. Here Marx had in mind especially being able to do both mental and manual work. To be prevented from exercising something so uniquely human as planning in imagination is to be prevented from realizing a human need.

The idea of communism itself implies the existence of unchanging attributes of human nature. It is defined as a society with certain characteristics such as absence of private property and division of labor that is congenial to human beings and in which they will become fully developed and lead happier lives. If human attributes continually changed, there would be no guarantee that such a society would fulfill that function. The trouble with class societies is that the special whims of the ruling class, not human needs, determine the nature of production. Hence the notion of communism assumes the existence of the static real human needs.[31] In *The Holy Family,* Marx spoke of the "contradiction between the human nature of this class [the proletariat] and its actual condition of living, which is the overt, absolute, and complete denial of its human nature."[32] He was still thinking in these terms years later, even when he abandoned some of the quoted expressions.

On balance, it is probably easier to argue for the thesis of static needs (which the Chinese ignored in Marx) than for the idea of malleability. But because the Chinese drew heavily on this latter Marxist idea as filtered through Russian lenses, we must consider the Russian modification of it.

The New Soviet Man
While retaining the Marxian idea of the social nature, the new Soviet concept dramatically departed from Marx on the matter of man's changeability. Until about 1930, the intellectual climate in the Soviet Union was favorable to the Marxist doctrine that people have unconscious needs that are unsatisfied by an uncongenial social environment (the division of labor and private property), and that if the environment is changed people will be able spontaneously to satisfy the need to express their individuality and to care for others. By the end of the decade, however, there were the beginnings of a relative shift away from talk of altering social relations of production so that good tendencies could naturally express themselves, to a focus on aggressively and rapidly molding people into a new kind of man.

In the first period, although Soviet writers spoke of instincts and reflexes rather than of needs, the operative principles were consistent with the Marxist view of human nature examined earlier.[33] Human beings were viewed as passive reactors to the social environment; there is no way to speed up dramatically historical changes in human nature. When an environment congenial to man's nature (in Marx's words, congenial to his needs) arises, desirable behavior will manifest itself as well. Man will change when the evil Czarist-created environment changes. Desirable traits do not need to be molded or infused into people. They are there awaiting expression.

Freud and Marx are not difficult bedfellows. Both rejected the position that an understanding of an individual's present conscious beliefs, feelings, and values is sufficient for understanding his behavior and choices. Both tried to refocus attention on the unconscious determinants of conscious thoughts. For Freud this meant childhood experiences, and for Marx, true needs of which one may be unaware and economic variables that can influence beliefs (social existence determines consciousness). It is not accidental, therefore, that the 1920s were years of positive reception for Freud in Russia during which psychologists downplayed present, conscious factors in human behavior.

The major shift after the 1930 watershed was toward the short-term creation of personality features characteristic of a "new man" by a highly directive or manipulative government. This shift was paralleled by the attempts rapidly to create socialism in the USSR, in spite of its educational and economic backwardness. Although adumbrated in Lenin's theory of uninterrupted revolution, the principles directly responsible for this new line were spelled out in Stalin's doctrine that it is possible to establish socialism in one country (Stalin, *Problems of Leninism,* 1926) without the help of more advanced countries, contrary to the warnings of Trotsky.

After the shift, conscious mental phenomena were regarded as far more important factors in understanding behavior than were unconscious ones. Obviously this went against the elements in Marx that tied him to Freud, especially the notion of needs. It is not surprising, therefore, that Freud became persona non grata as attention shifted to the more immediate conscious processes. Psychologists were required to speak of the psyche as a qualitatively new synthesis of matter, the laws of which are not reducible to physiology. This was in contrast to the behaviorism and inferences from animal to human psychology that prevailed in the 1920s.

The new Soviet concept of man contributed something to the conception that later emerged in Chinese Marxism. At its crux are two principles. First, man is a goal-oriented activist, conscious of future tasks and able to introduce changes in himself and in his material environment by pursuing them. Officials and educators who wish rapidly to change man's nature need to transform his conscious goals and values. Second, this consciousness of goals and ability to seek them is combined with a concept of free choice, making ordinary citizens responsible for their acts. I shall argue (chapter 2) that only the first of these principles made its way strongly into the Chinese concept of man. The idea of free choice came through in all its Soviet fuzziness, but it lacked philosophical centrality. We are now in a position to introduce that Chinese concept of man formally, mindful that it builds on the Marxist and Soviet notions of the social quality and changeability of human nature.

The Chinese Concept

The Social Nature

The *Analects* reports that Confucius said to a disciple, "One cannot herd with birds and beasts. If I am not to be a man among other men, then what am I to be?"[34] The innate dispositions that make man a social animal as opposed to a self-interested one have been treated as most important by Confucians since that time.

In classical Confucianism, the social nature included innate tendencies to behave in certain ways toward other people—for example, the tendency to feel and behave compassionately toward kin and others (*jen,* humanheartedness), the inclination to act respectfully to those older than oneself, and the tendency to form social organizations. It also encompassed an "evaluating mind" that discriminated between proper and improper courses of social action. The social dimension was regarded as unique to man, but human nature also included those needs or activities shared with other animals. Mencius drew the distinction between the two dimensions by speaking of the social as "the greater part [of the self]" or "the Heavenly nature" and the animal attributes as "the lesser parts."[35] A somewhat different bifurcation was made by Neo-Confucian thinkers, who also claimed that no person can escape the consequences of having a social nature. Chu Hsi wrote of the hermits and monks:

> The Buddhists and Taoists, for example, even though they would destroy the social relationships, are nevertheless quite unable to escape from them. Thus, lacking the relationship of father and son, they nevertheless on the one hand pay respect to their own preceptors as if they were fathers, and on the other treat their acolytes as sons.[36]

Having made a case for man's social essence they assumed that people who learned its principles and understood what conduct is natural to man would be likely to accept social obligations (filial piety, loyalty) conducive to the maintenance of the kind of state they idealized. Similarly, it was expected that those in official positions would view their responsibility as helping the cultivation of the people's social natures, to the same end of realizing a stable central kingdom. Thus, doctrines about the desirable function of government are directly linked to ideas about the nature of man. The right social tendencies are there, but environmental conditions can prevent their manifestation. The function of government officials is to aid their development.

The classic Chinese Marxist statement on man's social nature is contained in an essay Liu Shao-ch'i wrote in 1941 entitled "Man's Class Nature":

> Man has two essences: one is man's natural essence [*pen-neng*], including his physical constitution, cleverness, state of health, instinctive capacities, and so forth (for example, in medical science there are various types of physical constitution); the other is man's social essence, including his psychological state, thoughts, consciousness, viewpoints, habits, demands and so forth.[37]

Simply put, man's social nature refers to psychological (mental-motivational) phenomena. The term encompasses all mental activities both affective and cognitive that are social both in terms of their group origins and in terms of their potentiality for affecting other people.

Ever since Liu's essay, contemporary Chinese philosophers and psychologists have differentiated between man's biological and social nature. Bifurcation is a convenient device for assigning to the trivial biological dimension the self-regarding trait or interest in self-preservation (life, as a natural right) central to the liberal democratic concept of man. (This has actually been done in Maoist critiques of modern Chinese philosophers who have taken positions akin to the Western one.) The distinguishing characteristic is the social nature (*she-hui hsing*):

> That which determines why a person is a human being does not lie in his natural essence but lies in his social essence, in his social nature.[38]

In their view of man's social nature, individuals do not possess sentiments, goals, interests, skills, and knowledge prior to or independently of membership in a social organization. Rather, these are formed in society. Furthermore, the term conveys the fact that these matters routinely affect other people. Individuals derive the major features of their identities from the groups to which they belong. As Mao said, men must "belong to some party, some class, or some nation," and "man participates as a social being in every sphere of the actual life of society."[39] Mao praised Marx for going beyond the "feudal" position that man is a thinking animal to the doctrine that man is a social animal.[40] To say, as the Chinese do, that the group cannot be considered a collection of individuals is to underscore the point that the psychological traits just mentioned have no existence independent of any group. The opposing Western view of men as having identities, aspects of which are formed independently of a group membership, is immediately associated with negative behavioral implications (selfish traits):

> In a class society, each individual belongs to a definite class, or a certain stratum within a class. The abstract and independent individual is nonexistent. Thinking only of oneself is the bourgeois outlook.[41]

Each group to which a person belongs is in turn partially defined in terms of some other group. Members of a group will be said to share some common duties to another group or have certain shared expectations about what is due it from the other. Further, interests and beliefs about duties are said to be socially induced within the various social units to which the person belongs.

Under the Confucian influence in the past, a person might be thought of as belonging to the group "younger brothers," which is defined in terms of the group "elder brothers," and part of the definition of each consists of the duties it owes or the expectations to which it is entitled from the other. Today we would call these social roles. In contemporary China, individuals are identified in terms of classes or subclasses, such as lower-middle peasant, which is defined in terms of other groups (e.g. landlord or rich peasant). Each person belongs to a series of ever more comprehensive groups. The Confucian younger brother might belong also to the group of "superior men" (*chün tzu*) that is defined in terms of the morally backward "common people" (*hsiao jen*) and also to the group of culturally advanced Han people that is defined by reference to culturally retarded barbarians. Today a peasant will also belong to the more comprehensive class of Chinese people that is defined in part in terms of imperialists (that is, some elements of their common consciousness derive from the imperialist experience). Thus a person identifies himself in part relationally, in terms of position within a group that stands in a certain relation to another group. Although there is continuity with the dominant Confucian legacy in the belief that a person's identity derives in part from the groups to which he belongs, the claim that feelings, goals, interests, skills, and knowledge are social products, induced in the group, is a new one. Many Confucians believed that some of them are innate.

The Neo-Confucian concept of selfishness (*szu-i*) underlies Chu Hsi's critique of Buddhist and Taoist recluses. It suggests the impossibility of the individual separating himself from the social network, especially the family, with which he is naturally connected and for which he has innate feelings of affection (*jen*). (In some cases the concept is also meant to suggest man's inseparable relations to the physical substance of which all things are composed and to the natural patterns of change, such as the complementary pairs joy and suffering). Selfishness arises when these links are obscured in the person's mind. Thus, a person's identity is a composite of the duties and expectations discriminated by his moral mind that accord with given social positions, and of sentiments for those in the network. The sentiments are as important as the sense of duty in realizing stability in the group. (Professor Francis Hsü has addressed this same issue from an anthropological perspective.) The Chinese Marxist position likewise assumes that a complete account of a person must include reference to the groups to which a person belongs, though the groups have changed. These now are primarily social classes and their subdivisions, or else collections of people sharing ideas or a life-style. But that contemporary position drops the idea of innate affection for others as part of what a person is.

Chinese writers often use the term social nature interchangeably with personality (*ko-hsing*). Both terms include the same psychological dimensions, such as those mentioned in Liu's statement in "Man's Class Nature." But in some contexts social nature may suggest such attributes, simply *qua* attributes, collectively possessed by members of a given social class. The specific content of those dimensions varies from individual to individual, and personality captures the sense of uniqueness and variety. Thought is present in both social nature and personality. It has two meanings: rational belief or knowledge, and habit. Both senses are present in the terms being considered. Chinese Marxists claim that thought is class determined. Because thought in the strict sense of rational belief is said to control all other psychological phenomena included in the social nature, the expression "class nature" is often substituted for the terms social nature and personality.[42] When they defined the social nature in terms of mental phenomena that thereby stand as the object of state "transformational" activities, the

Chinese were bringing to a culmination the special place that consciousness has assumed in the Soviet concept of man.

There is a general tendency in Maoism for the link between man's social nature (thought) and the economic base (so essential in the Marxist definition of social relations) to be sometimes fuzzy, sometimes nonexistent, and never as necessarily linked as in classical Marxism. There is no denial that the social environment influences people's thoughts. On the contrary, the greatest attention is paid to the influence of regional practices and needs and group life-styles on the thought of citizens. There is only a lessening of the rigidity of connection between economically defined class and thought. Gradually, this has led into a periodic tendency to define class in terms of thought, rather than in terms of economic property relations. Thereby the door is open to great expectations about the work of educators who can concentrate on manipulating thought. In order to approach a classless society, it is not necessary to rely only on the more difficult task of altering socioeconomic relationships. Furthermore, one can redefine the possible social situations that can change ideas to include those to which it is relatively easy for individuals to gain access (as is done in talk of developing a proletarian viewpoint through work on a farm during summer vacation periods). In sum, the contemporary developments in the concept of the social nature also have implications for the malleability of man. Transforming thought can involve changing the social or class nature. And, contrary to Marx, the time required for the transformation of social natures is telescoped.

Changeable Particulars
While we have seen that there is some continuity between past and present on the essentially social nature of man, there is a significant rupture with the Confucian legacy on the subject of malleability. Going beyond Marx and even the Soviets, the contemporary Chinese view allows almost unlimited variation in the personalities and abilities of different people and of a specific individual over a period of time. In contrast, the Confucian position emphasized the existence of human attributes that are innate, that cannot be altered, and that therefore establish limits to educational possibilities. A well-known line in the Chou text, the *Doctrine of the Mean,* reads, ''What is decreed by Heaven is called the nature [*hsing*].'' This means that a person's nature being so decreed, cannot be altered through human action; it is a

"given" that exists from birth. Neo-Confucians also affirmed the fixed character of man's essential nature.[43] This claim should be distinguished from the compatible Neo-Confucian position that people have "a principle of changeability" (*yu k'o i chih li*), meaning that they are correctable through study to the point where the essential nature can manifest itself.[44]

In addition, these unalterable attributes are universal. There are definite limits to the kind of variation that can occur from one person to the next: "The sage and we are the same in kind." This position was not dominant in all periods; important figures in the Han dynasty such as Wang Ch'ung and in the T'ang such as Han Yü emphasized the differences in the natures of people. But the Confucian revival that matured in the Sung again stressed the uniformity of human nature. This position, summed up in this remark of Chu Hsi, has had a lasting impact: "The nature is principle, and principle is the same from Yao and Shun to the man in the street."[45] That is, men share a common nature and that nature does not change. Broadly speaking, principle (*li*) is unitary and is the same in all things.[46] From this standpoint, all men, like all beings, have the same essence.

In contemporary China, however, the unalterability and uniformity of human nature are rejected. Excepting for the physiologically damaged, no human being is fettered by innate or early childhood impediments to personality change or to the acquisition of a wide range of verbal and technical abilities. This is an official principle about human nature. This principle is modified from time to time in the casual speech of educators, in the training programs available for selected students in the sciences, and in the treatment of a small number of prisoners, but it remains unique and is the most influential assumption about man in the contemporary Chinese view.

Numerous facts account for this belief in man's malleability. One such fact results from the separation of human nature into a social and a biological dimension and a consequent relative lack of interest in the biological characteristics, except where they interfere with the social. Except for the views of Pavlov, the biological realm has been universally viewed as relatively immutable. Hence downplaying the biological means directing attention away from a major natural impediment to change. Another explanation of malleability derives from the Chinese adaptation of the Marxist theory of the unity of theory and practice. In the Chinese literature, "correct ideas" have been associated with both positive personality features and technical skills. The possibility of having correct ideas is not a function of the structure of one's grey matter or innate endowment:

Where do correct ideas come from? Do they drop from the skies? No. Are they innate in the mind? No. They come from social practice, and from it alone; they come from three kinds of social practice, the struggle for production, the class struggle and scientific experiment.[47]

Ensuring that people participate in the right kind of practice can do a great deal to foster desired change in them.

The third fact pertains to the all important behavioral implications of the idea of malleability. Belief in malleability makes people optimistic about changing their undesirable personality traits and acquiring the technical skills needed for modernization. This optimism can help turn the idea of malleability into a self-fulfilling prophecy. It is believed that people will put out the extra effort that may indeed bring about some of the changes. The Chinese people can be thought of as "blank" and as "a clean sheet of paper" not only in terms of being economically poor and partially devoid of a new culture still being built, as Mao meant when he first used those words, but also in terms of being open to changes in personality characteristics and abilities. In both cases, "blankness" is used to generate a powerful optimism about the chances for change.

A final explanatory factor actually serves to link the ideas of social nature and malleability. It involves the application of the Maoist theories of contradiction and practice to human nature. The general law of change and contradiction is described as follows:

Every form of motion contains within itself its own particular contradiction. This particular contradiction constitutes the particular essence which distinguishes one thing from another. . . . It can thus be seen that in studying the particularity of any kind of contradiction . . . we must not be subjective and arbitrary but must analyze it concretely. Without concrete analysis there can be no knowledge of the particularity of any contradiction.[48]

Human beings are subject to his law. They are also subject to its claims about "particularity." One consequence was that Mao was led to accept the standard Marxist position that human nature changes and that different social classes have different natures:

Is there such a thing as human nature? Of course there is. But there is only human nature in the concrete, no human nature in the abstract. In a class society there is only human nature that bears the stamp of a class; human nature that transcends classes does not exist.[49]

Thus there are no universal human qualities. However, in the Chinese case, there is a striking departure from the customary Marxist emphasis on the uniformity of the nature of members of the same class. The Chinese do accept the doctrine of certain class personality features. But they also point to the vast differences in all social natures, even those of people within the same class. The social natures of individuals are extremely malleable.

Maoist writings employ the term ''concrete'' with abnormal frequency. Reference is made to specific, individual cases, and ''abstractions'' or generalizations about groups are suspect. Historians, doubtless, can find explanations in the guerrilla days, when adjusting differently to different circumstances had great survival value. Students of the philosophy of language may find reasons in the possible absence in the Chinese language of entities comparable to ''universal'' and ''logical class.'' But from an additional standpoint, the theory of contradictions is the source of the focus on the particular. It states that individuals are subject to constant change and must be studied in terms of their unique variations. This is reinforced by that element in the theory of practice that stresses the relation between social practice and the psychological features associated with social natures. The Maoist view is summed up in these remarks:

> The concept of man lacks content; it lacks the specificity of male and female, adult and child, Chinese and foreign, revolutionary and counterrevolutionary. The only thing left is the vague features differentiating man from beast. Who has ever seen such a man? All we ever see is Chang the Third or Li the Fourth. No one has ever seen the concept of house in general either. They have only seen concrete houses such as a western style building in Tientsin and a house surrounded by a square courtyard in Peking.[50]

Mao's repudiation of universal human qualities led him not only to the usual insistence on men's differing class natures, but also to the decidedly unusual attention to differences among individuals within classes. One thinks not of man in general but of specific men. In one of the earliest official analyses of human nature (1941) by a leading Party theoretician, Ch'en Po-ta directed attention to personality variation within classes:

> Each and every individual's personality in a class society has a definite class nature, because in a class society everyone belongs to a definite class, and all go through life under definite historical conditions. The unity of class nature and personality is one side of the matter. On the other side, in various kinds of societies there is a variety (the number is not uniform) of different condi-

tions, different phenomena, different kinds of work for the people, different kinds of lives, and different kinds of struggles; and the concrete environments, large or small, to which each person belongs (social, natural), the concrete angles of life with which each comes in contact (social, natural), all have various and different special features. This will influence each person's personality in each sort of society. Some will have abilities leaning in one way, others in another way; some have interests tending in one way, others in other ways; and, with regard to each person's character, some are brave and some are weak, some are deceitful and some upright, some are grand and some petty, some are modest and some haughty . . . etc. In sum, the many sorts of social life determine the many types of human personalities.[51]

Our conclusion, then, is that when the Maoists speak of the changeability of man they often refer to changes that may take place during a short period of time in individuals. They are not necessarily referring to long-term changes in the natures of the species or of social groups, as did Marx. Nor are they limited to speaking of short-term changes in the natures of groups. They avoid substituting highly general theories of types of social nature or personality types (applicable to large percentages of the human population) for accounts of individuals. In China the door is open for more variety in the analysis of personality components. The notion of thought that is introduced into discussions of the social nature and personality transformation also reinforces the place of the particular in the Chinese concept of man. Thought is variable and fleeting. Having learned that man's social nature is conceived as mental phenomena, we can expect that public aspects of thought will be significant in our study of mind. Aware that changeability and particularity are linked, we can expect to find that the question of diversity or uniformity in the treatment of people by educators will be a key issue in the analysis of the malleability of man.

Our consideration of the concepts of man in the three societies has revealed three points that set the stage for the detailed study to which we now turn. First, in German Marxism and Soviet communist theory the Chinese found a portrait of man that was acceptably modern and that also enabled them to reject Western atomistic individualism. The latter view was common among some influential intellectuals but was uncongenial to the enduring Chinese assumptions about man. There was now another option.

Second, the Chinese drew on the idea of man the conscious activist in the Soviet theory of man's malleability, and they have given mental phenomena or consciousness a central place in any description of him. Inheriting the notion of man's social essence, they linked the attributes of malleability and social nature by defining the latter in terms of alterable mental phenomena. One of their own nonderivative introductions into contemporary philosophy thereby becomes a series of principles about the nature of "mind."

Third, in the Chinese view no a priori reasons exist to deny either the possibility or the desirability of almost unlimited creation (molding) of people's social natures to induce personality traits or skills. The absence of any belief in innate characteristics, such as those so important in the Western liberal concept, provides for the possibility of extensive molding.

Furthermore, neither German nor Chinese Marxism provides a conception of private attributes that should be immune from manipulation, either because man supposedly possesses natural rights or because of the purported psychic damage that is likely to result from "repressive" interference. Within the context of Chinese assumptions of malleability, there would be no justification for this kind of a priori objection to such manipulation. According to Western liberal theory, many ideas have no relevance for anyone but the individual thinker, and they are justifiably placed in the realm of the protected private self. For the Chinese, most mental events are potentially accompanied by promptings to act, and therefore are justifiably subject to manipulation by agents claiming to represent those who might be affected by the acts.

As for the ends to which this manipulation is to be directed, two points that are directly pertinent have already emerged. Because man is not self-regarding, he does not have to be motivated by the acquisition of goods or by pleasure maximization. The transformed personality can be equipped with other motives. Although the termination of the division between mental and manual labor is a high priority in Chinese social philosophy, the Marxian theory of static needs was not absorbed. This suggests that while creating the all-round person who does both mental and manual work is a praiseworthy goal in both philosophies, it is prized for different reasons. For Marx, manifesting a host of capacities is an intrinsic human need; for the Chinese, it is not.

In speaking of transforming social natures, we are talking about "perfectibility" and "educability." These terms can be used to refer to both Confucian and Chinese Marxist views about man. However, we can see some essential distinctions in the meaning of the terms in the different periods. Confucians and Communists both speak of the perfectibility of man because both believe educational factors to be more important in determining whether people actually will become moral exemplars than are minor differences in innate variables: no original sin, no different "callings," no major physiological fetters. This is an important element of continuity between past and present. On the other hand, the Confucians spoke of education as aiding the development and manifestation of specific inborn, desirable tendencies. Thus there are definite parameters to the kind of change that can occur. The educational techniques are influenced by the preexisting attributes to be drawn out. Operationally, the teacher's job is predetermined: to train the innate moral sense, leading it to intuit (i.e., accept) the Confucian moral code. The Chinese Marxist idea of malleability does not a priori lead the teacher to any particular approach; contemporary educational practices are not restricted by the student's antecedent attributes. The material is far more pliable, for better or for worse. The parameters of malleability are enormous.

The Chinese Marxist alternative to the essential features of the liberal democratic concept of man stands as follows: The psychological principle concerning the clustering of beliefs, feelings, and actions (chapter 2) and the malleability of the mind under social influences (chapter 3) replace factual claims about a private psychological realm. There is no place in the Maoist conception of the self for either a private realm of beliefs or for unique and innate inner forces that determine individuality. The concept of malleability also replaces assertions about natural man's innate motives and instincts (for example, that he is egoistic or aggressive). The substance of the chapters that focus on the educational role of government in transforming men's social natures (chapters 4, 5, and 6) is incompatible with the ideals of privacy and autonomy. The problem of man's psychological capacity for autonomy is left rather muddy in the Chinese works, as we shall see.

Chapter 2

The Nature of Mind

There is an aspect of the Confucian and Maoist concept of mind (or social nature) that provides a justification not only for the kind of government that should exist but also for the manner in which that government should exercise its duties. This aspect can be described as "clustering."

Clustering involves combinations of three mental phenomena: knowing, feeling, and promptings to act. Knowing involves both understanding the distinctions between things in the natural world that correspond to distinctions marked by language and recognizing moral principles. Some of these distinctions are regarded by the Chinese as normative. In the past, they were regarded as Nature's signals as to what object or course of action is superior or inferior, right or wrong, or proper or improper. Feelings are concomitant with the act of recognizing (knowing) or of acting in accordance with what is known. Joy, anger, pity, and so forth accompany knowing. Often, evaluations are also contained in the feelings. Certain feelings (e.g., joy) convey approval, others disapproval. Thus evaluation can come in either the act of knowing or the act of feeling. As a result of the enduring clustering of knowing and feeling (and the association of evaluation with both), there has been a blurring of the distinction between the mind's recognition of factual distinction and its making of evaluations. There is no factual knowledge that does not contain a potential association with an evaluation.

Finally, there is a prompting to act in a certain manner relevant to the knowing or feeling. Because they assume the probability of association between "knowing" and "promptings to act," educated Chinese have been sensitive to the behavioral implications of a principle or theory. They assume that if people learn a principle, they will also be inclined to behave in a certain way.

One of the themes of this study is the tendency of many Confucians and Maoists to merge what we call the realms of fact and value. There are two basic philosophical approaches to the question of why this merging occurs.

26

One focuses on the objects of knowledge. This approach would be appropriate for a work on Chinese cosmology or metaphysics. It might concern itself with the fact that, according to many Neo-Confucian thinkers, the objects of knowledge were principles that simultaneously provided both descriptive information concerning the changes that any object predictably would undergo and also prescriptive information about how it should behave. In much the same way, it would be interested in how, today, the dialectical law of the absoluteness of struggle between opposites tells one something about how objects are likely to interact and also how they should be encouraged to interact. In contrast, one strong Western metaphysical legacy with roots in Cartesianism treats all material objects of knowledge as characterized only by quantifiable extension and motion, causing the disciplines that study them to claim to be value free.

Rather than proceed along these lines, we have chosen to approach the question of the fact-value merger from the standpoint of psychology, i.e., in terms of the mind that knows rather than of the objects known. We therefore focus on the mental phenomenon that we describe as "clustering," and its implications.

The Confucian Cluster

If the tendency to cluster had suddenly emerged in Chinese Marxist writings of the twentieth century and had not been encountered previously, the phenomenon might be discounted as transient and trivial. But there is substantial evidence of its prior existence. Examining it will underscore the distinctive strength and importance of clustering in the Maoist concept of man. It is not a phenomenon that is evident in the discussions of knowing of all traditional Chinese schools. It is not evident in the form we will describe in Taoist and Buddhist discussions of the mind, nor is it something that one encounters in all Confucian texts. But it certainly is present in the works of Confucians whose writings were part of the routine study of educated Chinese for so many centuries preceding the modern era: Mencius and Chu Hsi. It is also reflected in some others, whose authors either influenced Chu Hsi (such as Ch'eng Yi) or were influenced by Mencius (such as Wang Yang-ming).

A comparison of the discussions of knowing in pre-twentieth-century Western and in Chinese philosophy reveals that the topics of most concern to the Westerners are rarely significant in the Chinese discussions. For example, the question of certainty and doubt is important to Westerners: Are there truths that cannot be doubted? What are the grounds for the knowledge we supposedly have when we grasp such truths? What is the relation between knowing something and the reasons we can give to claim knowledge? What is the relation between knowledge and belief? How do we weight the competing arguments in favor of intuition, sense experience, and awareness of the laws of logic in answering these questions? Another set of questions important to Western philosophy concerns the relation between our sense experiences and objects supposedly external to our minds: Do objects themselves resemble our perceptions of them? Do objects exist outside of and independently of our minds and experience?

Certainly, the Chinese philosophers were not unaware of some of these questions, but they were primarily concerned with two quite different questions. First, what can we learn through studying things that will tell us both how things are naturally structured to act and how they should act? That is, what we can learn about moral rules and also about objects—acorns, streams, planets, or people—that will help us evaluate whether or not they are acting properly. The other question is, what happens to a knower as a result of his efforts to know, that enables him to behave properly when alone or toward other people and things? Does he learn things about himself in the process of trying to know the natures of other things, and does that knowledge help him to behave more consistently with Confucian norms? Does he acquire feelings toward objects he knows that he should seek to duplicate in his noncognitive dealings with them in the future? In short, those who are interested in knowing are interested in making the right evaluations and in guides to action.

Knowing

Chou Confucians conceived of the human mind primarily as an evaluative organ, the function of which was to identify the normative qualities that are writ large in Nature, including human society. Their conception can best be described as one of an "evaluating mind."[1] By that expression, we refer to functions denoted by either or both of two terms: $^a i$, the sense that discriminates what is the proper course required as a duty in a given situation, and $^c chih$, moral knowing, the sense that discriminates right and wrong revealed as "factual distinction" in Nature, and that grasps general moral principles. Both Mencius and Hsün Tzu believed that $^a i$ is innate to man and distinguishes him from "water and fire, plants and trees, birds and beasts."[2]

The Neo-Confucians kept several aspects of the earlier beliefs about the mind's knowing operation, but they added some new dimensions. Because discussions of knowing in Neo-Confucian thought frequently employed the term *bli* (principle), we must start with some comments about *bli*. Social units retain their cohesiveness through the existence of sets of duties that individuals feel toward others and their expectations of obligations that others have toward them. Mindful of this phenomenon in human society, the Neo-Confucians applied it to Nature as a whole (inclusive of human society). They claimed that Nature is permeated by both social and cosmic patterns of interaction that never change and that if followed lead to a stable equilibrium.[3] These patterns may have been associated with rules governing the interaction, but it is not clear that such rules were always formulizable; in places Chu Hsi speaks of *bli* as revealed in a manner akin to enlightenment. These patterns and rules suggest the activity that is both natural and ethically imperative to each object or event in a given category. The ethical imperative derives from the contribution that a given object provides to the stability of the total order when it conforms to the pattern or rules. These patterns were called *bli* (principle). Theoretically, the pattern suggests behavior that objects will follow spontaneously when there is no outside interference. Thus that which causes an acorn to undergo the changes involved in becoming an oak tree is the *bli* specific to it, and its "duty" is to abide by the *bli*. Since the universe is an integrally organized whole, each object has a duty to the other component parts to abide by its *bli*. Otherwise, the other parts can be adversely affected. Ch'eng Hao said, "For all things there is a *bli*, conformity to which results in ease, violation of which in difficulty. If each follows its own princple, what burden will be imposed on its labors?"[4] The *bli* of a physical object or event also often suggests that there is some appropriate conduct of man toward it.

One can identify three kinds of knowing in Neo-Confucian thought. The first, which need not concern us in detail, is sensory knowing, stemming from direct acquaintance with stimuli that affect the senses. The other two forms of knowing involve understanding the *bli*. One is the grasping of principles by intuition (*chu li, t'i li*) or by inference from a number of cases (depending on one's school, or sometimes, depending on which passages one selects from the philosopher's text). The other kind of moral knowing involves being able to determine whether a particular thing is abiding by rules contained in the *bli*. The term *bchih* (to know) was often used in this connection, though it was also used to refer to the other form of moral knowing. In the mind of the knower, evaluations, based on the degree of congruence between actual behavior and the rules in the ᵇ*li*, were often closely associated with this moral knowing.

Although there are significant differences between the doctrines of Ch'eng Yi or Chu Hsi and those of Wang Yang-ming, nevertheless there is considerable continuity in their conceptions of the subject matter of knowing. Thus, Wang Yang-ming continued the spiritual descendancy from Mencius that had also characterized Ch'eng Yi and Chu Hsi, regarding moral knowing as the essential function of the mind: "The faculty of innate knowledge is to know good and evil."[5] In terms of the types of discriminations made by the mind, it is not easy to distinguish Wang's knowledge of good and evil from the moral senses to which Mencius (so influential in Neo-Confucianism) referred (ᵃ*i* and ᵇ*chih*). The most common example of innate knowledge used by Wang was that concerning children's obligations toward parents. Similar examples were offered in the *Mencius*.

At the same time, Wang distinguished between moral knowing and sensory knowing. He spoke of the latter as functions of moral knowing. Hence, "Innate knowledge does not come from hearing and seeing, and yet all seeing and hearing are functions of innate knowledge."[6] He used the same language to describe both sensory knowing and moral knowing, and the same language to describe the unity of knowledge and action that characterized them both. The two kinds of knowing are closely linked, but moral knowing is more important.

We are left with the conclusion that in Confucianism moral knowing is the most common and most important kind of knowing, that sensory knowing may share some aspects of the evaluative process, and that sensory knowing still differs in some unclear respects from moral knowing.

Feeling

Mencius said that "reason and propriety delight our minds just as the meat of grass- and grain-fed animals delights our mouths."[7] The feeling of joy signifies two things. First, it accompanies the act of acquiring moral knowledge or making evaluative distinctions, indicating that they are man's natural activities. Second, it conveys approval given to proper, right, or good actions or objects, just as the feeling of distaste conveys negative evaluations.

In most Neo-Confucian philosophical writings, feelings carry approval or disapproval, manifested in love, compassion, and empathy for an object or in hatred and anger at it. Moral knowledge achieved through grasping the ᵇ*li* comes in moments of enlightenment that bear some resemblance to the "awakening" of which Buddhists spoke. It is described as different from thought, in that thought moves (*tung*), and the enlightenment is tranquil. In the case of the ordinary person, it will follow a period of thought. The Sage achieves a rapid insight, not preceded by thought.

It is common to find the pursuit of knowledge in this sense being described as a cluster of feeling and knowing. It is both an attempt to empathize with or direct one's feelings of compassion onto the thing and to understand its ^b*li*. Drawing on Buddhist imagery, Chu Hsi used the term *t'i* (to embody) in this connection to convey both cognitive and emphathetic forms of mental penetration into things:

> "*T' i*" is similar in meaning to "making humanheartedness (*jen*) permeate all deeds everywhere". . .if there is one thing which it does not encompass, then it has not achieved a successful embodiment, and its inclusiveness is not realized. This is for the mind to have something outside of itself. Selfishness separates, so that things and the individual self stand opposed to each other. . . . "Therefore, if one's mind is external to things, it has not done sufficient to unite with the mind of Heaven." . . . "What is the meaning of *t'i*?" It is to place the mind in things and to examine their principles. It is just like "the investigation of things" and "the extension of knowledge." It is not the *t'i* of the phrase meaning "essence (*t'i*) and function."[8]

Some enlargement of the very concept of self, involving an experienced broadening of the ties linking the individual mind with the many things is involved in the grasping of principle and in the feeling of compassionate interjection of the self into things. Here is a classic example of the fact that accounts of knowing in the case of any philosopher, Chinese or Western, often are determined by antecedent acceptance of a given theory of reality. A Chinese previously committed to an organic conception of the world and its objects, with all of the interdependency of things in it that that entails, will be likely to give an account of knowing in which the knowing act cannot be completed without both cognitive grasping of principle and affective sympathy for the thing known.[9]

A phrase used by Chou Confucians as well as Neo-Confucians to refer to the sense that discriminates right and wrong or correctness and incorrectness is *shih fei chih hsin*. In so discriminating, this sense performs cognitive functions. And yet the same phrase suggests a sense that approves and disapproves. To *shih* something is to approve it, and to *fei* it is to disapprove it. These are matters of feeling. Thus the terminology reveals that the mind concurrently engages in cognitive distinction making and in affective evaluation.

Another term denoting knowing is ⁱchih. Chu Hsi's own use of this term continued the classical Chou Confucian tendency often to think of knowing as a form of evaluation, in which the mind decides whether some form of activity is proper or improper. At the same time, Chu Hsi's language suggests that in knowing, the ability to recognize something as good or bad or right or wrong (an ability people have as a result of being born with the ᵇli of "knowing") is also paired with emotional feelings of acceptance or rejection and approval or disapproval. Thus ᵇchih involved: having an ability (based on an innate unobservable principle) to discriminate between right and wrong; consciousness of specific distinctions; and feelings of approval or disapproval.[10]

What is the nature of these feelings? Chu Hsi specifically mentioned love, respectfulness, a sense of what is proper, a sense of differentiation, delight, anger, sadness, and enjoyment.[11] This is significant in two ways. When we examine the first four in this list, we find that two of them (the third and fourth) involve mental operations of evaluation unlike the emotional states referred to by the other terms. Yet all four are grouped together. Then Chu Hsi added the more usual list of feelings (*ch'ing*)—delight, anger, sadness, and enjoyment—to the other four. All are feelings. This reinforces the conclusion that in his view, moral evaluation (which necessarily is based on knowledge) and feeling in the customary sense are intimately associated, with no sharp bifurcation between them. Thus, evaluation involved both recognizing something as good or bad and also having an emotional response to it that reflects one's evaluation. The two are not separated.

In China, the idea that the feelings play an evaluative role is very old. In the "Great Preface" to the *Book of Poetry,* Wei Hung (fl. A.D. 25) spoke of poetry as a manifestation of people's sentiments toward the government. The feeling element in the mental cluster is also revealed in Wang Yang-ming's works, often intimately intertwined with the third element, the "beginnings of action" or promptings. Thus he says,

> Innate knowledge is nothing but the sense of right and wrong, and the sense of right and wrong is nothing but to love the right and to hate the wrong. To love the right and to hate the wrong cover all senses of right and wrong and the sense of right and wrong covers all affairs and their variations.[12]

He regarded the knowing and the emotional experience as arising almost simultaneously. The content of the following comment on a passage from the *Great Learning* is a bit farfetched for a Westerner, but the point comes through clearly enough.

> Seeing beautiful colors pertains to knowledge, while loving beautiful colors appertains to action. However, as soon as one sees that beautiful color, he has already loved it. It is not that he sees it first and then makes up his mind to love it.[13]

It is desirable that there be a correspondence between the knowledge of certain duties (or the embryonic acts described below) and certain feelings. A knowledge of filial duties should be accompanied by filial feelings; a knowledge of public duties by humane feelings. The fact that the correspondence is desirable means that it is not always realized. In the absence of such correspondence, the mind's task is to note the typically selfish nature of the feelings in such a case (the existence of selfish desires, or *szu yü*) and attempt to achieve the correct emotional accompaniment for the other mental events.

One important conclusion to be drawn from the clustering of knowing and feeling is that to know a moral rule was generally also personally to accept it for oneself. Feeling approval meant accepting it. A second conclusion is that from the perspective of some Confucians, the mind was routinely considered to have as among its most important and distinctive attributes feelings for other beings that project the self beyond the individual subject, perhaps leading to action affecting others. These feelings, when not obscured, help to solidify the individual's place in a larger network of relations. And this fact causes that Confucian conception of the mind to stand in contrast to those in the liberal democratic heritage in which the mind's insular nature is stressed. The contrast is in the emphasis.

Promptings to Act
In speaking of the association between promptings to act and knowing, we are talking about subjective beginnings of action that in some instances were regarded as having their own power to emanate from the mind into overt behavioral forms unless impeded by something else, such as a competing "thought." Thus we are not discussing specifically the doctrine of the "unity of knowledge and action," in which "action" more frequently refers

to publically observable acts. The presumption that these internal events will have outer manifestations may have roots in a general belief held during the Chou period, cited in the *Great Learning,* that "What truly is within will be manifested without."[14] Therein the maxim is cited as a warning to those who do not work to rid themselves of their evil tendencies but vainly seek to disguise them.

In Confucian works, the Chinese terms that I will render with the English "promptings to act" are most frequently ᵇ*i* or ᵃ*chih,* translated respectively as "intention" and "will." There is considerable evidence that these mental phenomena (and sometimes *szu* or "thought" as well) were regarded as emanating forth, such that they potentially leave the person's subjective realm.[15]

Because ᵇ*i* suggested an emanation whereby a private mental occurrence has a high probability of becoming a publically manifested act, much of Neo-Confucian self-cultivation centered on "making the ᵃ*i* sincere" (*ch'eng i*). In practice, the effort might involve following up a thought to hate evil intentions with a commitment to regenerate that hate every time a new evil intention appeared. But of course, the will (ᵃ*chih*) and the thoughts were also to be watched for the same reason. Thus Chu Hsi said that "There must be sincerity in thought [*szu*] and watchfulness in action."[16]

There are several explanations for the association of promptings to act with knowing (especially moral knowing) in Confucianism. The first lies in the conception of the moral sense (ᵃ*i*) with roots in Chou thought. ᵃ*I* carries not only the idea of discriminating the proper and the improper but also an awareness of an obligation to abide by the judgment in action. The early Confucians developed a sense of the mind as an internal law-giver or commander, that commands obedience to the moral judgments it makes. The emergence of this dimension of the mind resulted from the internalization of sovereignty. It involved the transition from an original view of the sovereign as Heaven, Shang ti (Lord-on-High) or the king, existing outside of the individual and sending down decrees (*ming*) to him, to the eventual view of a sovereign as also existing within the individual himself, issuing decrees to the individual.[17] When the internal ruler determined something to be right and a duty, that duty was like a command issued to the self. Thus there was a correlation between the dictates of the internal moral sense (ᵃ*i*) and the external Heavenly injunction (*ming*). The Heavenly injunctions were to practice certain acts, which were identical with the things that man, in the new conception, would command himself to do.[18]

^a*I* continued to convey the sense of "command to the self" in Neo-Confucian texts. The command makes action in accordance with a value judgment more likely than it would be if there were no such injunction. It does not have a motive force of its own. But Neo-Confucians frequently linked action of some kind (covert or overt) with it. Thus Ch'eng Yi (1033–1108) said that "^a*i* is knowing the right and wrong and following principle in action; this is ^a*i*."[19]

The second and related source of the association of promptings to act with knowledge can be found in the doctrine that there are degrees of knowledge, and that "real knowledge" demands manifestation. The knowledge in question is of duties incumbent on the person studying, and the promptings are to act in accordance with the knowledge. Ch'eng Yi spoke of knowledge as deep (*shen*) and shallow (*ch'ien*). The deeper the knowledge, the greater the possibility that the promptings will manifest themselves in public conduct:

> When knowing is deep, then action in accord with it will necessarily be perfect. There is no such thing as knowing what should be done and not being able to do it. Knowing and not being able to act is only a sign that the knowing does not go deep.[20]

The probability of overt action is a function of the degree of knowledge of ^b*li*, and feeling once more enters the picture in that the transition into action in accordance with ^b*li* is invariably accompanied by joy.

The Chinese position here is somewhat reminiscent of the Socratic doctrine that "he who knows the good does the good." The difference lies in the Socratic claim that ignorance is the source of evil, in contrast to the Neo-Confucian argument that it is selfish desires that cloud the mind. In any case, the Chinese speak of degrees of knowledge, varying in accordance with the amount of clouding.

Finally, the association of promptings to act with the mind's private knowing and thinking operations derives some strength from a general principle in Confucian cosmology. This is that there is an inherent dynamism in all things that permits them to run a course from imperceptible beginnings to publically observable full development. This principle was then applied to the mind's operations as well. The term used to refer to the imperceptible beginnings with their inherent dynamism was *chi*, which can be translated as "springs of action." Thus Ch'eng Yi said, "The Man of wisdom knows the springs of things; therefore, he tries to be true to himself at the earliest stir thought.''[21] The assumption is that the thoughts share this probability of issuing forth publicly. One had best be wary of evil thoughts and repress them before the manifestation in conduct occurs.

This theory can be textually traced back to the *Book of Changes,* wherein the "springs of things" were also clues to good or bad fortune. Neo-Confucian writers also were fond of quoting the following passage from the *Book of Changes:*

> The Master said, to know the springs of action [*chi*] is something spiritual. . . .
> The springs are the minute origins of movement. They are the first signs one
> sees of impending good fortune. The superior man acts as soon as he perceives
> the spring.[22]

Normally, when Chinese and Western commentators, past and present, have discussed Wang Yang-ming's doctrine of the unity of knowledge and action, they have examined it in terms of the enduring juxtaposition in Chinese intellectual history between what David Nivison called "knowers and doers.''[23] The distinction goes back to the *Book of History,* which says "It is not knowing but acting which is difficult.''[24] Thus the Chinese term action (*bhsing*) in Wang's theory has been understood in the sense of public deed. He certainly did use the term with that sense very often. And he took note of the fact that few of his contemporaries shared the thesis about the unity of knowledge and action.

However, having analytically extracted the general association of a *private* prompting to act with knowing, we are in a better position to explain why Wang put forth his doctrine. He was pointing to a fact about the private realm with which many philosophers could agree but which ordinary citizens were prone to forget. Thus the behavioral implication of his position gives the ultimate explanation. In Wang's view, the danger of theoretically isolating the concepts of knowledge and action is that people will think only of public, manifest action. They will forget the likelihood that promptings to act tend to manifest themselves, and they will not take the remedial course of being "watchful over themselves when they are alone.''

> The Teacher said, ''you need to understand the basic purpose of my doctrine.
> In their learning people of today separate knowledge and action into two
> different things. Therefore when a thought is aroused, although it is evil, they
> do not stop it because it has not been translated into action. I advocate the unity

of knowledge and action precisely because I want people to understand that when a thought is aroused, it is already action."[25]

In this passage, "action" is used in two different senses. In the line "has not been translated into action," it is used in the popular sense of overt behavior. In the line, "when a thought is aroused, it is already action," it is the private prompting. The association of private promptings with knowing and thinking was present in the doctrines of all Neo-Confucians. Wang was reminding those philosophers in their writings to take note of the two senses of "action," lest ordinary people fail to repress evil thoughts as they arise.

The Contemporary Cluster

The Confucian account of the detailed components of the psychological events involved in clustering differs from that of the Chinese Marxists. But the belief that such mental events as knowing and feeling and having promptings are closely associated is common to both. However, before describing the contemporary Chinese conception of the mind, we must note the existence of aspects of it that derive from classical Marxism and Soviet thought.

Chinese writings on the theory of knowledge have drawn heavily from Marx's historical materialism and from Soviet reworkings of ideas laid out by Lenin in *Materialism and Empirio-Criticism*. The former inspires the claim that the basic question of philosophy is that of the relation between thought (*szu-wei*) and existence (the material world, and, especially, its economic variables). Which came first and which determines the other? Whether or not one believes knowledge of something called "the objective world" is possible supposedly depends on one's answer to the question of the relation between thought and existence. Idealists, maintaining the primacy of thought, are said to deny the possibility of that knowledge; materialists take the other position. The importance of practice in determining the nature of thought and knowledge also comes from Marx. There are no static objects with which people work (practice), and there are no static ideas involved in people's knowledge. Lenin contributed the notion that the theory of knowledge is a theory of reflection (mental images are copies or reflections of objective things).[26] Thus ideas are not produced by the mind itself; the images that emerge are believed faithfully to resemble externals. Lenin also is responsible for the claim that in each age people acquire increments of truth (relative truth), with an absolute truth achievable as a distant occurrence.[27]

In China, these ideas provided the philosophical roots for the theories of cognition articulated first by Mao in *On Practice* (1937) and then in the 1950s by the psychologists associated with Peking Normal University. The latter developed the quasi-scientific detail to give body and contour to the framework contained in Mao's essay. Their major work is entitled simply, *Psychology*. In both of these works, knowing and knowledge is *jen-shih*.[28] By itself, the term is used interchangeably with "theory" (*li-lun*).[29] We are told that knowledge reflects and explains the "essences" and "laws" of things and that "the process of knowing (*jen-shih*) reflects the characteristics and principles of objective things; it explains the essence (*pen-shen*) of things."[30] The term "essence" most likely refers either to the particular internal contradiction that gives a thing its unique status, or to the relations existing between the thing and other objects. "Laws" are the dialectical laws of change applicable to the thing. Used in this way, the term *jen-shih* is the same as "rational knowledge."

Knowledge begins with sensation (*kan-chüeh*), which is awareness of individual qualities of a thing (primary or secondary qualities, i.e., shapes and sizes, or colors and sounds). The individual qualities are assembled as a whole identifiable object to which a name can be applied (e.g., apple, stone, wind-noise) and that accurately reflects the objective world in a process called "perception" (*chih-chüeh*).[31] Being aware of a set of perceptions that have identity as wholes is characterized as "perceptual knowledge," *kan-hsing jen-shih*.

Knowledge of any kind is acquired in practice. This means having direct contact with things in the course of trying to alter the material environment through production, class struggle, or scientific experiment. Perceptual knowledge does not go beyond being able to identify and name things. The higher kind of knowledge that involves recognition of the essence and laws of a thing is said to require that the perceptual knowledge be passed through a thought process, whereby it undergoes a "leap" and becomes "rational knowledge" (*li-hsing jen-shih*).[32] Rational knowledge reflects reality better than perceptual knowledge.

Through rational knowledge a person learns ethical principles and other truths. These can be acquired either through personal manipulation of the material environment (practice), followed by the other steps that eventuate in rational knowledge, or through instruction. On the basis of these primary truths, the person is provided with an antecedent standard for learning secondary facts or values about the attributes of specific objects.

In this secondary form of knowing one encounters a methodology that departs from the derivative and harkens back to earlier Chinese approaches. Knowing in this form often involves both identifying attributes in an object and also making value judgments. Such knowledge is said to be accumulated by acts of comparison between specific qualities of the object in question and those of another object that usually possesses them to a greater or lesser degree. The particular qualities being compared are suggested by preexisting principles provided by rational knowledge. The following statements by contemporary Chinese writers attest to their belief in this method:

> The method of comparison is a scientific method used in human thinking. It is also a scientific method by which men know [*jen-shih*] things. Without comparing one cannot correctly think and one cannot correctly know [*jen-shih*] things.[33]

> It is always through the method of comparison that the masses understand [*jen-shih*] things, accept reasons, and solve problems. The masses judge, think, speak, and act on the basis of concrete cases, personal experience, and on a foundation of concrete contrasts made within the realm of experience and practice. This is characteristic of the masses' method of thinking.[34]

> Only if a youth can understand [*jen-shih*] clearly the actions and qualities of other people can he easily and confidently talk about himself. We can see that in order to have students understand [*jen-shih*] their personal qualities and correctly evaluate, we must first guide them to an understanding of other people's qualities as well as lead them to use the moral standard employed in evaluating other people as a basis for self evaluation.[35]

The assumption that knowing and evaluation proceeds through a process of comparison is responsible for the important place of model individuals and organization in Chinese educational theory and practice, which we will describe in chapter 6. The other elements that constitute the largely derivative framework of this theory of knowledge are not in themselves of further interest to us. There is little point in worrying about such problems as the failure to provide criteria for extracting "the true" from a body of sense data or the lack of an explanation of the relation between ideas and objects. Our interest lies rather in being able now to identify and set aside the derivative matters, in order to separate out the contributions of the Chinese themselves to this theory of knowledge: clustering knowing and feeling, and knowing and acting.

Knowing and Feeling

Contemporary Chinese philosophers and psychologists associate knowing (*jen-shih*) and feeling. Because Mao himself had spoken of knowledge in terms of grasping something's essence and laws, knowledge and feeling have to be distinguished theoretically. But they are described as invariably occurring in tandem. There is no act of knowing that is not followed by a positive or negative emotional response. Feelings are directed back toward the object of knowledge, as attitudes. Thus the text of *Psychology* says,

> What is a feeling [*ch'ing kan*]? When a person knows [*jen-shih*] a thing or deals with a thing, he definitely is not coldly detached and without feeling. Towards some things he feels delight and towards others he feels a loathing. A certain kind of behavior elicits his happiness, and other kinds elicit his anger. Psychological processes like these kinds of delight, dislike, happiness, and anger are called feelings. Feelings are the attitudinal experience that a person has towards a certain thing. The process of feeling and the process of knowing are different; the process of knowing reflects the characteristics and principles of objective things; it explains the essence of things. But feeling is the attitudinal experience of a person towards the objective things that are reflected; it explains the attitude that a person has toward a thing. But feeling and knowing are intimately related. Feeling is produced in the wake of recognition, and also follows along and changes with changes in knowing. For example: We know the greatness of the Motherland, and then give rise to feelings of warm affection to it. As our knowledge of the Motherland increases more, our warm affection for the Motherland gets deeper.[36]

In addition, a complete account of a feeling or sensation will involve reference to some belief(s) with which the feeling or sensation has been intimately associated.

The path to comprehending this begins with an oft-repeated claim: All feelings have a social nature. That is, they have a class nature. In the Chinese Marxist lexicon, speaking of the class nature of mental events like feelings is another way of referring to the broader principle of the interrelationship of mental events.

Let us first consider the principle and then turn to typical examples involving feelings and sensations that are used to illustrate it. The Chinese diverge from other Marxists in the degree to which their orthodox line insists that all mental activities have a class nature. Philosophical and psychological discussions that reflect this orthodox line normally have begun with one or both of two statements by Mao and (until 1965) by Liu Shao-ch'i:

> In class society everyone lives as a member of a particular class, and every kind of thinking without exception, is stamped with the brand of a class. [Mao][37]

> A person's class nature is determined by his class position. A people's special character [*hsing ko*] and special class nature arises when for a long time they, as a definite group occupy a definite class position; that is, they occupy a definite social production position, producing, living, and struggling for a long time with a definite style; that is, producing their specialized life style, interests, demands, psychological set, thought, habits, concepts, outward bearing, and their specialized relations with other groups of people, things, etc., and their differences from other groups of people or mutual opposition. [Liu][38]

In contemporary China, to say that mental events carry a class stamp is to say two things. First, certain beliefs or feelings originally entered one's consciousness because one belongs to a certain social group and does certain kinds of work. Second, man's class consciousness controls much of his psychological activity.[39] This means that any specific mental activity such as a motive, goal, thought, or belief must be understood in a nexus, as influenced by other psychic phenomena collectively known as class consciousness.[40] The second of these two points is the one that is used to justify explaining every mental event in terms of its relation to others, and to oppose the psychologist's focus on individual psychological faculties by themselves.

We now turn to specific examples of the supposed influences of class on mental events and seek to identify precisely how this relates to feelings and sensations. First, it is claimed that the same stimulus will cause different reactions in different people as a function of the class to which they belong. Thus, in a colorful illustration drawing on folklore, we are told that it is untrue that a member of the bourgeoisie and of the proletariat will both experience fear if they encounter a tiger in the mountains. The latter, especially a member of the Party, will not. Nor is it true that ill health will cause depression in all persons. On his deathbed a worker will not feel depression.[41] People of different classes may at different times and under different circumstances experience responses that people call by a single name. However, because different factors give rise to the responses, the responses themselves are different. The depressions or fears of two people are "qualitatively different."[42]

Second, even though there is sufficient overlap in the responses of members of different classes to the same stimuli to cause us to use a single term to describe the response (perception of redness, sensation of heat, feeling of love), the content of the response is made different by other psychic events in the person's mind, and this is sufficient to cause the responses to be qualitatively different. (Needless to say, those other psychic events are parts of class consciousness.) Thus the love of country by members of different classes is said to be different because of the ideas associated with the feeling of love in them. The sensation of heat from the sun will be different in members of different classes because of other elements in their consciousness. In a direct causal relation, a proletarian idea may actually cause a worker to feel less heat than that which would be felt by someone else. A red patch causes different people to think of different things and makes the perceptions qualitatively different.[43]

Philosophers speak of the impossibility of adequately studying one feeling in isolation from other mental events. Consider the following reference to many people's reaction to the same poem:

> Do not all men have pleasure, anger, sorrow and joy? Yes, but the point is the concrete contents of pleasure, anger, sorrow, and joy are different for persons of different classes. Persons of different classes may be moved by Li Hou-chu's verse, but the feelings aroused by this verse are not the same. And such is precisely an expression of the social character of man. . . . It follows from the above that the feelings aroused by Li Hou-chu's verse are not the same for person's taking different standpoints and that with different states of mind they appreciate this verse from different angles. Why? Because of differences in class position, in upbringing, and in experience; in short, differences in human nature.[44]

The author is claiming by implication that two sorrows (or any other two relevant feelings) are not the same, because they are caused by different objects or associated with different ideas.

In all of these cases, the response is different only if one believes that an adequate account of a response requires inclusion of other mental happenings or external stimuli with which the response is associated. This alone makes the Chinese view intelligible. As far as feeling itself is concerned, an adequate account of a sentiment contains both a statement of what the sentiment is (e.g., sorrow) and also a factual description involving, among other things, the subject's understanding of the circumstances in which the sentiment arose. The latter element, clustered with the former, makes the sorrow of one person different from the next.

The general orientation of those who regard feelings and sensations in these terms is most explicitly evident in the following critique of a study of color and shape preferences among children. The essence of the criticism, contained in the following statements, most succinctly gives away the perspective on how to regard mental events:

> Even within the sphere of experimental psychology, the authors have not studied the mutual action of man's sense organs on one another and the interrelations between man and color and shape. Instead, they have adopted an isolated, abstract method of study. . . . The same color in different things can produce completely different reactions from a person. . . . There is nothing in the world that exists in complete isolation by itself. . . . Man's preference for color is developed under certain conditions of living. . . . The differences in color preferences between different persons is determined by different personalities formed as a result of different social practices and different life histories.[45]

Chinese philosophers and psychologists often say there is no such thing as pure feelings. This means that one should consider the cluster, not simply the sentiment in a vacuum. It also means that feelings are vehicles for evaluations. The only feelings that are regarded as worthy of attention are those that carry some evaluation and are themselves therefore subject to praise or blame.[46] Sometimes reference to such feelings is provided in two two-character phrases used to describe explicitly moral feelings. An example would be "feelings of admiration and envy" (*tsan-yang ho hsien-mu ti ch'ing-kan*), indicating both approval and a secondary feeling experience.[47] Sometimes the context conveys the message: To establish proletarian feelings with a person is to like each other and approve of each other.

Just as in the Confucian case, the correct feelings may not actually accompany knowing certain facts. The individual has a responsibility to insure that such a proper accompaniment is realized.

Knowing and Acting

The other distinctively Chinese dimension to the theory of knowledge is the intimate connection between knowing something and having an inclination to act in accordance with one's evaluation of it. One way that this connection is revealed is through a consideration of the meaning of *jen-shih* itself. Another way is through a study of the relation between statements about knowing and about having covert motives. A final way emerges in a consideration of the concept of *szu-hsiang* or thought.

Contextual analysis of statements employing the term *jen-shih* reveal that it oftens carries the sense of both to understand or recognize, and to accept.[48] (This "acceptance" element was first noted by Robert and Ai-li S. Chin.) I use the term "accept" in the sense of having a commitment to act in accordance with what is known and approved or disapproved. In the statement, "Most cadres have already known (*jen-shih*) the great meaning (*i-i*) of participating in physical labor and moulding themselves in basic units," knowing involves accepting for themselves.[49]

Even in those cases where no explicit reference is made to meaning (*i-i*) in the sense of value or significance, the notion of acceptance or approval is often still associated with knowing.

Once having *jen-shih* [recognized and accepted] simply the quality of thought of the proletariat, one can then educate the common people.[50]

Helped by the branch of the association, I *jen-shih* [recognize and accept] that I must first have revolutionary thought; this is very important.[51]

The same applies to another frequently encountered term meaning "to understand."

Only if we truly work for the masses will they finally *liao-chieh* [understand/accept] us.[52]

. . . in order to *liao-chieh* [understand/appreciate/accept] the people deeply, we must integrate ourselves with them forming one body, so that one's work will be done well.[53]

Let us consider the second kind of evidence that suggests a clustering of knowing and having promptings to act. Philosophers and psychologists generally repeat Mao's statement in *On Practice* that rational knowledge (*li-hsing jen-shih*) is the reflection of the essence (*pen-shen* or *pen-chih*) and laws of a thing. Their discussions of the object that is known begin to depart from these Marxist views when at other times they refer to conceptual knowledge as involving knowing the meaning (*i-i*) of something. Knowing the meaning often refers to understanding the value or significance of the thing for human beings. Furthermore, knowing the meaning is normally accompanied by an internal prompting to make one's conduct in some way consistent with the value reflected in the meaning. Chinese analytical studies have adopted the Western term "motive" (*tung-chi*) as a tool for attempting to understand this prompting. The Chinese terms for meaning are unusual in so often and so clearly having the sense of value or significance.[54]

Statements that refer to meaning (value/significance) as the object of knowledge (*jen-shih*) typically take the form:

> Fully understanding [*jen-shih*] the significance [*i-i*] of carrying out the mission, the cadre-fighters were not afraid of hardship, fatigue . . . and gained good results in planting and improving lands.[55]

To know the meaning (*i-i*) of something in this particular sense is to know two things. One is how the thing in question affects or is related to some other thing (such as another job or the realization of a goal). This is revealed in the common pattern that takes the form, "*X*, vis-à-vis *Y*, has an important meaning." The "meaning" informs us that *X* works in a certain way to induce some change in *Y* or in people's perception of *Y*. The other thing that the meaning tells us that this change is of some value or disvalue. Thus we find such contrasting qualifications of meaning as "*X* can be of completely positive meaning, or it can be of completely negative meaning" (. . . *chu yu chi-chi i-i, yeh k'o-neng chu yu hsiao-chi i-i*).[56]

All of this is background for pointing to evidence that knowing the meaning of something also includes the idea of having a resolution to act. The evidence can be found in Chinese studies of motives. The term used for motive (*tung-chi*) is a Japanese import (*doki*).[57] The term is not used in Chinese psychological studies with the precision that it has in Western texts. But the confusion in usage is itself revealing, because when it is used it calls attention explicitly to the existence in Chinese of an idea that would be understood but never clearly articulated were it not for the new availability of the term *tung-chi* from Japanese sources. The idea concerns an element of consciousness that incites one to act. (A recent philosophical dictionary from the Chinese Marxist perspective defines motive as "the subjective wish in people's action." Motive and objective result have the form of a dialectical unity, in that "a result is the manifestation in action of a motive," and a motive is "the director of action [that leads to] a result.")[58] That element of consciousness is normally present whenever one knows (*jen-shih*) the meaning of something if meaning contains the sense of value.

It is possible to examine the interrelations between knowing, meaning, and motive. The most explicit studies of the matter by Chinese themselves pertain to the grasp of moral rules by primary-school-age children. They are said to be able to know the social meanings of their acts, and at the same time to be able to take the social meanings as their own motives. Their motives are then depicted as "moral motives belonging to their knowledge" (*jen-shih shang ti tao-te tung-chi*).[59] Elements of consciousness that prompt one to act (motives) are associated with knowledge, rather than with desire, will, or feeling. The implication is that when one knows right or wrong and good or bad one will also have a prompting to act consistent with that knowledge. There is, however, no guarantee that a particular prompting to act will be successfully realized in overt behavior, in view of the fact that competing promptings also occur. Probability of success depends on something called "internal moral experience" (*nei-hsin ti tao-te t'i-yen*), in which knowledge of moral rules derives more from personal comprehension of the reason for them than from recognizing rules as injunctions laid down by other individuals such as parents; this comes with age and training.

Statements about having correct knowledge of a purpose or meaning are also used interchangeably with statements about having a correct motive. For example, in another study, the authors used statements about children having a correct knowledge of the purpose or meaning of study (*tui tu-shu mu-ti ti jen-shih cheng-ch'üeh ti yu X%*) as though they have the same content as statements about children having a correct motive for study (*cheng-ch'üeh ti tu-shu tung-chi*).[60] Knowing a purpose and having a motive are not distinguished.

Finally, evidence for the clustering of knowing and action emerges from a consideration of the term "thought" (*szu-hsiang*). The term has a strict and a loose sense, and the former overlaps in meaning with several other terms that pertain to cognition, thereby serving as the focus for our consideration of clustering. In the strict sense, thoughts are beliefs about the nature of the material world (including human society) or about values that are used by the individual to learn more about the world. They are like hypotheses based on factual evidence, with one exception: they normally entail the prompting to act. Like other cognitive aspects of consciousness in Leninist epistemology, thought is described as "a reflection of objective social, political, and economic reality."[61] This points to the origin and possibility of its conveying accurate information about nature and society. Further, it is the outcome of a deliberative process in which other beliefs about the world play a role. The Leninist view of all knowledge as incremental until absolute knowledge is achieved is maintained. Thus, although *szu-hsiang* has the tentative nature of any hypothesis, it denotes a conclusion that all the facts seem to indicate at the moment. One Chinese philosophical analysis distinguishes as follows between the two terms most often translated as thought:

> *Szu-wei* refers to the process of abstractly summarizing when people reflect things in the material world through their brain. So it is the process of thinking how to do something. *Szu-hsiang* is the end result of reflection, the outcome of abstract summarization, i.e., after a procedure has already been thought through.[62]

The thoughts or beliefs that emerge from such deliberations serve as instruments for gaining further knowledge (*jen-shih*) of the world in the same way that hypotheses do:

> What kind of thought [*szu-hsiang*] should we use to know and grasp the laws of this objective world?[63]

> Marxism is the world-view of the proletariat, and it is also their thought-weapon [*szu-hsiang wu-chi*] for scientifically knowing and revolutionarily reforming the world.[64]

When used loosely, *szu-hsiang* refers to mental phenomena that are not innate but that are also not the result of any deliberative process and normally have no effectiveness in eliciting additional knowledge about the world. As such, the Chinese characters are best translated as ''desire'' or ''attitude'' or ''habit.'' For example, in one source we learn that thoughts, especially those bad ones that have their origin in the old society, become habits.[65] Strictly used, thought overlaps considerably with the knowing component of clustering. Loosely used, it reveals a similar degree of overlap with the value-laden feeling component.

In *On Practice* Mao describes rational knowledge as theory (*li-lun*). *Szu-hsiang* in turn often doubles for theory, in that a series of beliefs that in one place is called theory will in another be called *szu-hsiang*. There is considerable overlap in the meaning of *szu-hsiang* in the strict sense and rational knowledge or theory. Both are ''reflections'' of the objective world, contain conclusions that available facts indicate, serve to gain further information about the world, and originate through practice. This overlap permits us to apply any conclusion about the association of thought with the beginnings of action also to knowing, as evidence of the knowing-action cluster. Our recent Chinese Marxist philosophical dictionary actually defines the term thought (*szu-hsiang*) when philosophically employed as "rational knowledge of objective things."[66]

In both its strict and loose sense, thought is often understood as activating and then directing behavior. Not all thought eventuates in action, but there is a strong tendency for it to do so. To this extent, there is congruence in the content of "knowing a meaning" and "having a thought." Both expressions (when thought is understood in the strict sense) refer to kinds of knowledge that are intimately associated with action. In the case of *szu-hsiang*, the explicit statements referring to the role of thought in action are of the following type:

All human acts are directed by thought consciousness.[67]

Thought is the director of action. Whatever kind of thought there is initially determines what kind of action will follow.[68]

This conception of the relation of thought and action differs most immediately from that in our own culture in that we do not regard all actions as involving conscious awareness.

Our examination of "knowing a meaning" indicated that such knowing was often associated with having a motive (*tung-chi*) to act. There is evidence that having thoughts is also linked with having motives. For example, the terms motive and thoughts are often used interchangeably: "They can only see that some people who are motivated by individual fame and profit [*ko-jen ming-li tung-chi*] can achieve a successful result, but they do not see that those people would work even more, faster, and better to save more money or material if they had less thoughts of individual fame and profit [*ko-jen ming-li szu-hsiang*]."[69] Or, we may be told that "gratitude is the kind of thought [*szu-hsiang*] that can be the motive [*tung-chi*] for positively taking part in revolutionary struggle."[70] Elsewhere, the context of statements reveals the goal orientation in *szu-hsiang* that is an integral part of having a motive: "They emphasize democracy but neglect centralism; they stress freedom but neglect discipline. They lack the goal/motive/thought [*szu-hsiang*] of really serving people."[71]

We can sum up our findings thus far and indicate their relevance to the basic theme of this study. Knowledge can be about both facts and values. Feelings that bear evaluational reactions often accompany knowing or holding beliefs. The beginnings of conduct are promptings to behave in a manner consistent with the evaluational reaction to the object of knowledge.

Acting and the Will

Our examination of terms used in Confucian works to denote "promptings to act" included ªchih, usually translated as "will." The modern term is *i-chih*. A Westerner is likely to think that the process of freely willing (choosing) to act is often involved somewhere in the covert mental beginnings of action. These two facts constitute sufficient grounds for us to investigate whether or not the notion of "freely choosing" is involved in these promptings. The question has significant policy implications. Traditionally in the West, for example, the doctrine of "free will" has put responsibility for acts primarily on the individual actor, with consequent influences on the interpretation of deviant behavior (criminal justice systems) and the role of education.

The Chinese drew selectively from the new concept of man as a conscious activist that emerged in the Soviet Union in the 1930s. The new Soviet conception of mind included a distinction between an inner realm of consciousness and a separate external realm of matter. The Cartesian flavor that pervades this conception of mind stems primarily from the "copy theory" of perception, initiated by Engels and developed by Lenin in *Materialism and Empirio-Criticism*. Crucial to the copy theory is the notion of a distinct external world that is cognized or mirrored in the mind, and that remains separate from it. Lenin also had turned the Marxist observation that the proletariat increases its knowledge of its historic role as it becomes more revolutionary into the very different thesis that consciousness in the sense of understanding the actual conditions of one's time can be a major factor in one's ability rapidly and successfully to achieve revolutionary goals.[72] Writers ever since have been fond of quoting Lenin's remark that "The consciousness of man not only reflects but creates the world."[73] Another pillar of the new view of man was Engel's *Dialectics of Nature*, published in 1925.

Soviet philosophers apply to this distinction between matter and reflecting consciousness the additional distinction between "internal" and "external" conditions, both of which must be accounted for in any explanation of human action. External (material environmental) factors, on which the determinist would focus, must be mediated through internal, covert ones. The internal conditions include goals and interests.

Free choice is located in consciousness and made possible by the existence of the internal conditions. They permit people to avoid being buffetted by immediate external occurrences and instead to select choices in accordance with long-term goals. Man has creative consciousness in that through choice selection based on goals, he can alter the course of history and not be a slave to the material variables of the moment. These variables are said to be mediated through the internal conditions, which prevents them from moving the person like a billiard ball answering the shove of a cue.

Soviet philosophers muster philosophical arguments to justify free choice. Each arrangement of matter moves itself (each brain is such an arrangement), and each level of arrangement has some laws of its own, not being totally explainable in terms of a lower level of arrangement. Thus human consciousness cannot be totally explained in terms of instincts or neurological phenomena that could be identified in lesser animals. The Soviets have never abandoned the Marxist doctrine of the social conditioning of mental events and use it when it serves their purposes. Authority for the reintroduction of free choice and individual responsibility, on the other hand, can also be found in Lenin's *Materialism and Empirio-Criticism.* Lenin quoted approvingly Engels's statement that

> Freedom of the will, therefore, means nothing but the capacity to make decisions with real knowledge of the subject ... Freedom, therefore, consists in the control over ourselves and over external nature which is founded on knowledge of natural necessity.[74]

He then proceeded to comment,

> For until we know a law of nature, it, existing and acting independently and outside our mind, makes us slaves of "blind necessity" ... The mastery of nature manifested in human practice is a result of an objectively correct reflection within the human head of the phenomena and processes of nature, and is proof of the fact that this reflection (within the limits of what is revealed by practice) is objective, absolute, and eternal truth.[75]

There are at least two problems with this concept of mind. The Cartesian overtones (symbolized by the distinction between inner and outer) are inconsistent with Marx's disavowal of these dualisms in which one pole is an external, extended separate world and the other pole something that thinks.[76] Furthermore, the Soviet discussions tell us nothing about how we can differentiate between the parameters of "immediate situations" that need not control us, and other material situations that do determine the goals we have (social determinants of consciousness). And the process of internal "mediation" is left unclear.

Problems inherent in the Soviet attempts to cope with the problem of the formation of consciousness are evident if one examines only briefly the shifting official line itself. The zigzag from behaviorism of the 1920s through the free choice orientation of the 1930s has been repeated.[77]

If anything is clear in the Soviet analysis of man, it is that there is an acute muddle about whether or not man is an autonomous actor and what precisely such an actor would be. Out of this muddle the Chinese accepted the idea that people consciously pursue goals and that rulers should be concerned with education as it affects the formation of those goals. Leadership efforts to provide people with appropriate goals will be effective, and people can have confidence in the changes that they undergo as a result of remolding. Thus, the new Soviet man provided a point of departure for the Chinese concept in both its telescoping of the time period of "human nature" transformation and also in its introduction of consciousness as one of the leading foci of those transformation efforts.

But the Chinese have also had to carry over some of the Soviet muddle about free choice, when they have bothered with the concept at all.

In their explicit statements, the Chinese would agree with the following claim by Soviet authorities that in attempting to control man the object of one's efforts should be his conscious thoughts:

> Soviet psychology is in contradistinction to bourgeois psychology in this regard—bourgeois psychology takes the "unconscious" as a point of departure, as though it were the central core of man's personality, but Soviet psychology . . . has indicated the dominant role which conscious influences play as compared with unconscious influences . . . Soviet pedagogy holds the principle that it is the conscious personality of man, his conscious behavior, and his conscious discipline that are to be molded.[78]

But the very inconsistencies in the Soviet theory itself lay little obligation on the Chinese to treat carefully and seriously the references to free choice, with their explicit conclusions about responsibility. They trace the origin of acts to thoughts.[79] When talking about why people have bad thoughts, Chinese philosophers frequently rely on rather strict interpretations of that controversial statement in his Preface to *A Contribution to the Critique of Political Economy* that in the final analysis "existence determines reality." They define existence in terms of family, work, artistic products, and educational practices. In other contexts, this statement of Marx plays no such central role.

From a cultural perspective, the Soviet philosophical and psychological works have been preoccupied with freedom of choice because the authors live in a society that is European and that has been subjected to the doctrinal legacy of free will, original sin, and individual responsibility. Confucian thought has no place for the ability of man to select his own values or the duties/expectations that accrue to a given social role. The concept of autonomy in this strong sense is absent. Confucian thought does have a place for the ability of man to choose the way in which he goes about realizing those values or duties.[80]

When the Western philosophical concept of free will entered Chinese philosophic discourse during the first part of the twentieth century, it was understood in terms of the intuitive moral sense that comes down in the Mencian stream of Confucianism. Its Western significance in the cosmological debate over determinism and the moral debate over abuse of choice, leading to commission of sin, were not prominent in China.[81]

Politically, as Raymond Bauer showed, the concern with freedom of choice in the USSR exists because of Stalin's desire to blame and punish individuals rather than to hold responsible the social environment that he himself managed. The Soviets have been at pains to say that their claims about free choice are not the same as those contained in the "idealist's" doctrine of free will. But the distinctions are fuzzy and, in each case, the implications for holding individuals directly responsible are about the same.

Philosophers and psychologists in the People's Republic have been much less interested in the topic of freedom of choice than have their Soviet counterparts, though they do talk about choice making and Mao himself used the distinction between internal and external conditions.

As Fung Yu-lan once said, "[Ideological remoulding] depends on your own efforts, although others can be of help. Chairman Mao has taught, 'external causes become operative through internal causes.' This is indeed the case with ideological remoulding."[82] Just as there is relatively little study of the problem of freedom of choice in China, so is there also relatively little philosophical discourse about individual responsibility. Chinese accounts of deviancy contain extensive references to environmental variables, though they are not devoid of remarks about personal accountability. It is a matter of emphasis.

We are not saying that all Chinese Marxists deny the ability of men freely to choose. Nor are we saying that there has not been periodic fluctuation in the degree to which the origin of deviant acts is traced beyond the individual to social practice or prior societal influence. We are saying that there is no formal and explicit introduction of the concept of individual responsibility in a philosophic sense as was done in Soviet thought in the 1930s. The significance of this fact for our study is that in the hands of the formulators of doctrine, it increases greatly the ruler's obligation. Human evils or transgressions are not so easily explained away as a product of misuse of free choice by individuals. Instead the state bears a burden of ensuring that a preponderance of good thoughts exists in the brains of the citizens.

Clustering and Language
One of the most commonplace observations a person could make about China past and present is that language occupies a special place in the culture. Chinese scholars spend considerable time talking and writing about the nature of language and the relation between words and realities. There are many reasons for this. In the past, one was the difficulty of the written language, the written form of civil service examinations, and the consequent association of literacy with special economic or political privilege. In the twentieth century, since the May Fourth period, a key to social change has been seen to lie in the substitution of a written language much closer to the spoken and devoid of the old ideals of maximizing conciseness of expression, and use of classical allusion. Both the broader acquisition of new technical skills by large numbers of people and also the minimizing of old status barriers depended on seeking educational universalization. That depended on the adoption of a new, easier written language.

Yet there is an additional explanation for the special interest in language. This is a consequence of the linking of facts and values discussed in this chapter. Chinese often respond to the words of others as if, in addition to merely describing events, the words also convey value judgments. This is a universal function of language, but the Chinese have long been more sensitive to it than others. The recognition of this fact about language was theoretically embodied in the Confucian doctrine of the rectification of names (*cheng-ming*). According to it, to use a word like "king" to refer to a person was both to describe a social position and also to indicate approval of the manner in which a person is occupying it. Similarly, in contemporary China there are demands that certain terms be used in a comparable manner.

Actually, one does not need to go any further than the terminology used to describe the nature of man himself to find the tendency to cluster the factual and evaluative senses of terms. In 1959 professors from East-China Teachers' University and the Shanghai Teachers' College held long discussions preparatory to writing a textbook on psychology. There was a long debate on the definition of will (*i-chih*). A number present repudiated the notion that all people have a will, because to do so would be not only to make a psychological description of them but also to convey moral approval of the manner in which all people pursue goals. "The act of the reactionaries is not in accordance with the People and therefore is not an act of will; otherwise the destructive activity of the counterrevolutionaries would also be a strong expression of will power."[83] The literature is rife with similar examples.

Disputes in China can often be resolved when one accepts the opponent's wording, because accepting the words entails accepting the moral judgments contained in them. This is especially evident in the literature of confessions and self-criticisms. Autobiographies must be constantly rewritten until, among other things, the wording is correct from the cadre's standpoint. Using certain descriptive statements about oneself, such as reference to the class to which one belongs, is regarded as equivalent to moral condemnation of oneself.

But beyond the specialized use of individual words, one can find evidence of the fact-value association in the interpretation of statements as a whole. One need only look at the interchanges in any philosophical polemic. For example, consider the opposing dialectical views of Mao and Yang Hsien-chen that were so much discussed in the 1960s. Apologists for the former normally included in their remarks some variation on Lenin's statement, "The unity of opposites is conditional, temporary, transitory, relative. The struggle of mutually exclusive opposites is absolute, just as development and motion are absolute."[84] To paraphrase such a statement as the Maoists did, was not only to describe a fact about how things in the world work, but also to convey one's approval of conflict as morally correct. In contrast, stressing the unity of opposites ("two combine into one") in a description of dialectical laws was regarded as also an expression of moral approval of long-term reconciliation between social groups. Or, in another example, to describe all people as sharing certain attributes is regarded as concurrently containing the moral judgment that all people are equally "good."[85] The significance of many of the philosophical polemics in China is lost on foreigners because they are accustomed to focusing only on the apparent descriptive content of the language used to lay out Marxist cosmological claims and fail to understand the politically significant moral stands that are also being communicated.

Understanding this dual function of language adds a new dimension to any explanation of the Chinese demands that intellectuals learn and utilize in their works the language of the peasantry, and that academics in the natural sciences, including psychology, sinify the language they use in lectures, recordings, and publications. To use the language of the peasantry is to take a step toward both describing and evaluating the world as they would. To sinify one's scholarly language is to affirm one's national identity by adopting Chinese values.

Our analysis of the Chinese concept of mind reveals one of the reasons why there is no place for a "private self" or a realm of beliefs that should be protected by a tolerating government. An adequate account of any mental event like knowing or believing requires its placement in a nexus and a description of it in terms of other mental events with which it is associated. All beliefs about the world are potentially clustered with promptings to act that can affect other people when manifested. But there is an intermediary step between knowing and the beginnings of action.

Feelings that convey approval or disapproval are also clustered with facts. When there is approval or disapproval, there is also acceptance or rejection of the matter in question for the self. The prompting to act follows upon the acceptance or rejection.

Any scientific or philosophical judgment on the merits or defects of clustering is outside the scope of this book. Yet it is worth citing the following remarks from the current standard *Handbook in Social Psychology* that point to a conclusion congenial in approach to the one we have just examined:

> Philosophers at diverse times and places have arrived at the same conclusion, that there are basically three existential stances that man can take with respect to the human condition: knowing, feeling, and acting ... Within the scien-

tific study of attitudes, the trilogy came early and stayed late . . . The question arises of how closely the cognitive, affective, and conative components are related. If all three give approximately the same results, one should perhaps apply Occam's razor to reduce the redundant conceptual baggage . . . The results indicate that the three components are quite highly intercorrelated.[86]

When coupled with the belief in malleability, the tendency to associate knowing distinctions with both value-laden feelings and promptings to act leads to a particular conception of the role of the state. It is viewed as having a duty to ensure that in the thoughts of the people proper evaluations and promptings regularly accompany recognition of factual distinctions. Thus its primary role is to "cultivate" the peoples' minds. Therefore, contrary to some Western liberal democratic theory, it is not proper for state agencies to concern themselves only with the so-called externals of behavior, as suggested by the old English legal maxim: "The thoughts of man are not tryable; the devil alone knows the thoughts of man."

Chapter 3

The Malleability of Man

If chapter 2 highlighted an element of continuity with the Confucian past (clustering), this chapter focuses on a significant rupture. That rupture can be found in the idea of malleability that gives content to the notion that human nature changes.[1]

"Human nature changes"—a vague statement acceptable to Marx and to Engels, to Stalin and to Mao. The point is: what is it that changes, under what conditions does it change, and what is the nature of the change? Curiously, the most effective way to go about finding the answers to these questions in the case of contemporary China is to examine the ferment in three different fields (philosophy, literature, and psychology) on one topic—the presence or absence of universal human characteristics or nontrivial traits. As usual, we can gain more understanding of the topic by examining the behavioral implications of the claims that there are or are not universal human traits than we can by searching the Chinese sources for the experimental evidence or the logical arguments offered in support of the claims. After examining the behavioral implications we will have some insight into why this topic has saturated publications in all three of the fields mentioned, far outdistancing any other topic.

The Chinese immediately associate the panhuman with the innate and the innate with the unchangeable. Throughout their Confucian history at both the sophisticated and the popular level people linked the notions of universal traits ("The sage and we are the same in kind") and the notion of innateness. The associated Confucian claims were that all people share the same major attributes, and also that the unique attribute of man, *jen* or humanhearted-ness, is innate (*hsien-t'ien ti*). There is no theoretical reason why some common traits cannot be the result of similarities in the natural environments of all people, but in China what was universal was also innate.[2] Today discussions of innate characteristics are suspect because they suggest that which is unchangeable. The Chinese leaders want to change people, and to

57

have them change themselves, into "new men" having the virtues that proper clustering achieves and also into people with skills needed for development tasks. Hence the stress on malleability, which, along with clustering, is the second human attribute that shapes the role of government.

The Problem of Innate Characteristics

Philosophy and Literature
In the fields of philosophy and literature, the major controversy about innate characteristics has centered on the subject of humanism. In a manner remarkably similar to their Confucian predecessors, many contemporary philosophers and literary people labeled as "revisionists" have fused doctrines about a universal human nature with an ethic of humanism. The Chinese phrase used to convey the association of these differing notions is "the humanism that emerges from human nature" (*ch'u yü jen-lei pen-hsing ti jen-tao-chu-yi*).[3] "Humanism" still suggests a set of moral imperatives, intuited by an innate moral sense that also characterized Confucian humanism. These are various obligations to love all other people or to treat them benevolently. The moral imperatives, of which everyone whose mind is not clouded by selfishness should be aware, are associated with innate feelings of sympathy (*t'ung ch'ing hsin*) for others, also commonly held by all people.[4] Many of the recent advocates of a humanism with roots in the Chinese tradition are content to make vague references to the common features of human nature and to the fact that that nature is "good."[5] As it has for twenty-five hundred years, the word "good" suggests the existence of innate tendencies to act compassionately on behalf of others.

One implication of this "goodness" applies primarily to the changeability of groups. This dangerous implication is that people who believe in it will try to tolerate their oppressors out of kindness rather than struggle with them and transform them. The Maoist whip normally used to slap down this kind of thinking is, "We do not apply a policy of benevolence to the reactionaries."[6]

Besides a kind of universal sympathy, there is a host of other traits that various deviant philosophers and writers identify as common to all people. Some maintain that there is an instinctive love of family and friends.[7] Pa Jen (Wang Jen-shu, former member of the editorial board of *Wen-yi pao* [Literature and art daily] and a diplomat) pointed to other common sentiments:

Sentiments are things that are shared and similar among people. Hunger, thirst, sex—these are things that people commonly demand. People all like the fragrance of flowers, the song of a bird. They share a common hope to continue existing, to be warm and have enough to eat, and to develop. . . . We can say that these demands, likes, and hopes have their roots in the common nature of mankind.[8]

The popular philosopher Feng Ting of Peking University claimed that the survival instinct is common to all, In his own words,

The most basic and most common characteristic of living things is the preservation of life. This is shown first of all by their turning toward or away from external stimulus, i.e., by their avoiding or welcoming an external stimulus.[9]

His view is similar to that of Pavlovian-oriented psychologists who treat biological phenomena rather than social attributes as the essential dimension of man. His critics insist that the "hopes," "yearnings," "strivings," "wishes," and so forth that Feng Ting treats biologically (as in "striving to gratify one's needs") should be treated as social phenomena.

Pa Jen's critics claimed that his views implied that members of the proletariat should focus on developing human sentiments they already possess, instead of transforming themselves. Feng Ting was most often attacked because of the static quality of the life he idealized. It involved "being well fed and clothed, living in a spacious and clean house, enjoying love, and living in amity with his wife or her husband, parents, and children."[10] This too is catering to and enriching the existing urge for life rather than transforming people's minds and turning them into new men capable of doing mental and manual labor.

Periodic denials that humanism is a Chinese product appear in the Chinese media, most vociferously in answer to studies by compatriots pointing to its indigenous roots. A frequent claim is that it is a capitalist import which made its way into China during the May Fourth Movement (1917–21).[11] However, the term "humanism" is most commonly used in English to refer to the antitheistic spirit of the Enlightenment in which the goal for which men were urged to strive was reoriented away from bliss in Heaven to increased happiness on earth, something to which each individual has a natural right. Reliance was to be placed on human effort rather than on divine grace in achieving that happiness. Certain ideas associated with humanism in this sense (for which the more appropriate term is *jen-wen chu-i*) were introduced to China during the May Fourth period. But the form which humanism (more precisely, humanitarianism) (*jen-tao-chu-i*) took in China in the 1950s and 1960s, with its stress on a love for all people grounded in common innate sentiments, affirms its Chinese origins.

The special character of the Chinese interpretation of humanism is revealed in their critiques of Russian and European Marxist discussions of humanism. The Chinese read into these foreign philosophical statements their own traditional association between the theories of human nature and the humanistic ethics, in which "love of all people" was made the central norm.

> The birth of scientific communism was a great leap in human thought. Now the revisionists have tampered with the teachings of scientific communism, and reverted to the preaching of human nature in the abstract and of "love of humanity," which Marxism-Leninism transcended long ago, and to such slogans as "man is to man a brother. . . ."[12]

Even more indicative of the uniqueness of the Chinese obsession with humanism and its behavioral implications is the fact that humanism cannot be found among the nine or ten most frequently encountered deviations of revisionists identified by the Soviets.[13] Even the term "humanism" has a different connotation when used by Eastern European revisionists from that which *jen-tao-chu-i* has in Chinese. In contemporary Europe, humanism has more to do with freedom than anything else. These Marxists contrast "dialectical materialism" and "humanism." The latter, they feel, is a noble ideal leading to the end of human slavery (by bureaucracies, in modern socialist states) and the emergence of people as free, creative beings in the sense in which the young Marx used the words.[14]

There are only two ways to explain why almost every major philosophical and literary discussion of man in China ends up on the theme of humanism. One is that it represents the strongest legacy of the past that must be destroyed. The other is the behavioral implications of belief in a universal human nature and in the humanistic ethics: people will focus on the innate and downplay the possibility of change in themselves. Furthermore, in the interest of being kind to others they will not struggle with them in order to change them. People who believe in such universal traits as feelings of compassion for all others will also attribute to all people the ability to intuit a moral obligation to act benevolently to others. This is treated as a universally valid norm, and it spreads the reticence to change others to all who accept the existence of the intuitive norm. All such beliefs are opposed to the doctrine of malleability. They inhibit the transformation of men's minds.

The literary and philosophical issues concerning human nature have been reflected in very real policy disputes at high levels of government. The central issue here has been whether to minimize (from considerations of ''humanity'') or to perpetuate the ''class struggle,'' in the sense of subjecting large numbers of intellectuals and officials to intensive thought remolding and the mass of the population to an increase in political study. Pa Jen was able to publish his works about a common nature because of the encouragement of party figures like Shao Ch'uan-lin (once secretary of the Party Committee of the Chinese Writers' Union) and others closely associated with the Shanghai Academy. Shao was strongly criticized in 1964. After the Great Leap, high officials in the Ministry of Education opposed using Mao's works as basic teaching materials in middle school political courses, and in May, 1963, Feng Ting was chosen as editor-in-chief of the work *Dialectical Materialism* that was to take their place. The attacks on Feng began in 1964 and have continued. Several of the dates on which high leaders advocated playing down the class struggle have been identified, and those points have been followed by heightening of the antihumanism campaign. (For example, Liu Shao'ch'i claimed on April 27, 1957, that capitalists had changed, and so class struggle could be minimized.) If the statements made in the preceding paragraph explain why humanism per se is such an important and lasting topic in China, these political events help explain why the topic has emerged with such fury during certain specific years.

Psychology

Chinese psychologists and philosophers are fond of quoting a passage from Engels that says,

> Simply stated, animals merely make use of the external natural world, using their own being to change it, whereas man makes use of the changes he has wrought in order to force the natural world to submit to his goals, in order to control it; this is the major difference between man and other animals, and that which causes the difference is labor.[15]

They are fond of this passage because it offers a convenient authority for attacking any biological characterizations of the essential attributes of human nature. These usually involve at some point references to experiments with dogs or rats and inferences from their behavior to humans. To anyone familiar with Confucian remarks on the basic difference between man and beast (centering on man's evaluating mind and humane heart), this concern does not come as a surprise. But a casual glance at the works of Chinese psychologists during the first decade after 1949 reveals Pavlov as the heroic figure, and he, it would seem, is guilty of biologizing if anyone is.

Strictly speaking, in the Soviet Union up to the present, Pavlovianism has been regarded as belonging primarily to the domain of physiology and not psychology. However, in 1950, fourteen years after his death, the teachings of Pavlov were officially adopted in the Soviet Union as also forming the basis for psychology.[16]

In the autumn of 1953 three Russian psychologists went to work at Peking University, Peking Normal University, and Peking Athletic College.[17] Thus began the intensive study of Pavlov in China that lasted until 1958 (a year marked by increased Sino-Soviet tensions and the rise in impact of Maoist doctrines). The major centers were at the first two of these institutions and at the Institute of Psychology of the Chinese Academy of Sciences. The Chinese specialists involved were mainly senior faculty members, many of whom had done graduate work in the United States and England. They wrote basic texts, compiled course syllabi and course materials, disseminated information to provincial normal schools through journal articles, and did some rather unoriginal laboratory research into the activities of the higher nervous system. Under Soviet influence, the leading Chinese psychologists fused Pavlovianism and the Leninist reflection theory so as to constitute the scope of psychology. The processes whereby the brain reflects the objective world are sensation, memory, imagination, and so forth. These were regarded as conditioned reflexes or "temporary nervous connections." The psychologists regarded their task as to study these processes biologically.

In the long run, the rise of Pavlovianism presented a case in which the Chinese approved of the idea of malleability but eventually found serious problems with the implications of neurological plasticity. Pavlov's classic statement on the matter was:

> The chief, strongest and most permanent impression we get from the study of higher nervous activity by our methods is the extraordinary plasticity of this activity, and its immense potentialities; nothing is immobile, intractable, everything may always be achieved, changed for the better, provided only that the proper conditions are created.[18]

This statement is often quoted by Russian educational psychologists, who have some influence in the translation of theories about man into educational practices. Soviet views of malleability focus on the limitless changes to which the human nervous system is subject. There are great possibilities for men to acquire conditioned reflexes and also for these to be transformed into unconditioned reflexes. The implication of the Pavlovian thesis for Soviet educational policy is that innate differences between people supposedly associated with differences in intellect are minimized.

The doctrine we are discussing, then, is one of malleability within certain physiological limits. But the trend has been to minimize the limits and emphasize the plasticity. There are a number of arguments offered for this, all evident in the study "Heredity and Upbringing," by a Soviet analyst. First, the flexibility of the nervous system, to which I have referred before, is stressed: "But the nervous system does not remain static in its development. Conditions of life and of upbringing can reinforce or shelter the nervous system. Native abilities by no means determine future personality characteristics.[19] Second, physiological characteristics are always referred to as "potentialities" which sprout only in the proper environment.

> Each child is endowed by nature with some individual physiological characteristics which represent potentialities. . . . What is being transferred by heredity is not ready-made abilities, but only the prerequisites for their development; that is, certain physiological characteristics of the organism which demand further development are transferred from parents to children in accordance with biological laws of heredity. These hereditary prerequisites may develop, but they may wilt, depending on prevailing conditions, the nature of the educational influence, and the whole system of upbringing and teaching to which a given child is exposed. . . . Hereditary inclinations determine neither the whole process of the child's growth nor the realization of his individual potential.[20]

Third, the continued emphasis is, in fact, on the educational environment, rather than on innate characteristics.

> In the formulation of a person's view of the world, the decisive ingredients are the environment, educational goals, and the normal development of the child, not biological heredity.[21]

The final two reasons do not purport to be scientific explanations, but rather appeal to the psychological and political implications that people often draw from the doctrine of innate characteristics. The fourth reason, then, is the negative effect on children.

> It is wrong to give children the impression that unsuccessful attempts indicate lack of ability; they may lose belief in their strength and be unwilling to make further effort.[22]

Finally, it is argued that the idea of innate differences in intelligence has been used as a capitalist tool to deny equal education to workers and their children.

Similarly, during the period of Chinese borrowing from the Soviet Union, Chinese psychologists were also at pains to stress the neurological plasticity of man. The major work on personality[23] during this period was *How to Understand the Personality of Students (Tsen-yang ch'ü liao-chieh hsüeh-sheng ti ko-hsing)* written by Chang Chih-kuang, Professor of Psychology at Peking Normal University. She drew heavily on a distinction between four basic dispositional (*ch'i-chih*) types in people: choleric, vigorous, phlegmatic, and melancholic. The four types are based on three innate characteristics of the nervous system: (1) its ability to establish a conditioned reflex when presented with a strong stimulus; (2) balance/imbalance, or, on the one hand the ease with which it can be influenced by either a positive or negative stimulus, or on the other its tendency to be more excited by or more inhibited by positive or negative stimuli; (3) flexibility, or the capacity to produce the same reflex to a new stimulus. Finally, four neurological types differentiated by Pavlov are associated with the four dispositional types: aggressive and unrestrained, active and effective, quietly determined, weak and timid. But once having pointed to the innate basis of dispositional types, Professor Chang went on to affirm their plasticity. People can change types. When she talks of abilities, in order not to suggest that they are immutable, she calls them "subjective conditions" (*chu-kuan fang-mien t'iao-chien*). Character can be changed under the influence of school environment, group activities such as Youth League, outside reading, one's occupation, and the propaganda presented in radio and theater.[24]

The same analysis applies to other scholars who start from a discussion of the physiological categories common to all people (such as "temporary nervous connections"). Although they speak of innate factors that have a bearing on dispositional types, they always end by affirming the plasticity of the nervous system and thus of the types.[25] They make it clear that intellectual acumen (*t'ien-ts'ai*) is not determined by the innate qualities of the nervous system.[26]

In sum, in their analyses of human nature neither the Soviet psychologists nor the Chinese who were most influential in the 1950s can be accused of ignoring the malleability of man. But from the Chinese standpoint, the behavioral implications of analyses in physiological terms were such that beginning in 1958 the physiological approach was denounced for "biological determinism" together with ignorance of human changeability.[27] Typically, the attack was not directed at the scientific validity of the Pavlovian position but rather at its effect on people. Pavlovian principles have never been repudiated, and, indeed, have retained some role in a variety of disciplines. However, any attempt to drag them into discussions of human nature, personality, or the field of psychology is "biologizing man" (or "creaturizing man," *pa jen sheng-wu hua*, or, *jen ti hsin-li sheng-wu-hua le*).

In psychology, "biologism" is the same error that can also be found in the other fields of philosophy and literature: attributing universal human qualities (in this case, physiological attributes). In the Soviet Union a distinction is made between "biologism" and Pavlovianism. The former involves the claim that a behavioristic account of human behavior is a sufficient and complete one, and the latter involves no such claim. Soviet warfare against "biologism" is not warfare against Pavlovianism. In his later works Pavlov left no question that he was aware that school children are not dogs. In China, however, the distinction is not clearly made. An attribution of universal human qualities is believed to be associated with both "biologism" in psychology and with Pavlovian principles when applied by psychologists. The behavioral implications of belief in universal traits are regarded as so dangerous that both approaches to psychology are rejected. The implications are the same as those stemming from claims about common features in all people made by philosophers and literary figures: they cause people to focus on the unchangeable and to think that man is not malleable.[28] And all that is important to the Chinese is the expectation that people will associate common traits and the unchangeable.

The Chinese psychologists believed the problem was that people would be led by the Pavlovian inferences from dogs to humans to think of physiological variables somewhat common to all animals as therefore fixed and relatively unchangeable. They would forget about the "plasticity" of the nervous system and think only of the universal animal traits. If psychologists dragged the theory of nervous system types into studies of human conduct, they would be ''creaturizing man.''[29] Instead, psychologists should concentrate on the attribute unique to man: his social nature or thoughts. People can more easily comprehend its changeability. They will more rapidly understand the variability of man's social nature as a function of obvious social life differences in people's thoughts from class to class and also of people within a class.

The second behavioral implication of Pavlovian theory ties directly into its physiologically based notion of plasticity: except for those who have suffered some neurological damage, the material constitution of every person's nervous system is similar in the sense that each is capable of developing an almost endless variety of ''temporary nervous connections.'' The differences between people in possession of this ability are far less significant than the almost universal ''extraordinary plasticity of this activity, and its immense potentialities.'' Now from the Chinese standpoint, the negative behavioral implication of this claim is that it leads to too much emphasis on uniformity of educational experience. That is, if scholars talk of people sharing common physiological capabilities like this, educators will assume that exposing students to the same organized stimuli (teaching techniques and content) will result in their all achieving approximately the same levels of knowledge or skill. Too little attention will be paid to the differences in students' background or social life as this affects their ability to learn. (Later in this chapter we will note the factual basis for this expectation.)

Another way of describing the danger of discussing man in terms of his nervous system is that it causes people to lose sight of the ''whole man.'' This danger is not present, it is held, when the focus is on man's thought. Forgetting the whole man, people will be led to study the forms of consciousness (emotion, perception, memory, etc.) and to ignore both the origins of its content and also the ways in which that socially induced (class induced) content affects the whole range of the person's psychological life. Once again, it is the behavioral implications that count. Practically speaking, people will start treating everyone in a similar manner. They would think that because the forms of consciousness of Russian workers are the same as the forms of Chinese workers, the same policies can apply to the working conditions of both. Believing that there are physiologically determined childhood stages measured by age group in the development of the forms of consciousness, they would act as if all children of the same age group should be treated similarly.

Beginning in 1958, pace-setting younger Chinese psychologists and educators, while not rejecting the idea of the plasticity of the nervous system, redirected attention to "changeability" in a new sense. In so doing, they aligned themselves with the developments in philosophy and literature, in which attention was redirected from universal, innate human drives (e.g., survival) or sentiments (e.g., compassion) to man's social nature, which was defined in terms of thoughts.[30] The essential differences between people is said to lie not in neurologically based dispositional character types, but in their subjective class standpoint or thought.

Chinese psychological writings point to two characteristics of thought that mark it off as man's essential nature. First, it is a "higher level" of consciousness than perceptual knowledge, which is the highest level attained by other animals, because it is capable of reflecting the essence or internal contradiction of things. Second, it is subject to evaluation as good or bad; physiological reflexes are not. The Chinese insist that distinctively human activities be capable of being viewed from an ethical standpoint. Thoughts are often good or bad, or complex combinations of the two. Hence the Pavlovian influenced psychology syllabus used in classes at Peking Normal University was criticized for discussing personality in terms of dispositional types in which no distinction of good or bad is possible, and other studies reject the typological approach on the grounds that they tell nothing about who will become good or evil.[31] In addition, it is impossible to compare, for example, the aggressive activities of a dog with those of a human, because an evaluation (such as "courageous") is always a part of the human description, never a part of the dog's. This is forgotten by Pavlovians or physiologists who analogize from lower animal to human behavior.

Another characteristic of thought that accounts for its being man's essential attribute is that it often manifests itself in the kind of interpersonal action that is also distinctively human. Not all thoughts manifest themselves; there are conflicts between competing thoughts (desires) in which only one emerges in action. But when the manifestation (*piao-hsien*) occurs, it is a form of social- and class-influenced conduct. And the manifestation is likely to occur because of the association of thought with a prompting to act.

Thought is said to give a richer, more complex portrait of individual characteristics than do the physiological attributes. Educators who concentrate on thought therefore will be more likely to take into account specific environmental and personality variables of the people they educate, leading to better results in personality transformation and in achieving equality of opportunity. In other words, the negative features of an excessively uniform approach, which tends to expect people from both enriched and deprived backgrounds to have the same ability to cope with educational materials, will be reduced. Most important, there is no longer the danger that concentration on universal physiological features (such as conditioned responses) or traits common to large segments of humanity (such as physiological "types") will cause people to concentrate on the innate and forget the malleable.[32]

Pavlovianism has a secure place in Chinese science in spite of the violent attacks on its dominance of the study of human psychology. Many of the extreme and intuitively unsound claims put forth during the initial attack have been repudiated or forgotten.[33] But primacy is still given in any study of personality or character to the socially determined content (thought) as opposed to the physiologically measurable processes of reflection through which the content is "mirrored."

The officially commended reorientation of these psychologists and educators represents an introduction into the scientific sphere of the Maoist recognition of the great differences in the social environments even of people within the same class. Instead of speaking of the plasticity of the nervous system or the scientific study of how to present facts to all students, the new approach was to talk about changeability in two senses. One has to do with malleability of thought, and, hence, personality and value orientation. The other concerns malleability of skills, which follows upon changes in thought, and is supposed to occur in a manner consistent with the new value perspective. In this reorientation, China's psychological theory converged with the trends in philosophy and literature.

The Malleability of Thought

In the Chinese response to Pavlov, with its new emphasis on thought, we find the bridge between the idea of malleability and the topic of the previous chapter, a link between the two central dimensions of the Chinese concept of man.[34]

From 1958 to 1960 and since the spring of 1964, the trend among educators and educational psychologists, especially the young pacesetters glorified in the media, has been to stress the malleability of "internal causes," such as knowing this purpose or meaning (i-i) of activities, or having a positive feeling toward doing something.[35] Although educators and educational phychologists may have given token admission to the fact that the internal causes include physiological factors (such as the brain) and psychological laws (for example, those governing remembering), in practice they generally referred mainly to "thought."[36] Herein lay a departure from the theory of the period of Soviet influence when it was held that "The internal conditions are the structure and state of the cerebral cortex, the developing level and operating laws of the mental processes, the general tendencies of class tendencies of the consciousness."[37]

From whatever standpoint one might think of man, then, be it philosophical, literary, or psychological, a new perspective had emerged by the end of the first decade of the People's Republic. The new approach provided the theoretical underpinning for both differentiating between individual personalities within classes and for advocating some diversity in educational strategies. This was certainly not the first time that Chinese theoreticians had pointed in this direction, but this was the first time that this aspect of man was singled out for exhaustive consideration with consequent alterations in the treatment of human behavior in all disciplines and relevant agencies.

Among other things, molding man's plastic nature aims at the creation of proper thought clusters. Effort is directed to thoughts in the sense of knowledge of ethical principles, scientific hypotheses, and meanings. It is also concerned with thoughts in the loose sense of feelings of acceptance and approval or rejection and disapproval. The creation of new personalities and new skills is a product of both kinds of thought transformation.

Malleability of thought centered on the individual or student being manipulated by any kind of instructor. The Maoist sanction most often quoted in support of this is from *On Contradiction:*

> The fundamental cause of the development of a thing is not external but internal; it lies in the contradictoriness within the thing. There is internal contradiction in every single thing; hence its motion and development . . . and [materialist dialectics] hold that external causes are the condition of change and internal causes are the basis of change, and that external causes become operative through internal causes.[38]

Malleability was now discussed primarily in terms of facilitating the resolution of struggle between contradictory thoughts in the person's mind. This facilitation is a primary task of the educator, to be achieved, among other ways, through the reinforcement of so-called "positive points" within the contradictory situation. When the struggle is over, the change has occurred. Man has been changed. The term "contradiction" is extremely vague in Chinese Marxism. It can refer to matters that are mutually incompatible (if one applies, the other cannot also apply). The resolution of the contradiction involves the conquest of one of these by the other. The term can also refer to tension between two positions, a situation resolved by an alteration in one or both poles. For example, in the educational situation this might involve a conflict of goals where both are to some degree acceptable, but the implementation of one is seriously hindered by the pursuit of the other.

The teacher is supposed to apply the method of "one divides into two" (*i fen wei erh*) from Maoist dialectics.[39] In every individual there are both positive and negative points. In his talk at the "Hangchow Conference" in 1965, Mao said, "Our comrades are also of a dual nature; that is, they are at once correct and fallible. Don't you have a dual nature? I myself have a dual nature."[40] The instructor's job is to discover the positive and build on them in order to overcome the negative, or to detect negative thoughts and aid the individual to deal with them. For example, a model teacher was cited in 1959 for recognizing and redirecting the virtue of bravery certainly present in a delinquent who terrorized his class with a snake.[41] Even "advanced people" have negative thoughts, and so the educational work carried out on a model worker in a weaving plant involved constant attention to her mental "defects."[42] An instructor of some kind is regarded as absolutely essential in the manipulation of thought in order to accomplish change in the individual. The change does not come spontaneously. Obviously, to deny the possibility of a person spontaneously changing is not to remove all burden of self-effort from the individual and place it on outside agencies. The term "self-reform" (*tzu-wo kai-tsao*) appears in discussions of the changing of the individual's thoughts. It bears some points of resemblance to traditional Taoist and Confucian descriptions of "self-cultivation" (*hsiu-shen*) and "self-transformation" (*tzu-hua*). The major difference is in the degree of submission to formal outside instructional agencies required in contemporary China. The traditional conception left far more leeway for the individual to carry his own burden of personal educational reform.

There is nothing inherently mysterious about these actions of teachers in China. They fall under the heading of the socialization that occurs in any society. Their distinctive feature is the degree of training of the teacher himself in such practices, and in the degree of the teacher's planning and purposiveness in carrying out that socialization. Much less of the socialization is haphazard.

In addition to the manipulative activities of the instructor, there is another variable in understanding how thoughts are subject to change. They are remolded when the individual participates in certain forms of "social practice." The usual references are to manual labor as the great furnace that forges proletarian thoughts in students and others. This is extremely important, and it is used to justify productive farm or factory labor for almost everyone in China today, as it was by Khrushchev in 1958 in the USSR.

In the broad sense, social practice is often used as an umbrella term for all the activities in which a person participates and the many educational influences to which he is subject. Thus the visitor to China will be told that "we reject the metaphysical view that people are born bright; they become bright through social practice." Social practice here can refer to schoolhouse instruction, tutoring, persuasion to work harder, and so forth. Intellectual backwardness is explained in terms of the poor and uneducated milieu from which a person came and from inadequate social practice.

A second subject of malleability, related to the first (thoughts concerning especially matters of ethical principle and desire), arose as a result of the 1958–60 period of reorientation. Human nature is also changeable in that, as a result of changes in an individual's "thoughts," new abilities and skills can be forged.

However, there is a muddle in this case. There is said to be a necessary connection between thought and behavior. The latter is spoken of as *piao-hsien* (lit., manifestation). It is the manifestation of covert promptings associated with thoughts. By changing thoughts one changes behavior. The muddle is a result of the fact that *piao-hsien* can refer to two things; so the question that arises is: What behavior? On one level it is the "selfless," "persevering" and "courageous" behavior that manifests correct thoughts in the strict or loose sense. But on another level it is being adept at various technical skills. The first change that an individual undergoes (in thought) is the sine qua non for evolving new skills and abilities in the course of production or technological practice.[43] Thus man is changeable in this second sense in that skills and abilities following from right thoughts can be induced. This is the first point to be made about building skill acquisition on a base of transformed thoughts. The second is that skills that involve factual knowledge *should* be so built, for reasons that go beyond learning efficiency. The link to the proper foundation of normative thoughts ensures that that knowledge will always be associated with the proper feelings and promptings to act. Simply stated: The skills will be applied in a manner consistent with the official rules and goals.

The doctrine of the malleability of skill applies to the acquisition of routine factory and school skills. It also applies to skills and abilities that do not seem routine to the Westerner. Some examples illustrate the point rather dramatically. The following pertains to the capacities needed for becoming a good pilot:

> To learn flying well one must first be adept in the control of one's feelings, and struggle against certain incorrect ideological trends. To do so one needs strong will power. . . . Thus the excellent will power possessed by the proletarian fighter makes it easier for him to become an outstanding flier. . . . The various psychological dispositions which are closely related to aviation are rapid and correct sensual judgment, flexibility of reaction, etc. . . . These qualities are not pre natal, and much less are they immutable. They are gradually evolved and developed in the course of the accumulation of experience. For example, certain sports activities (such as ball games, sprinting, skiing, parachuting, and gliding) can train a person's flexibility, courage, and capacity for sensual judgment.[44]

Furthermore, creativity (*ch'uang-tsao-hsing*), or the ability to make inventions and innovations, can also be learned, as the following quotation attests:

> Having investigated the laws of creative thinking, the psychologists have not only smashed the heresy of bourgeois psychology, which regards creation and invention as the products of accidental "inspiration," "sudden comprehension," and the like, but have also been instrumental in promoting creation and invention, as well as in encouraging the movement for technological reform.[45]

As another example, the following statement concerns a model carpenter, credited with ninety-seven kinds of technical innovation: "All innovations are created by the laborers in their production struggles and scientific experiments. None emerge only from the empty thoughts of the inventor's Heaven-sent brain."[46] Model workers routinely attribute their ability to create innovations to thought first, and knowledge of technique second.

This position on the inducing of creativity contrasts with that operative during the mid-1950s under Soviet influence. The *Labour Laws and Regu-*

lations of the People's Republic of China (1956) provided a system of monetary rewards and administrative methods for evaluating innovations in order "to develop workers' and researchers' initiative and creative ability." The *Provisional Regulations Governing Science Awards to be made by the Chinese Academy of Sciences* (1955) established monetary and honorific awards aimed at "inspiring the positive and creative talents of scientific research workers . . . for serving the construction of the country."[47]

There is another positive feature that derives from the doctrine of malleability of thought. In addition to skill change, the manipulation of the individual's thoughts is intended to achieve another production dividend of interest to Western industrial psychologists. This is to intensify dedication to work, in much the same way as Calvinist teachings have been observed to do. Psychiatrists have dealt sufficiently with the zealousness that emerges from religious conversion to throw a certain light on the state of the transformee, which bears some resemblance to the enthusiasm of the "reborn" convert. But there are other factors operative too.

Recently students of the motivation of industrial workers, such as Frederick Hertzberg of Case Western Reserve University, have examined the psychological effects of fragmented production processes and other aspects of modern economies, and they have offered solutions. Some of these have been implemented. There have been alterations of the assembly line in some Swedish plants, a rewriting of certain job descriptions in telephone companies so that one worker handles all phases of a task, and semiautonomous worker-teams in certain automobile factories. In the latter, workers have some choice in the arrangement of part of the production process.[48] Some of the causes of worker boredom, absenteeism, alcoholism, and sabotage that brought the psychologists on the scene are remarkably similar to those discussed by Marx over a hundred years ago, at first under the topic of alienation.

There has never been much interest in the idea of alienation among Chinese. The *Manuscripts* had only a brief and limited circulation, back in 1956–57, and in the Chinese translation the term alienation was often interpreted differently from the way in which it has been understood in the West, being devoid of any reference to the psychological consequences of the division of labor. The Chinese have not profited from Marx's insights, supported by the contemporary studies just mentioned, about the state of mind of the worker participating in a fragmented job. There seems to be little interest in reducing such assembly-line-style fragmentation. Rather, the

Chinese focus on the division of labor in its objective mental-manual manifestation. In this connection they have utilized certain techniques that are consistent with some of the approaches other than reducing job fragmentation advocated by Marx for eliminating the feeling of alienation. These include some degree of popular participation (mental labor) by workers in some production decisions in the name of the mass line.

But on the basis of their theory of thought malleability, they have also covered an important base not covered in Marx's own account of alienation. The inadequacy in Marx's account lies in his discussion of the psychological dimension or feelings of lack of control in alienation. He had a naive belief in the possibility of eliminating from modern society the "manufacturing" division of labor that supposedly gives rise to it, and he had too restricted an explanation to the causes of alienation. He did not realize that industrial society brings its own causes of alienation, such as the rootlessness felt by people who move frequently from job to job, who have lost the guidance of family units and stable customs. Nor did he understand the enduring fears that are simply part of the precarious nature of all human action and life.[49] There is no reason why the disappearance of classes will have any effect on these feelings. It is unlikely that the division of labor will ever be more than minimized in any society. But that need be a matter of grave concern only if we have as limited an understanding of the causes of the feelings of involuntary action as did Marx. For, although we may not be able to eliminate the division of labor, we can cope with some other causes of that feeling.

In the Confucian classics, tranquility is the standard description of a healthy mental state. And the writers were quite precise about the way to achieve it. The *Great Learning,* for example, informs us that having a firm value standard which enables one to identify primary and secondary priorities is its sine qua non. In contemporary China this insight is perpetuated. "Having a firm standpoint" is one key to possessing the most desirable psychic condition. The other key is actually being able to live as one's standpoint would dictate. Some of the educational influences to which all Chinese are subject are intended to provide the standpoint. Additional teachings are aimed at explaining the meaning or purpose of one's work. Feelings of acceptance and approval of that work are expected to cluster with knowledge of its meaning. In other words, through fostering the appropriate clusters they teach that it is possible to live and work with one's skills and within the limitations of one's present condition in a manner congruent with one's ethical standpoint. (Chapters 5 and 6 will examine how this is accomplished.) Ultimately, success is achieved when transformation of thought is accomplished. The transformation includes knowledge of ethical principles and knowledge of the meaning of one's work (both matters of thought in the strict sense) and acceptance and approval of it (thought in the loose sense).

Reverting to Marxian terminology seldom used in China, we can pinpoint the Chinese discovery as follows: a person is likely to feel partially free, in control, and unalienated when he has a clear sense of what is good, and when he understands how the use of his skills and his other activities are consistent with what he believes is desirable. That is, when he understands their meaning. Westerners talk of feelings of freedom and Chinese traditionally spoke of feelings of tranquility. These were culturally different ways of describing the psychic state of the person who is able to act effectively because he knows what paths he approves of and is able to follow one of them.[50] There is no need for everyone to share all of the same views on the good life, and, indeed, the more severe the division of labor among many different occupations the less likelihood there will be that this will occur. The other part of feeling in control and unalienated, discussed elsewhere, is a product of some degree of participation in (not necessarily impact on) those decisions affecting a work organization that are open to mass input.

Since a cause of poor motivation is identified as lack of a clear and firm value standpoint and lack of appreciation of the meaning of one's work, the Chinese corrective measure does not require any tampering with the fragmented tasks or division of labor within a *production process* (it does involve participation by workers in certain managerial discussions). In our society a similar situation is the espirit de corps existing in certain military units, manifested in the dedication of individuals whose jobs are fragmented parts of a whole and who have little input into basic decisions about what they will do. Their dedication has its roots in their acceptance of the organization's teaching about what activities are good and their ability as individuals to use their skills in a manner consistent with those judgments.

It is generally known that the Chinese are skilled at the arousal of hatred to inspire outbursts of energy, as their promotion of "telling the bitterness" of the past attests. But the Chinese contribution to our knowledge of the solutions to worker alienation is much less appreciated. There may be various ways to achieve results similar to those the Chinese believe they are achieving. But in China, the approach rests primarily on a belief in the malleability of personality.

By focusing on the malleability of thought, the Chinese were able clearly to define the subject matter of educational efforts. From our analytical perspective, it is routinizing the formation in all citizens of the fact-value-prompting clusters discussed in the previous chapter. From their perspective, and using their terminology, it is the resolution of thought contradictions. This in turn provides a base of correct values on which is built the acquisition of technical skills that henceforth are to be applied in a manner congruent with the values.

Implications for Educational Policy

The two contrasting conceptions of malleability had concrete implications for educational policy. The Soviet conception, based in the nervous system's plasticity, led to educational uniformity; the later Chinese conception, fluidity of thought, led to a modified sanctioning of diversity. Or, one could say that one reason for the Chinese ultimately downplaying the universal trait of plasticity of neural activity lay in its behavioral implication: it would cause educators to rely on uniform teaching techniques and materials, with dangerous consequences for rural education and the egalitarian ideal. With the emergence of a new sense of human malleability, a spirit of some diversity did indeed intrude into the policies of a state that had always prized centrist controls.

The Soviet position was that, except for the brain damaged, all children ideally should be exposed to the same educational environment because all can profit from it to approximately the same degree.[51] Whether or not children will develop new abilities and skills depends ultimately on their being exposed to proper teaching practices.

The belief that as a result of the plasticity of the nervous system, proper teaching methods are able to introduce changes therein constitutes the "scientific" rationale for the ideal of uniformity in curriculum and teaching methods for all students in the Soviet Union. Economic necessities have permitted the continuation of specialized technical schools. However, except for these, all middle schools in the Soviet Union are "comprehensive," offering the same broad curriculum in the sciences, foreign languages, history, geography, Russian, and so forth. Each school serves the entire age group regardless of individual differences in "level of attainment." There is no tracking; all students cover the same material at the same rate. Although some schools are known, in fact, to be better than others, the aim is to make a given standard uniform in all.

The thrust of research in educational psychology has been directed to the question of the optimum manner of organizing and presenting materials in order to bring all students up to the common standard.[52] But in actual fact, Soviet educators themselves, in self-criticisms, were maintaining until the early 1960s that there had been more romanticism about the vague role of education in promoting the brain's development than clear thinking about the ways in which teaching actually influences mental developments. And they had paid too little attention to the student's own "internal qualities."[53]

During the 1950s, along with borrowing from the Soviets the theoretical basis for the belief in the malleability of human nature, the Chinese also took over its implications for educational theory—the ideal of uniformity. Pavlovian assumptions about the plasticity of the nervous system, personality formation, and the molding (*tuan-lien*) of abilities were adopted, almost in toto.[54] In other words, the Ministry's goal was to provide a uniform curriculum in all regular schools. The same materials were to be taught to all of the children of the same age-level at the same rate. In addition, the same teaching plans were to be used by all teachers of the same classes. The Chinese educators assumed that all children could make the grade because of the new favorable social climate and the implementation of proper teaching methods. All students were to develop into the same kind of "all-round man"; they were to become fully developed (*ch'üan-mien fa-chan*) in the spheres of general academic knowledge of all kinds, knowledge of production, technology, morality, aesthetics, and physical education. The Chinese educational materials consistently spoke of the desirability of achieving a certain homogeneity in personality development. There was no need, so the argument ran, to give undue weight to the individual's interests or abilities; both are malleable.[55] Educational psychologists busied themselves studying "typological features of the nervous system" whenever the concern with individual differences arose.[56]

From the official standpoint, an illegitimate attack (still viewed as illegitimate today) on the uniformity principle was first mounted in 1955 and erupted strongly during the Hundred Flowers period.[57] The slogan for the attack involved adding the phrase "teach according to the individual's abilities" (*yin ts'ai shih chiao*) to the previous guideline of "all-round development." Many of the proponents of this massive illegitimate attack were Western-educated teachers. However, there is strong evidence that certain officials in the Ministry of Education were covertly in sympathy with it. During the period 1954–57, a select number of schools were secretly designated as experimental units to implement the principle of varying the curriculum in accordance with the individual's differing abilities and interests. These attacks on uniformity, coupled with their usual insistence that people take account of innate differences in intelligence and abilities, reemerged during the period of liberalization, 1961–63.[58]

This illegitimate demand for termination of the Soviet approach, with its uniformity principle, was attacked in the 1950s as being a continuing echo of the John Dewey-Hu Shih educational theories. First, as understood by the Chinese, such theories maintained that innate factors are crucial in determining many of the abilities that individuals can acquire and that the primary function of education is to promote the natural growth of the innate factors that vary from person to person.[59] (The irony is that John Dewey stressed the malleability of human nature in opposition to the theories of the so-called conservative Darwinians.) Second, acting in accordance with such principles gives priority to the individual's present interests and abilities rather than to the "demands of the people," i.e., to the economic and social aspects of modernization.

Much of the argument against the pseudo-Dewey line hinges on the malleability of interests and abilities. One does not need to take an individual's present, stated interests as an unchangeable given, so the argument runs; new interests and talents can always be created in accordance with state requirements.[60] Commentators are fond of pointing to the specialists who changed fields during the anti-Japanese war. None of this is meant to deny the very real differences in people's momentary interests and abilities. Another argument (voiced in the 1950s but more pronounced during the Cultural Revolution) is that abilities are things that can only be shown through the actions of a group. Writers speak of the knowledge and ability of the group, and of individuals as being "incomplete" apart from it. People who do well are not supposed to claim credit, for their success is only a manifestation of the group's achievements, which works through them.[61] Personal significance is derived through the success of a group. A burden of responsibility also falls on others in the group to aid the slow learner. But in the end we are left with a rejection of the centrality of the principle that each person's unique individuality should be allowed to develop. Karl Marx would weep.

Beginning about 1958, Maoist opposition to the uniformity approach without succumbing to the pseudo-Dewey line took center stage. At its core was the claim that uniformity carried a pro-urban bias, with two negative consequences: it slowed the spread of educational opportunity to the rural areas, with harmful effects on the egalitarian ideal of the revolution; and it hindered increasingly the amount of rural manpower with basic-level training in scientific agronomy. Another and related reason for the Maoist opposition to the uniformity ideal was the desire to gear some part of the courses to local production needs. This meant varying the curriculum between city and countryside, and between differing rural areas. The uniform curriculum was not producing area specific job skills.[62]

The new official slogan associated with the Maoist attack on the uniformity ideal was "teach according to the man" (*yin jen shih chiao*).[63] This meant two things: that teachers must be sensitive to the varying thought configurations of their students, and that teachers and educators must be sensitive to the varying cognitive backgrounds of their students.

Instructors should investigate the whole complex of a student's desires, goals, and so forth, paying attention to the struggles occurring between them and how this affects the skills the student already has or is trying to acquire. Thus, "People's thought is always concrete, varied, and continually changing and developing. Our educational work can only be efficacious if we implement a variety of educational works, meticulously contrived in accordance with the thought conditions of each individual."[64] This general principle applies to both inschool and extracurricular thought molding. A popular maxim was called forth to identify it: "every lock has its own key" (*i-pa yao-shih i-pa so*). This also meant that teachers were encouraged to vary their presentation of material in accordance with the attitudes of people in their areas. The curriculum too can change somewhat from place to place. It is assumed that parental attitudes are absorbed by students and affect their work, or the pupils, some of whom may be adults, may have "feudal attitudes," such as not wanting to study with a young or a female teacher.[65] In some regions peasants may not wish their children to go to school, feeling that what is learned is impractical and that the children's labor is required in the fields. Model teachers there are praised for concentrating their lessons on those matters that peasants can find immediately useful and meaningful.[66] In the classroom the principle means that the teacher should constantly strive to relate the content of a book under discussion to the specific thought situation or family background of the individual student, or assign work with this in mind.[67]

In theory, the Maoist educational guideline insists that we cannot simply speak of educating persons; we must speak of educating members of a certain class, or farmers in a given region, or longshoremen, or a specific child from a specific background.[68] Some aspects of educational content, therefore, will vary in accordance with each of these types of differences. One of the reasons for the partial decentralization strands in Maoist policy is to facilitate this kind of variety in content by giving some local people some voice in curriculum.

Emerging from the conflict between the new line of diversity and the deeply rooted centrist tendencies were new policies after 1970 that drew on both sources. They contrasted with the uniformity of the first decade, and yet they represented a definite withdrawal from the strongly localized initiative of the period from 1964 to 1970. If we take primary and middle schools as examples, a period of local experimentation was concluded with the requirement that certain sections of many courses be the same in all regular schools. Thus portions of the textbooks on Chinese history, mathematics, Chinese language, and geography were to be the same. But allowance was to be made for a portion of the material covered each semester to be specific to provinces or to urban or rural areas. For example, only twenty of the thirty lessons to be covered in a Chinese language course had to be uniform throughout the country; the remaining ten would focus on tales of heroes and models from the local province. The use of additional texts of a local nature to meet local needs was always permissible. Further, in mathematics and the natural sciences, teachers were to have the right to assign written exercises that would be more appropriate to urban or rural experiences and production needs. The courses in basic agricultural knowledge and basic industrial knowledge would change from place to place depending on the actual crops and production specific to that area. Provinces would always be permitted to introduce new, more efficient ways of teaching a subject. Thus there was to be local input at the start, even though democratic centralism prevails in the end. Materials used in universities are subject to more provincial variation than are those used in lower grades.

In addition to a toleration of limited diversity, the spirit of the new period encouraged irregular scheduling of class meetings where needed to accommodate the unusual work habits of herders or boat people, or other special circumstances. Extra funds were to be made available to the poorer school districts as well.

In sum, the new orthodoxy advocates an education in which special attention is paid to people's thoughts (forging correct values, goals, and attitudes) and which takes account of their varying cognitive levels and probable knowledge needs. It is accurate to describe the Chinese position as a belief that inner causes (correct thoughts, wishes) can have important effects in changing the material world.

The Chinese malleability theory contains a deeper and more comprehensive confidence in the changeability of people than is found in the Soviet Union. In principle, thoughts can always be altered. The Soviets have taken a more conservative position on the legitimate expectations of inducing change. A. V. Lunacharsky, the First Commissar of Education of the Russian Republic, conveyed this point:

> We can mold a child of five to six years into anything we wish; at the age of eight to nine we have to bend him; at the age of sixteen to seventeen we must break him, and thereafter we may say, "only the grave can correct a hunchback."[69]

The Chinese retort would be that there need be very few "hunchbacks" in any society.

In addition, there are major Maoist departures from classical Marxism. It is not the way a man produces that is the primary determinant of his nature or his thinking. It is the kind of education he receives, of which laboring is just one kind of educational experience. In addition, the new man is not defined as one who has the full development of his individual capacities. Rather, he is one who has a different set of values from that which he used to have, and some development of the three capacities he shares with all people; for physical, intellectual, and moral growth.

The centrality of the idea of malleability in Chinese Marxist theory can be viewed in part as a product of revolutionary optimism. Just as it may be believed that a people can rapidly be transformed from being "poor and blank" to being advanced, so may individuals be similarly changed.

Like any other central Maoist concept that we examine, malleability may dominate the theoretical literature, but this does not mean it is never challenged in sentiment, policy advocacy, or practice. Rural practice, reinforced by vagaries in the official policy of remembering class struggle, has continued to cause old class designations to stigmatize individuals long after the classes are eliminated. The research of Martin Whyte and William Parish, Jr., indicate that bad class labels have been handed down even to paternal grandchildren, making such individuals special targets during campaigns. Their class origin may be cited against them in consideration of their entry to upper middle school or university, of their request for welfare or cooperative medical assistance, entry into the militia, or search for a marriage partner.[70] Not only do such practices ignore the official principle of malleability, but they also ignore the aim of campaigns intended to apply that principle, such as ones stressing deeds or manifestations (*piao-hsien*) rather than family background. In the mid-1960s, Chou En-lai laid out the thrust with the statement that one cannot choose one's family, but one can choose one's road.

As emphasized in the Preface, we are concerned with the Maoist concept of man. Indirect opposition to aspects of malleability are also reflected in rather sophisticated debates over economic theory. In the early 1960s, for example, one of the prominent economic voices was Lo Keng-mo, and one of the popular topics was the nature and connection between productive forces (tools or level of technology, raw materials, labor force) and production relations (matters concerning the interrelations between workers, managers, owners; matters concerning distribution of income). Lo took the anti-Maoist position that changes in the forces are a precondition of any changes in relations and in cultural matters or those pertaining to thought. Visually, the three are related like a pyramid, with the forces as the base. In other words, changes in workers' thought may be delayed a long time as changes in the forces gradually evolve.[71] There is no evidence in these debates about the size of Lo's following.

The enduring importance of the idea of malleability is not to be found in any dimension of the idea itself. Rather, it lies in the psychological effect that belief in malleability probably has (and, in China, is officially required to have) on those who subscribe to it. The belief that people are educable is a self-fulfilling prophecy which may produce the effort or the climate that makes possible some change for the better in individuals. The importance of such a psychological attitude can be illustrated by an example from the United States. Discussing the impediments to prison reform and the continued high rates of recidivism that demonstrate the failure of American penology, a leading psychiatrist isolated what he has come to realize is a key to the failure of so many attempts at reform:

> We do not really believe, most of us, that they can be rehabilitated, that they *can* change for the better, or that it is worthwhile making the effort.[72]

Would a self-fulfilling prophecy of malleability make some difference in the matter of penology?

In the realm of education, there is a well-known study entitled, *Pygmalion in the Classroom: Teacher Expectation and Pupil's Intellectual Development,* that examines increases in the learning of ghetto children in the United States as a function of their teachers' high expectations.[73] Although the data in the study have been criticized as defective, the affirmative answer that the authors give to the question of whether "teacher's expectations of their pupils' performance may serve as self-fulfilling prophecies" has been increasingly supported by other students.[74] Many teachers have never seriously examined one of their basic assumptions, i.e., that certain children have innate or otherwise unchangeable limitations in their abilities, and that it is of no use for the teacher to expect more of them. The psychological implications of the doctrine of nonmalleability are as powerful as those of the opposing position.

Contrary to their orthodox Confucian ancestors, Chinese theorists today make such statements as

> When a person is born, he does not have a bad or a good nature. The kind of a person he will grow up to be depends entirely on the kind of education given him by his objective environment.[75]

Of course, they share with their predecessors the faith in the wonders of education. However, it would be erroneous to regard the Chinese conception of the mind as simply the proverbial blank sheet of paper. As we noted in the previous chapter, it is assumed that writ large on the paper from birth are tendencies to cluster knowing factual distinctions, feelings that carry value judgments, and promptings to act. This innate disposition to cluster helps explain the belief in malleability. Since knowledge (*szu-hsiang,* or consciousness) is linked to attitudes and ultimately to action, anyone's attitudes and behavior can be altered by changing his knowledge or consciousness. These interwoven attributes of man, when combined with the otherwise malleable characteristic of the human personality, form the background for the Chinese doctrine of the function of government. The responsibility for state nurturance of the mind is linked to its claylike plasticity, within the limits of the mind's innate tendency to cluster. The beliefs of people will probably be associated with promptings to act in a manner congruent with their judgmental feelings. The nature of those acts must be determined as much as possible in advance for the sake of the group so that the clustering occurs in a goal-directed, controlled rather than haphazard manner.

Chapter 4

The Function of Government

There is an intimate connection between ideas of human nature and doctrines about the desirable function of government. In premodern Chinese political thought, the outside analyst can identify the phenomenon of clustering and the idea that people are perfectible through education as twin supports for the view that fostering the development of the people's social nature is a desirable function of government. In contemporary China, the notion of malleability has entered the picture to provide a third bolster for that function, serving to add new dimensions to the idea of perfectibility. The common core is the absence of belief in innate or early childhood impediments to the manifestation of highly desirable personality traits and the presence of optimistic assumptions about man's possibilities.

All of these points pertain to the psychological foundations of the theory of government. As such, there is a limit to what we can infer from them: namely, that a central function of government will be treated as the transformation of the social natures of the citizens, and that some of the time the explanations of this function will involve reference to these psychological foundations. We cannot infer that the major explicit statements about the function of government will always be stated in terms of these background assumptions. Rather, it predictably will be stated in terms of categories and principles that are regarded as orthodox by Chinese Marxists. These include some drawn from Marxism-Leninism (in particular, the categories of theory and practice and democracy and centralism) and one from China's own revolutionary experience (the mass line). But Mao defined and systematically worked these orthodox terms and ideas into a doctrine in complete harmony with a conception of the state required by the psychological doctrines examined in the previous chapters.

It is natural to associate the idea of verbal instruction or the use of models with our statements about state fosterage. But verbal instruction and model presentation in schools and study sessions constitute only an especially important part of the picture. Fosterage also is accomplished through changes in what Marx would call the social relations of production: by involving workers in some managerial decisions; by forming ''three-in-one'' groups of workers or peasants, technicians, and cadres in which a certain amount of role switching occurs; and by requiring office workers to do manual labor. Like verbal instruction and model presentation these changes also have as a goal the transformation of people's social natures (in these examples, creating the trait of the willingness and ability to do mental and manual labor). As Mao wrote long ago:

> What do we have to give to the people? . . . It is to organize them, lead them, help them to develop their production, improve their material welfare, and, on this basis, gradually uplift their political consciousness and cultural standard.[1]

Similarly, all the steps that have been taken in the direction of minimizing inequalities of distribution (chapter 8) have included character transformation as a goal. The negative trait of egoism, as a craving for personal wealth and status, is associated with the existence of wide income gaps. But as in the case of malleability, the Maoist voice has not been the only one heard. The economist Lo Keng-mo explicitly claimed that in certain kinds of enterprises, such as coal mines, it is not possible to make changes in production relations. That is, the mode of distribution of wages and/or relations between managers and workers cannot be altered until there are changes in the production forces, or tools and raw materials. This would mean, in contrast to the Maoist position, that it is not possible to depend on such relational changes now as a bolster to other state fosterage efforts used to transform people. The explosive Maoist retort would be that if the relations are not changed, the forces will once more take on characteristics of a capitalist stage (see chapter 3, note 7).

None of this is to claim that the idea of proletarian dictatorship is unimportant in understanding the role of government in China. Indeed, this derivative element in Chinese Marxism is also important. At times, it may act to justify further forms of manipulation and indoctrination. Forceful action in the name of the ''dictatorship'' may be necessary as a first step to insure that such changes as worker participation in managerial discussions actually are allowed to occur. At times, coercion by the proletarian dictators of so-called class enemies actually takes front stage in official statements about the government's primary aims, conflicting with the government's more benign educational policies touted with equal vigor another day. Our claim is simply that enduring from the pre-Communist period and still sustained with considerable strength by its relation to the contemporary assumptions about human nature is another view of government, that of fosterage. Even though submerged from time to time, it is also present, potentially in tension with the doctrine of the coercive role of the dictatorship of the proletariat. Although we focus on the fosterage function in this chapter, we must admit at the outset that the most accurate portrayal of the role of the state in Chinese Marxism would refer to this tension.

Marxist and Soviet Theory

In German Marxism, the closer society evolves toward communism, the less directive or manipulative of the lives of the citizens the state becomes. Its coercive nature is increasingly minimized after the victory of the proletarian revolution. Actually, at no time in German Marxism does the state gain the central explanatory position in accounting for the fate of the human condition. The primary cause of man's unfortunate condition under feudalism and capitalism is said by Marx and Engels to be the division of labor (and then social classes) rather than any special feature of the state. The latter does enable the privileged to continue their exploitation of others, maintaining a legal system that keeps the poor poor.[2] During the period of transition to socialism, the state becomes an apparatus for the proletariat to exercise its dictatorship over the bourgeoisie, and it is a highly manipulative, coercive mechanism. As communism is approached, however, two external changes in society are occurring which, once achieved, diminish the necessity of an interventionist state: the elimination of the division of labor and of private property. The coercive state apparatus gives way to administrative functions.

Classical Marxism draws a distinction between man's personality and his needs, and views that ideal society as that in which the individual is able to fulfill his capacities. The needs are always there. Coercion is necessary to end the division of labor and the property system that prevent people from realizing them. However, once the proper social relations exist, the values people acquire in those relations will permit them to find satisfaction in expressing their needs. State intervention is minimal after successful revolution at every point in the Marxist analysis. The emphasis is on creating social institutions congenial to static dimensions of human nature and to free expression of individual capacities. In contrast, the Russian view has little place for individual fulfillment in its portrait of the ideal society. Continued state education and coercion are practiced and justified in orthodox theory. Human nature is not defined in terms of needs.

During the 1920s, the most prevalent portrait of man and of government in Soviet philosophical and psychological circles was more consistent with the classical Marxist stress on enduring human needs than was a new doctrine that emerged in the 1930s. The main point of continuity between the classical Marxist and Soviet conception of the 1920s was: human nature changes for the better automatically when social institutions are changed, and also when people struggle in a manner that changes their consciousness. In tandem, an anarchistic spirit pervaded the views of these Russians on the role of the state. There was a good deal of talk about the state withering away after economic changes and class elimination take place. Law codes were seen as having only short-term usefulness: ''We refuse to see in law an idea useful for the working class. . . . Religion and law are ideologies of the exploiting classes . . . we have to combat the juridical ideology even more than the religious,'' wrote one jurist.[3] Schools were often loosely run on a nonuniform basis under the assumption that if students have something interesting to do, they will develop and become cultured.

Nevertheless, with one exception, it is doubtful that the conception of man theoretically operative during the 1920s had a substantial impact on ordinary Russian citizens at that time. One reason was the gradual change in outlook of Lenin himself, symbolized in the differences between the anarcho-syndicalist views of *State and Revolution* (1917) and the pessimistic demand for a highly manipulative state apparatus in *Left Wing Communism, An Infantile Disorder* (1920). Actually, the worker's control of factories and self-government by soldiers, advocated in *State and Revolution,* were implemented for only a few months after the victory. ''Temporary'' measures to ensure state survival in the face of civil war and economic ruin (''War Communism'') were retained as a means more rapidly to attain communism. And the need for straight coercion and party control of the masses in the ''dictatorship of the proletariat'' was reinforced in Lenin's mind by failures of the Communist movement in other countries, where it was crushed or took the soft road of parliamentary process. Institutional changes were not sufficient; direct party manipulation of the people was essential to guarantee progress in utopia. Hence the transition from worker control to the secret police, federal commissars, and mass organizations.[4]

Only in the schools of the 1920s was there widespread concrete influence on the people of the belief that individuals will be changed when their social institutions are changed. Adumbrating developments in China thirty to forty years later, part-work part-study institutions were organized in an attempt to eliminate the division of labor between mental and manual labor.

The new portrait of man that emerged in the 1930s in the Soviet Union helped to define part of the content of the manipulative function of government from that point on. If men, conscious of goals and purposive in their pursuit, can telescope changes in nature and society, one state function is to teach them the proper goals. Thus propaganda and training in *voispitania* (upbringing) have become the means for attaining this end. But far more than in China, the state has come to be viewed as a set of omniscient individuals with unique access to the Truth, or, more modestly, through whom History works.[5] Their function, then, is to discover Russia's current needs in the context of their more fundamental knowledge of the morphology of history, and to shove the rest of the country in the directions indicated.

One can trace this latter approach to Lenin's claim about workers prior to the proletarian victory, that

> The history of all countries shows that the working class, exclusively by its own effort, is able to develop only trade union consciousness. . . .[6]

The workers must be led by "scientific socialists," most of whom came from the bourgeoisie originally. The workers are not capable of attaining "consciousness" in the sense of an accurate appreciation of history or the problems of the present.

Throughout Soviet writings the reader encounters remarks about each person's enormous potentiality for development. Such remarks appear inconsistent with the limited possibilities just described for most citizens to acquire theoretical knowledge. In fact, Soviet references to human plasticity normally are speaking about any one of four things: (1) that there are no innate I.Q. differences between nationalities or classes, and, most intelligence testing is biased in favor of some educationally privileged group; (2) personality is determined primarily by environmental (including school training) factors. Thus, both inherited factors and early childhood experiences (such as the Oedipus complex) should be downplayed if they suggest something unalterable in the personality; (3) the individual's motives and interests are not fixed at birth but can be molded into congruence with the demands of the state; (4) correct teaching materials have a great deal to do with the ability of students to learn new skills. They are more important than innate abilities. None of these four is inconsistent with the claim that certain people in the USSR have a superior understanding of the course of history, of the problems of the present period, and of the best policies for dealing with them. The essential characteristic in the new concept of man can still remain; man the purposive builder of socialism, who is conscious of his goals and able to free himself from the constraints of the moment by pursuing them. Quite simply, one can be a goal seeker without having extensive knowledge of why the goals are appropriate. That knowledge can be and usually is limited to a few.

Contemporary Chinese Theory

The Chinese have absorbed Soviet justifications for a manipulative and coercive post-Revolutionary state. Yet crucial differences between their positions remain. In China, included in the concept of malleability is an additional element: given the changeability of personality and the receptivity to the acquisition of skills implied by the four Soviet principles, theoretical knowledge can be rapidly attained by most citizens. It is attained through a combination of practical activity and classroom instruction under the guidance (fosterage) of the state, if personality change proceeds in tandem.

The two dimensions of the concept of man in China examined in the previous chapters serve as the dominant foundation for the doctrine that the primary function of the state or ruler is fosterage of the social natures or minds of the citizens. That doctrine stems partially from the phenomenon of clustering. The fact that knowing and feeling frequently have action consequences moves these ostensibly private events of knowing and feeling outside the exclusive concern of the individual. They become a matter of society's concern as well. Hence, as the instrument of the group, the state assumes an obligation to ensure that individuals' beliefs, theories, and feelings are of a kind likely to elicit promptings to act in a manner conducive to the well-being of society as a whole.

The other dimension of the concept of man in China from which the fosterage function is derived is malleability. In Confucian terminology, remedial action (personality transformation) was described as "recovering the original nature" (*fan hsing*). There are no innate impediments to achieving more desirable personality traits. The other side of the same Confucian coin indicates a significant attribute with which man is born: all people have a mind that is capable of learning. This belief reinforced confidence in the potential success of state fosterage.

The common ground between Neo-Confucian and Maoist positions is not the presence or absence of innate abilities, but rather the optimistic assessment of man's potential for seeing the light, in the absence of unalterable defects of endowment. The existence of this potential places a burden on rulers to ensure that the learning occurs.

In addition to the psychological foundations and the Confucian legacy of perfectability, the fosterage function owes a third debt, to the guerrilla experience, for the concept of the mass line. With its obligation on officials to listen to the masses, reflect, and then teach them, this doctrine plays a central role in the explicit formulation of the educational duties outlined later in this chapter. At present our concern is merely to consider the various sources of strength for the idea that the government can and should rapidly use schools, required experiences in social practice (especially labor), and changes in "social relations" to produce new persons. One of several reasons for the regular selection of Marx's *Critique of the Gotha Programme* for study has been to reinforce priorities: Character transformation takes precedence over other goals, such as distributional equality. The new person is described in these terms:

> This kind of laborer is a completely new man who can do things cultural and martial, can serve in a high or low position, can not only successfully do mental labor but also manual labor, and unite the expert and the laborer, the intellectual and the worker-peasant.[7]

A final explanation for the belief in the fosterage function derives from the Chinese applying to the goal of creating a new man that telescoping of time that Marx and the Russians had applied to developing a new economic order in Europe. In Marxism and Russian communism we find a variation of the idea that backwardness contains the seed of rapid progress.[8] Marx felt that an advanced society impinging on a less developed one would cause it to move through necessary historical processes more quickly than it otherwise would. Socialist ideas from England and France had penetrated a partly feudal Germany attracting some of the workers. Although a bourgeois revolution would still be necessary, if properly led the workers could force their capitalist allies in the antifeudal revolution into turning feudal estates and large industrial establishments into public property. This would telescope the transition from capitalism to socialism. Around 1905 Trotsky and Lenin independently worked out a doctrine having some embryonic similarity to that of Marx, but they associated the rapid transition with events that made total nonsense of Marx's and Engel's historical materialism as it has traditionally been interpreted (see pp. 102–3). Lenin and Trotsky claimed, in effect, that a small number of people could first make revolution and then use their position to create the highly developed industrial base that in historical materialism should have preceded the revolution by the workers and that is an essential concomitant of socialism.

If the Bolsheviks inverted the temporal order for the creation of a socialist level industrial base, the Chinese have inverted the order for the creation of the "new man." Their approach asks: Why cannot those same revolutionaries first make revolution and then, long before the socialist level of economy is achieved, use their position to begin forging through education the new man whose imminent emergence is also associated with socialism? One does find this latter idea in Russia, but it is especially pronounced in China. Once again, the reasons are contained in the assumption that the human psyche is blank and malleable, as well as in the fragile relation believed to exist between men's social natures and the purely economic conditions in which they live. This telescoping of changes stands in marked contrast to the gradual transformation of people associated with the major Marxist writings, discussed in chapter 1.

The discussions of man's rapid transition from an undeveloped state into the "new man" echo something of the traditional dialectical movement from weakness to strength. The classical Taoist works put the doctrine in the context of the reversal of opposites:

> "To remain whole, be twisted!"
> To become straight, let yourself be bent.
> To become full, be hollow.
> Be tattered, that you may be renewed.
> Those that have little, may get more.[9]

In Confucianism, the principle that in weakness is the seed of strength often meant that the objectively (militarily) weak but virtuous ruler would attract the people of his enemies to himself through his example, thereby becoming stronger.[10]

Let us conclude this discussion of the foundations of fosterage by considering the vocabulary and imagery used to describe it. In China there was a long history of conceiving the ruler-ruled relations as patriarchal, i.e., between the people and a ruler who is "Son-of-Heaven" and "father of the people." Although it was proper to speak of the "government's" function, referring to fosterage carried out by the ruler and his official deputies, at times, Chinese writers referred to one person's acts. That is, the fosterage by the emperor himself rather than by the entire governmental apparatus. The same holds today. Whereas in the United States we denote by "government" a collective body and speak of its protective relation to the people, Chinese writers often substitute the single person (such as Mao) and speak of his fosterage relation to the Chinese masses; as in the expression "nurtured by the sunshine, rains and dews of Mao Tse-tung's thought . . ." the masses, etc., etc. (*tsai Mao Tse-tung szu-hsiang ti yang-kuang pu-yü hsia . . .*).

In addition to *pu-yü* (to nurture), the other terms that literally convey the sense of fosterage in Chinese are *yang-ch'eng* (to nurture), and *p'ei-yang* (to cultivate). The latter is used to refer to general educational efforts directed at the populace as well as to specialized "cultivation" given to prospective models and party members. Since long before the ascent of the Chinese Marxists, educators have been compared to farmers, having a duty to learn and apply what is best for the plant. This was one of the favorite images of Ts'ai Yüan-p'ei (1868–1940), the leading educational official in early Republican China. He was continuing a practice used by the earliest Confucians, who commonly analogized between governing and farming, and between human development and plant development. People are transformable, and changing them is the ruler's duty, in an educational manner described in the *Book of Rites:*

> When a ruler is concerned that his measures should be in accordance with law, and seeks for the assistance of the good and upright, this is sufficient to secure him a considerable reputation, but not to move the multitudes. When he cultivates the society of the worthy, and tries to embody the views of those who are remote from the court, this is sufficient to move the multitudes, but not to transform the people. If he wishes to transform the people and to perfect their manners and customs, must he not start from the lessons of the school? The jade uncut will not form a vessel for use; and if men do not learn, they do not know the way in which they should go. On this account the ancient kings, when establishing states and governing the people, made instruction and schools a primary object.[11]

The *Doctine of the Mean* spoke of the sage "assisting the transforming and nourishing powers of Heaven and Earth."[12] Neo-Confucian writers stated that "The gentlemen . . . should act for Heaven in its work of governing and nourishing the people."[13]

Today, we not only encounter the references to "the nourishment of Mao Tse-tung's thought" but also the common use of agricultural imagery:

Saplings can only grow and become useful timber if they are constantly under the care of the gardener. If we want to bring up children and train them to become successors to communism. . . .[14]

Even when the specific agricultural language is not being used, contextual evidence indicates that the rulers are still perceived as fostering the people's development when they are properly carrying out their responsibilities. Mao said that he wished to be remembered as a teacher, thus conveying his vision of the proper function of rulers.

Having noted the philosophical foundations and language of fosterage, we are in a position partially to fill in its theoretical content. That is a mixture of elements from the past and from twentieth-century Maoist principles. The former contributed the broad definition of education as including formal and nonformal training, and a long tradition of educational obligation felt by officials or those inspired by Confucian orthodoxy. The latter provides a theory of the origin and ultimate consumption of truths conveyed in the training.

Traditional Patterns

If the primary function of rulers is fosterage, the question arises as to how many people actually are affected by their educational practices.[15] The answer is exceedingly complex when one is referring to premodern China, and precision is impossible at this point. Yet we can say that a complete answer would include reference to three points. The first is official government schools. The relatively small proportion of the population ever directly affected by these schools might lead one to question the importance of fosterage in traditional China. However, the scope of fosterage expands significantly when the other two topics are introduced. The second is unofficial schools, the curriculum of which was patterned after that in the official schools. Such schools would not have existed to the degree they did without both the official and general social approval of Confucian education that stemmed from the concept of fosterage and the privileges that may accrue to some of those who received it. The third is education carried out by village elders, magistrates, and parents. Education was broadly conceived to encompass all attempts to transform the social nature of man, within or outside the schoolhouse, and so this too must be mentioned in any discussion of the breadth of fosterage. One can rightly ask: Do not similar people play a role in the socialization of children in all societies? Yes, to varying degrees. But in China, they were required to play it and would be held more than routinely accountable for deviant behavior perpetrated by their charges that supposedly reflected their own negligence in nurturance. Therefore we must look beyond the formal school. By doing this we can discover factual information to round out the picture we already have from Confucian theory concerning the broad terms in which education was viewed.

The T'ang period is an appropriate starting point for talking about official schools. The "institutes" and "halls" that provided advanced education (*ta hsüeh*) at the capital were, with one exception, open only to the offspring of people of specific ranks. For example, the Imperial Institute accepted children of members of the third rank and up and the Grand Institute accepted those whose fathers were of the fifth rank and up. But the Institute of the Four Gates not only allotted five hundred places to sons of officers of the seventh rank and up but also made room for eight hundred commoners (*shu-jen*). During the Sung, commoners were able to enter the Grand Institute through competitive examination. During the Ming, when the Imperial Institute and the Grand Institute were combined, some of the students came up from the county level schools through examination. But there were also alternative gates. High officials in the civil bureaucracy could choose one son to enter the school directly. Members of families of those of lower ranks who died in connection with a government enterprise could also send a son. Commoners could purchase admission. And there were provisions for foreigners (such as Koreans), members of border region minority groups, unemployed youths who had inherited titles, and for the offspring of people who had made great contributions to the state.[16]

In addition to the schools at the capital, there were counterparts by Sung times at the prefectural, provincial, and county levels. The curriculum was Confucian, similar to that in the capital schools, although there were significant variations in quality. A strong impetus for establishing them came in 1045 with an imperial decree that a county could establish a school if there were over two hundred students available for enrollment. Most of these schools were upper level. One source states that during the Ming there were over seventeen hundred of these regional schools, with a student population of seventy-six thousand, and that in the Ch'ing, although the number of schools remained about the same, the student population decreased to twenty-seven thousand. During the Ming, the state also gave some support to regional schools of Yin-Yang Studies (concentrating on the *Book of Changes*), medicine, and military arts. As early as 629 there had been a decree ordering the establishment of regional medical schools.[17]

The government also subsidized some scholarly academies (*shu-yüan*) beginning in the Sung. The Ming emperor T'ai Tsu ordered the creation of "community schools" (*she hsüeh*) to provide moral training to the rural masses. They were to be financed by local magistrates, who were to select their teachers from among resident exemplars of good conduct and scholarship. The curriculum was to be modeled after that of the Imperial Academy, emphasizing especially loyalty to the throne and the study of biographies of virtuous models. In the Ch'ing, their number was expanded as a result of K'ang Hsi's so-called "sacred edict," and, once again, the teaching of loyalty (to the Manchus) was stressed. Subsidies were usually provided for poorer students. At the same time, however, in the first part of the Ch'ing, many of the *she hsüeh* terminated formal teaching, only to revive in the late nineteenth century, when they hired *sheng-yüan* degree holders as teachers. This period of dormancy helped stimulate the growth of private schools, to which we now turn.

The initial blossoming of nongovernmental schools that offered basically a Confucian curriculum occurred during the T'ang, when government schools declined as a result of the weakening of state power itself. These community controlled schools (*hsiang hsüeh*) did provide some education to commoners.[18] However, one should not infer that the education was sufficiently sophisticated or the importance of aristocratic connections so minimal that such schools provided much of a channel into the capital schools and the civil services.

Acting in a private capacity in Academies (*shu yüan*), Confucian scholars both disseminated their own philosophical and political positions and also taught groups of students that might number one hundred. The academies emerged at the beginning of the tenth century and retained a quasi-independent status until the end of the Ming. Several hundred academies are known to have existed in the sixteenth century, some of which stood clearly opposed to the existing government.[19] During that century academies took over institutions that had been parts of the official school system, when they served as registration centers for holders of the First Degree and ceremonial buildings for Confucians and local gentry. Retired officials often did the teaching. Prior to the Ch'ing, many of these academies were financed by local groups. The tuition was low, sometimes free, with students getting a stipend (called "candlelight money"). In addition to degree holders and children of official families, the student body included bright youths recruited by scouts. In spite of their quasi independence, the academies' staffs normally were products of the Confucian educational process themselves and continued to have close links to the bureaucracy. In addition, the education offered was in its core content traditional Confucian fare like the Four Books, the Five Classics, and poetry.

One should not underestimate the education that took place outside of government schools through the efforts of Confucians acting in homes in a private role as teachers, or through the impact of their ideas. Obviously, many of the Confucian teachers taught because they had failed the examinations or had been removed from office. But the Confucian principles helped determine the appropriate profession for them to enter. And at the popular level one can never ignore the pervasive stimulus to study or the Confucian dictum that every person can become a sage.

Some of the officially jobless Confucians served as teachers in "charity schools" at the primary level (called *i hsüeh*) that might be financed by a clan or group of gentry.[20] As community schools (*she hsüeh*) that had been subsidized by the government became centers for ceremonial activities, the charity schools took over more and more of the local educational functions during the Ch'ing period.[21]

Finally, no consideration of the extent of education in traditional China should ignore the informal learning that affected many who had no hopes of entering an official school or the civil service. As far back as Han times village elders were obliged to give Confucian sermons periodically to their fellow villagers. They preached about filial piety, chastity, compassion for those in distress, and scholar officials who could serve as models for the people.[22] In later periods, they were required to read to the people imperial edicts that had a didactic purpose. The Shun-chih emperor (1644–61) of the Ch'ing, who revived a system of mutual moral-reinforcement (the village-covenant system, *hsiang yüeh*) by villagers, put forth "Six Edicts" to enlighten the people. A holder of the lowest examination degree (*sheng-yüan*) and village elders were supposed to address the people in a community twice a month and read to them the edicts, which enjoined them to be filial, to educate their children, to honor the aged, and so forth.[23] At other times, the primary school teacher was supposed to give the community lectures.

Texts directed at the education of common folk were produced on a wide scale in the T'ang. These were called *Meng ch'iu,* and they were in existence before A.D. 746.[24] Tales of officials, prime ministers, scholars, generals, immortals, and emperors filled their pages. Proportionally, most were personages of the Chin and Han dynasties. The themes ran the gamut of the desirability of diligence in study, of the dangers of disloyalty, of rulers who loved their subjects, and of the blessings and tragedies of the harvest.

Tadao Sakai has traced the evolution of popular encyclopedias originally intended for civil service candidates. First appearing in the Sung, they contained sections on preparation for examinations, poetry, history and customs, children's education, and household affairs. By the Ming period their audience and hence their content extended to all classes, within the usual limitations of illiteracy or poverty. They often contained passages such as ''for ready reference in daily needs of the four classes.''[25] Once again, the content of such popular educational works was primarily ethical.

Sakai has also pointed to the spread among all classes during the Ming of popular morality books (*shan shu*). Virtue is rewarded, vice punished. But the main point in these books is that people of differing classes have different obligations, and any assessment of a person's moral worth must take into account what is appropriate for his status.[26]

The conclusion one must draw from the variety of educational media in premodern China is that the range of people affected by some of the forms of instruction (not necessarily written) was substantial. Fosterage in accordance with Confucian principles was occurring on a large scale even when it was not financed directly by the state itself. And the number of individuals who benefited from private or official formal schooling, especially during the Ch'ing period, is much larger than most Westerners have believed. These distinctive cultural facts about China are effects of the special value placed on education in a country that regards the fosterage of minds as the major function of those in authority.

The Maoist Prescription

It has been necessary to present the material on traditional patterns in order to meet a predictable objection drawn from Chinese history—that very few people attended imperial schools, which seems inconsistent with the claim that Confucians regarded fosterage as the key state function. Using a far less extreme case, the objector could also point to the existence in the People's Republic of some high level opposition to rapid expansion of formal schools at the cost of lowering the quality of training at the upper levels. The same principles we have described in premodern China point to the proper perspective for understanding fosterage in contemporary China. Education involves more than communication of factual information to create skills; it aims primarily at character development. Thus education and moral education are not differentiated. Furthermore, it is erroneous to think only of the schoolhouse when considering vehicles for character development and the state's performance of its function. Our task for the remainder of this chapter is to examine the theory of fosterage as it is worked out in contemporary terms, as a basis for the subsequent discussion of the situation as it actually applies today within and outside the school.

Otherwise stated, we must go beyond the legacy of traditional, legitimate governmental intrusions in education to find an additional explanation for the fosterage role of government in Maoism. The philosophical underpinning of fosterage can be found in the Maoist theory of knowledge. Relevant aspects of that theory in turn form a central dimension of the "mass line," or of the Chinese perception of democracy in the polarity of "democratic centralism." Hence the fosterage role feeds right into this important political concept. But the mass line does not stand alone. "Centralism" is ultimately invoked to ensure that the final authority which is entitled to identify the truths that have originated with the masses, which should be returned to them in more sophisticated form, is the party leadership.

There is no evidence more striking of the fosterage purpose of the center or for its theoretical content than the on-going relation between Maoist epistemology and the Maoist theory of the function and methodology of leadership:

> In all the practical work of our Party, all correct leadership is necessarily "from the masses, to the masses." This means: take the ideas of the masses (scattered and unsystematic ideas) and concentrate them (through study turn them into concentrated and systematic ideas), then go to the masses and propagate and explain these ideas until the masses embrace them as their own, hold fast to them, and translate them into action, and test the correctness of these ideas in such action. . . . Such is the Marxist theory of knowledge. [1943][27]

As Oh-Hyun Shin so brilliantly demonstrated, an analogy between a person engaged in learning and a single or collective group of leaders links the two doctrines.[28] In learning, a person engages in practice (producing perceptions), then employs reflective thought in the brain (conception) to formulate theories on the basis of the perceptions. He then applies the theories in practice, which will refine the theories again, raising their truth value, in a continuing cycle. By analogy, the leaders work with, live with, or talk with the masses to gain ideas (akin to deriving perceptions from practice), return to their headquarters to articulate and systematize what they have learned from the masses (akin to reflection in the brain, leading to conceptualization and theory), and then convey it to the masses for action (akin to testing in practice). Of course, as individuals, each member of the masses and each leader does both perception and conceptualization.

Leaders improve the cognition of the masses by themselves performing the role of a processing plant (as the single or collective brain of the people), where proletarian consciousness is produced in the form of theory, as opposed to unsystematic ideas. But the leader(s) must return with such theories to transfer them to the masses through education (the second level of practice) and through having the masses participate in policy implementation, about which they are simultaneously educated (as in changing the social relations of production). From an epistemological standpoint, the final test of correctness of the centralized ideas or theories lies in the masses' implementation of them. Conception must be returned to practice in the form of policies, programs, and lessons in their meaning. This final requirement is achieved by the leaders in their fosterage role (then the cycle, beginning with the feed-back of new practice, starts again). "On Practice" and the doctrine of the mass line, when interwoven, contain much that is original and fundamental in Maoist thought.[29] Mindful of this, one can easily grasp how firmly anchored in basic Maoist doctrine is the educational function of government.

In the first stage, the leaders attempt to solve class, production, or scientific problems with ordinary workers (practice). This purposive involvement provides them with knowledge of the particular historical conditions of their epoch, and with an understanding of the interests of the masses. In the second phase, the leaders summarize what they learned through practice and then integrate that information with what they have already learned through their study of the universal truths of "Marxism-Leninism Mao Tse-tung Thought" (for officials at the second level).[30] This produces "rational knowledge," meaning theories, principles, and policies. In accordance with a distinction made by Mao in a short essay entitled, "Where Do Correct Ideas Come From?" (1963), the achievement of rational knowledge is called "the first leap," i.e., from matter to consciousness.[31]

The third phase is the actual nurturance by the leaders; the protracted educational effort (with books or models or in new social arrangements) whereby they attempt to cultivate the people's social natures, causing them to grasp the theories, principles, and policies, and to form the proper clusters. Once the people grasp the ideas, they will necessarily implement them and thereby change conditions. This process is logically prior to the Maoist claim that the people and the people alone are the motive force in the making of world history. Phase three of the continuous cycle is the transition "from rational knowledge to revolutionary practice," and it is described as "the second active leap," i.e., from consciousness to matter. Mao wrote:

> . . . while we recognize that in the general development of history the material determines the mental and social being determines social consciousness, we also—and indeed must—recognize the reaction of mental on material things, of social consciousness on social being and of the superstructure on the economic base.[32]

This "second leap" applies to the goal of creating a new man (who in turn creates a new society), the telescoping of time that Marx and the Russians applied to developing a new economic order in Europe.

In philosophical terms, the process whereby leaders become agents of social transformation has since the 1960s been called "the dialectical identity between thinking and being," which has become a central theme in the Maoist theory of knowledge.[33] It points to a claim concerning the effectiveness of returning theoretical knowledge to the masses (in short, the scope of their educability). This claim has been at the center of high-level political debate in China. The claim is that all efforts put into educational nurturance ("thinking") can be matched by quantitative or qualitative outputs in the social and economic realms ("being"), providing that people have such traits as "knowing the meaning" of their work.

The terms "thinking" and "being" come from Marx, and the most famous passage in which they appear is in his Preface to *A Contribution to the Critique of Political Economy:*

> The mode of production in material life determines the general character of the social, political and spiritual process of life. It is not the consciousness of men that determines their existence, but, on the contrary, their social existence determines their consciousness.[34]

"Thinking and being" in the Maoist phrase are equivalent to "conscious-ness" and "existence" in this translation from Marx. Marx is quite specific regarding the meaning of each. Existence refers to the two economic conditions of production that gradually conflict with each other, property relations (governing ownership) and forces of production or kind of technology. The former gradually becomes a hindrance to the development of new levels of technology, and the struggle leads to transformation of the economic conditions. Consciousness refers to "the legal, political, religious, aesthetic, or philosophic—in short, ideological—forms in which men become conscious of this conflict and fight it out."[35] The Maoist interpretation departs from Marx's both in its definition of consciousness and in its affirmation of the dialectical identity of consciousness and being, with less stress on the temporal priority of the latter over the former.

The term "consciousness" is one of the vaguest in Marxist vocabulary. Lenin sometimes used it in such a way that ordinary workers were capable of having it, as when it referred to their anger at their condition under capitalism and to their acceptance of party direction. At other times it was characterized as a unique possession of party members, as when it refers to such things as a knowledge of the states through which history will move, and understanding of the present historical age and its particular contradictions, and an ability to work out suitable plans for dealing with those contradictions.[36]

In Chinese, "thinking" (or "consciousness," *i-shih*) refers to the same things it does in Lenin's discussion of party members, plus a knowledge of how to apply general principles to concrete, local conditions. The term that describes the content of consciousness in the aggregate is "Marxism-Leninism Mao Tse-tung Thought." However, there are differences between the earlier Marxist and the Chinese usages. In China, it is regarded as crudely originating with the masses, from whom it is learned and articulated by the few leaders. After successful nurturance, it becomes the rational possession of the masses as well. Mao described the situation in these words: "Once the correct ideas characteristic of the advanced class are grasped by the masses, these ideas turn into a material force which changes society."[37] Thus one can rephrase the function of government as cultivating in the people the ideas that will enable them to change society.

Actually, the third phase refers to either one of two different events: simply putting a policy or theory into practice, or "the turning of ideas into a material force." The meaning of the latter requires analysis, both because of the vagueness of the words themselves and also because this is what many writers are talking about when they refer to "Maoist voluntarism." In some discussions it denotes the extraordinary psychic energy that a properly educated people bring to their work. This energy is believed to have its origin in several sources. The confidence that the leaders have in the people's ability to perform miracles is expected to act as a self-fulfilling prophecy, causing the people to exceed routine production goals. The people's spontaneous obedience to directives in which they play a consultative role is believed to increase overall efficiency. The people are selfless, and the selfless who work for the group good set higher standards than those seeking personal reward. Finally, and most important, those who know the meaning of their work have high morale that increases their productivity. All of these consequences of leadership nurturance produce "material force" in the sense of unusual work effort. In other contexts, there is a rather different meaning; "turning ideas into a material force" can refer to achieving a qualitatively superior or innovative result in work as a consequence of applying a superior problem solving methodology. That methodology is also a product of proper educational practices, and once again a set of procedures is believed to feed into it. One is self-reliance. Another is the general availability to the people of scientific principles through simplified instruction. A third stems from people being habituated to making the transition from textbook theory to practical application, with the result that their book knowledge is useful to them. Finally, everyone's problem-solving ability is increased through the pooling of knowledge that exists when technical models travel from place to place and guild secrets are opened up in the spirit of the public interest. More innovative workers exist as a result of the nurturance.

An important conclusion emerged from this clarification of "turning ideas into a material force." It is inaccurate to portray this as the doctrine that human *will* is more important than objective economic variables in determining historical change. Such a description completely ignores the cognitive elements so often involved. These may include a factual understanding of the interrelations between jobs (part of knowing the meaning) or they may include a grasp of simple, scientific problem-solving methodology. In any case, there is normally something more than will involved, and that is why education is so time consuming and pervasive.

The elaborate Maoist theory of nurturance cannot coexist in the same system with the Marxist materialist conception of history as it is often interpreted. This traditional interpretation demands that historical stages be characterized by at least four traits. First, the class that is to be dominant in the stage to come must lead the revolution that ushers in the new age, and it must remain the class holding political power once the revolution is complete. Second, all economic developments appropriate for a given age must occur in it before the next one emerges. As Marx says in his Preface to *A Contribution to the Critique of Political Economy:*

> No social order ever disappears before all the productive forces for which there is room in it have been developed, and new, higher relations of production never appear before the material conditions of their existence have matured in the womb of the old society.[38]

Third, there is a time lag between economic occurrences, in which relations of production come to fetter forces of production, and the reflection of them in consciousness in the form of ideology. Fourth, the historic stages are of long duration.

The Maoist attempt to change China rapidly is inconsistent with every one of these. The proletariat is in charge of the state during part of the presocialist phase, rather than the bourgeoisie. Socialism is declared achieved before the industrialization associated with capitalism has had a chance to flower. Elements of ideology often precede rather than follow the appropriate economic changes. And the time span necessary both for the presocialist phase and for the creation of new persons with the traits appropriate to a communist state are very short. How Marxist Chinese Marxism would remain if these are inconsistencies and if historical materialism were rejected is a problem that the Chinese, obviously, never face but that is of no small interest to an outside observer evaluating Chinese philosophy.

Some recent studies of Marx find a more congenial place for Maoism in that Marxist tradition. They claim that Marx did not believe in a strict progression of historical stages for every society, but only for Europe, allowing flexibility in the predictable evolution of a society like China. Also, they focus more on the continuous interaction of consciousness and matter than on a narrow interpretation of "matter determining consciousness."[39]

According to Maoist writings during the Yenan period and after 1955, the primary instruments of fosterage are a small number of individual leaders (especially Mao himself) rather than the party or members of the proletariat. Both of the latter require constant moral and technical nurturance from the few leaders. They are not capable of being vehicles for the transformation of society without it. This is contrary to the views of Lenin, who believed that party members already had technical and organizational skills necessary to building socialism. In China, rank and file party members can become second level interpreters of correct principles to others, while still subject to continuing education themselves.[40]

At the secondary level, wherein lower officials devise implementational policies in accordance with national guidelines, there is much discussion of the return cycle back from "matter to consciousness," which means treating policies or theories like hypotheses, to be revised if expected occurrences do not materialize. There is less of this at the top level.

To claim that the formulation of the principles conveyed through state nurturance rests with a few individuals is not, in Maoist theory, to assert that those few have any innate superior intellectual capabilities. Rather, they have had the proper background of practical involvement with the masses in solving problems, combined with the theoretical training needed to integrate and interpret those practical experiences. The masses are the ultimate source of knowledge, and the masses can absorb significant amounts of rational knowledge that the rulers, in their fosterage role, pass on to them.

One of the two most striking differences in the concept of man in contemporary China from that of the Soviet Union, based in the Chinese idea of malleability, lies in the view that ordinary people are capable of achieving accurate knowledge about philosophical issues and concrete social and technical matters. On the one hand, they can obtain it directly through their own involvement in problem solving. Their wisdom needs only to be adequately articulated by people who emerge from their midst (such as the present leaders). Furthermore, that wisdom can be articulated by professional philosophers and others after returning to their offices from a cooperative working experience with the people. On the other hand, when taught, the masses can understand matters relating to the "essences" and "laws" of things. The malleability of ordinary people again underlies their ability to master through study theoretical material of all kinds. This means that the nurturance of the leaders should not be limited to manipulating motivation without providing understanding. Mao remarked in 1966, "It is to the advantage of despots to keep people ignorant; it is to our advantage to make them intelligent. We must lead all of them gradually away from ignorance."[41] The ability of people both to learn important truths through practice, which must be "concentrated" by the leaders, and to comprehend the theory passed down to them from the top is stated in these words by Mao, "[We] must learn from the masses, formulate our policies, and then educate the masses. Therefore, if we want to be teachers, we have to be pupils to begin with."[42] Mao was fond of saying, "The lowly are most intelligent; the elite are most ignorant."

If the epistemological foundations of state fosterage in China reinforce the "democracy" side of democratic centralism, the centralism component is by no means neglected. It exists with the requirement that the official Peking interpretation of truths supposedly emanating from the masses be agreed to by all. But it is by no means intuitively clear that central decision making on this matter is intrinsically desirable. Indeed, there has regularly been tension between the centralism and democracy dimensions of the polarity, sometimes suggesting that the central interpreters are less than omniscient.

In the final analysis, the most important function of government is fosterage. If for Marx, actually serving as "the vanguard of the proletariat" is sufficient for socialist leaders to claim legitimacy, in China it has also included, along with protecting China from foreign enemies, "being in the service of the people."[43] The most important service the leaders feel they carry out is fostering the development of the people's social natures.

The human significance of the differences in philosophical beliefs between two societies can often be found in concrete cultural practices. In the case in point, the Chinese reworking of the Leninist seed concerning proletarian consciousness is unique in its assertion that ordinary people can achieve accurate knowledge involving theory tested in practice. There are two practices in China not found in the Soviet Union that are directly associated with this. One is the use of the mass line. Like the idea of fosterage, the doctrine of the mass line serves to create tension with the otherwise coercive, centrist, tendencies that derive from Soviet ideology. The other is the quantity and quality of political and moral education to which all people are subject, in order to ensure that every kind of technical knowledge taught will be related to intelligible moral knowledge, paving the way for an understanding of its meaning. In addition, such training ensures that people will have not simply zeal for work but also cognitive awareness of such things as the interrelationships between tasks to be done. Maoism does not glorify will and exclude factual knowledge in its vision of the basis of human power.

Like so much of Maoist thought, the fosterage conception of government is inspired by elements from Confucianism, from Marxism-Leninism, and from the guerrilla experience. Confucianism in its Mencian form suggests that people are perfectible if rulers provide the "rain and dews" to nourish them. Leninism suggests that telescoping of change is possible and permits the question: if true of creating an industrial base, why not true of creating new men too? The guerrilla experience (this element contributing most to the explicit formulation of government's role) provides the mass line, which, when combined with the Marxist ideas of theory and practice, insists on rulers transmitting theory to masses. A complete account of the conception of the state's role should point to these three sources of inspiration as well as to the psychological foundations discussed in previous chapters.

The Maoist theory of fosterage is unique in Marxism in the confidence it assigns to the learning capacity of ordinary citizens. High level policy disputes have arisen as a result of certain aspects of this position that are normally cloaked in purely philosophical language about the relation of "consciousness" and "matter." The contemporary implementation of fosterage in and out of the schoolhouse is the subject of the next two chapters, as is a consideration of the specific theories appropriate to each place. Having examined the principles of fosterage and their application, however, we can still insist on knowing what precisely is involved in "transforming the minds of people." Is fosterage really education, or "persuasion," as they call it? Is "coercion" also involved? If so, what form does it take and what does its existence imply? In chapter 8 we will attempt to answer these questions in our evaluations of the strengths and weaknesses of the Chinese approach.

As a final word, one should note that fosterage is important in China today as in the past in giving rise to what is often the first and most significant step by officials in facing any urgent political or social problem: radical alterations in the educational system and intensive extracurricular study by ordinary citizens. This is consistent with the belief that deviant acts are traceable to improper thoughts. Such a response can be described as the education panacea, carried out by officials sensitive to supposed shortcomings in previous acts of state fosterage.

Chapter 5

The Role of the Schools

Among the most successful plays produced during the National Modern Drama Festival in Peking in 1956 was "Bright Skies" (*Ming-lang ti t'ien*).[1] One of its central characters was an American doctor named Jackson who founded "The American Medical College" in Peking and then turned over his data on health and disease in China to "imperialists" for bacteriological warfare in Korea. Run of the mill plot. But there is an important episode in which the audience learns that Dr. Jackson had murdered a woman suffering from rickets because of a scientific interest in studying her deformed bones. The message was one to which Chinese have been exposed in various forms in Confucian and contemporary China: that specialized knowledge not guided by proper moral principles is dangerous. A similar thought was conveyed by a former Peking student, recently arrived in Hong Kong, who remarked about a Cousteau documentary on undersea life: "I suppose I found it interesting, but I could not recommend it because it had no educational significance." That is, it had no moral guidelines for using the knowledge about sea life to serve the interest of human beings.

Both examples indicate a common concern that clusterings of knowing, feeling (evaluating), and promptings to act occur in a desirable, predictable manner. When the government carries out its fosterage function it attempts to ensure that people will associate facts with the proper evaluations and will be primed to take the proper actions in relation to those facts. It is not necessary that this instruction occur in special courses designated as "political study." Chinese writers often refuse to distinguish political and moral education.[2] Thus they do not always make quite as clean a differentiation as Westerners are accustomed to encountering between, say, study sessions spent reviewing official decrees, and classroom time spent learning about mathematics and how the student should utilize mathematical knowledge. Both are aspects of the process of nurturance.

The target of the fosterage is the malleable social natures of the citizens.

> Some people believe that children will become good naturally when they grow up.... This is wrong.... A youth's development from infancy to adulthood depends entirely on the kind of education that the objective environment (parents, family, school, and society) bring to him.[3]

As one can see from this statement, the education that nurtures is conceived in the broadest sense, referring to training that occurs in the schoolhouse, the home, the work organization, the theater, and the public news media. The present chapter analyzes the principles developed in previous chapters as they apply to formal education. We shall first describe an important heritage from the Confucian tradition—the legitimacy criterion—and then outline the lessons provided by the Soviet experience. The stage is then set for a detailed analysis of the development of educational theory and practice in modern China.

Confucian Heritage: The Legitimacy Criterion

One of the most important consequences of clustering has been the development of a criterion which we have called the "legitimacy criterion," that has affected the content of education and scholarship in both Confucian and contemporary China. The phrase "legitimacy criterion" is not a precise translation of any single Chinese term. Rather it is the closest one can come to capturing the operational meaning of several different Chinese expressions used at different times. Thus in pre-Republican China, the term *tsung-chih* (platform of leading principles) was most frequently used, whereas since 1949 the term *fang-chen* (guideline) has been rife. In essence, this criterion means that in order to be considered a legitimate part of any curriculum, material must be conducive to learning or implementing the rules or goals contained in an orthodox ethical system. Its aim is to ensure state control over clustering. It requires that the learner be conditioned to associate facts with normative principles that have been officially approved. Thus, the criterion rejects the division between factual and evaluative educational information and insists that they are usually inseparable.

The most common goals of study stated by Neo-Confucian philosophers were to become a "sage" (*sheng-jen*) or "to be an ideal person" (*wei jen*).[4] A sage is a person in whose mind facts and values are always properly associated. There was general agreement among Confucians on the need for a legitimacy criterion to ensure that study does build ideal persons, although there was considerable variation in the views concerning the manner in which study and other forms of cultivation leading to sagehood should be carried out.[5] There was also disagreement about what type of material satisfied the conditions of the criterion.

In their roles as government officials, the Confucians necessarily had to articulate their view of the function of education in a different manner from that which they would employ as philosophers addressing individuals. It was to train people to serve the dynasty (*yang shih*) through the inculcation of administrative, literary, and ritual knowledge required of state employees. But the materials used in such training programs still reflected the philosopher's legitimacy criterion, though with special stress on the theme of loyalty to the ruler.

The existence of a criterion determining educational legitimacy caused all subjects in an approved Confucian curriculum to contain moralistic commentaries. The origins of this criterion antedated the ability of Confucian officials in the Han to achieve political power. The most obvious example is the nature and love poetry of the *Book of Odes*. Confucius himself helped to start a tradition of regarding these poems (a few of which actually are didactic) as guides to moral instruction.

> For the *Songs* will help you to incite people's emotions, to observe their feelings, to keep company, to express your grievances. They may be used at home in the service of one's father; abroad in the service of one's prince.[6]

Sometime around the middle of the second century B.C. one or two scholars named Mao issued a version of the *Odes* which came to have great influence. In its brief introductions to each poem and glosses on individual words, it explained the moral meaning of a poem. A joyful song indicates the composer lived in an ordered society. Or, using metaphorical interpretations, for example, a jilted lover is said to stand for a mistreated official complaining to his ruler about the abuse he has suffered.[7] There was a gradual evolution from the scholar's tendency to find didactic messages in all texts that custom taught were a rightful part of schooling, to the explicit pronouncement that all literature should convey ethical teachings.

Although there was a return to the respect for a literature that was free from moralizing during the Six Dynasties Period (A.D. 220–589), the criterion was merely somewhat dormant. And although Chu Hsi (1130–1200) eliminated some of the Han Dynasty's more tortuous political interpretations of love poems in the *Odes,* he too affirmed that they were largely didactic.

Confucians were ambivalent toward mathematics, some regarding it as of minor importance and others disagreeing. As one of the ancient "Six Arts" (Ritual, music, archery, charioteering, calligraphy, mathematics) it had the weight of tradition behind it, at least at the elementary level. But the rigor with which some of these arts were taught by Confucians is problematical; classical precedent may not always have been honored in fact.

When mathematics was taught in either the orthodox Confucian curriculum or in the specialized institutes, the Confucian justification normally took one of two positions. Either it was conducive to moral self-development ("sageliness within") by introducing one to regularities in accordance with which the universe operates, so that one could harmonize his own behavior with the natural rhythms. Or, it was of utilitarian value in pursuit of the value of "serving society." Yen Chih-t'ui of the Northern Ch'i dynasty (A.D. 500–577) gives us an example of the former rationale:

> Mathematics is also an important part of the Six Arts. Since ancient times, Confucian scholars who discussed the ways of Heaven [*T'ien-Tao*] and who set the calendar all mastered it. But it is something one can become enlightened about as supplementary; it is not something that one should specialize in professionally.[8]

Mathematics was important to Confucians as an aid in designing the new calendar with which every dynasty began, and as an aid to the parallel design of the almanac. The almanac set the appropriate times for government supervised planting, for playing certain kinds of music, and for performing endless other acts that had to be done at the right time in order to ensure that happenings in the human sphere were harmonious with those in the heavenly realm. But the term "calendar" also suggested temporal sequences that the individual should observe in his own conduct, and Yen Chih-t'ui was addressing himself primarily to the benefits that accrue to the individual in his own attempts to bring his conduct into harmony with the rhythms of nature. A Confucian who articulated the other justification of mathematics as something useful in serving the people ("kingliness without") was Lu Shih-i, who lived in the early Ch'ing. He wrote:

Mathematics is one of the Six Arts. It appears to be not of great moment, but actually is a matter of considerable pressing importance. All questions about nature, natural regularities, water conservation, military methods, and agriculture, need to use mathematics. If you do not know it, or are acquainted with it without having mastered it, you cannot talk about being of some use to society [*yung shih*].[9]

As might be expected, the great synthesizer Chu Hsi has generally been interpreted by subsequent Chinese commentators as appealing to both these justifications for studying mathematics. In this view, mathematics can be justified in its elementary forms for inclusion in the curriculum as conducive to sageliness within and kingliness without. At the higher levels, where it becomes more theoretical, mathematics becomes increasingly difficult to justify in accordance with the Confucian legitimacy criterion. Certainly Confucians could not look favorably on one who specialized in it. It is revealing that late Ch'ing scholars such as Liang Ch'i-ch'ao tended to categorize advanced mathematics as "Western learning," as though it were outside the parameters of legitimate Confucian subject matter.

Even the ostensibly specialized technical curricula were saturated with ethical training. Thus, the military program in the Sung included a course on loyalty, requiring the daily study of biographies of model figures, and in the Ming it included study of the *Analects, Mencius, Five Classics, Seven Books,* and the *Biographies of the Hundred Generals.*[10] Medicine, called the "benevolent art" was regarded as among the emperor's welfare responsibilities to his subjects and a field about which any filial scholar should know something in order to care for his parents. Medical instruction in government schools included the study of biographies of Confucian doctors (*ju i*), who had some literary background and practiced in order to help others rather than to gain financially.

Because the present book concerns contemporary China, the illustrations that would most convincingly demonstrate the continuity of Confucian and Communist interest in employing a legitimacy criterion should be drawn from the latest possible moments of Confucian practice. Confucian theory was never consistently implemented in practice; the legitimacy criterion was not always observed. But in the face of the foreign cultural threat, for many decades after 1840 the Chinese manifested a conscious commitment to enduring Confucian principles like the criterion, that in previous periods may sometimes have been neglected.

Examples can be found in both the regulations of individual schools and the pronouncements of educational officials in the second half of the nineteenth and early twentieth centuries. In these documents, the term most often used to convey the idea is *tsung-chih,* which means "platform of leading principles," "purpose," "standard," and is usually used in phrases such as "the purpose of learning . . ." (*li-hsüeh tsung-chih*). Thus in issuing renewed regulations for schools in 1903, Chang Pai-hsi, Jung Ch'ing, and Chang Chih-tung wrote, "The leading principles [*tsung-chih*] of learning, regardless of what level of school it is, should be to take loyalty and filial piety as the root and the Chinese classics and history as the foundation. This will ensure that students will in mind return to purity and uprightness."[11]

By 1910 when government regulations were issued for so-called "reformed private schools," at the lower level mathematics had been added to the minimum curriculum. But the ordering of that four-part curriculum by priority is revealing: Self-cultivation (*hsiu-shen*), national language, the Confucian classics, and mathematics. Invariably, the self-cultivation section of the curriculum is listed as the most important part of the schooling.[12]

There were qualitative differences between the elementary and upper level education received by youths in late imperial China, but they reflected primarily supposed differences in a child's intellectual powers before and after the age of fourteen. In addition to learning to read and write (often using simple Confucian texts), elementary education involved a form of behavior conditioning in which the child memorized songs and poems about proper deportment or about models of proper deportment. After fourteen, there was more stress on the student consciously selecting and then emulating models by himself.[13] But at both levels the purpose of the training was the same; to become an ideal person from an ethical standpoint.

It would be incorrect to suggest consensus among educated Chinese on the optimum way to carry out education or on the degree of disdain with which specialized technical training was regarded. We have been discussing dominant cultural trends, not matters of universal belief. The existence of an element in Confucian doctrine like the legitimacy criterion does not mean that historically it was always observed. The Confucian-oriented civil service was not always populated by generalists steeped in the classics. (Robert Hartwell has described the financial experts in the Sung government and Madaleine Zelin has pointed to the role of the specialist in the eighteenth-century bureaucracy.) The legitimacy criterion simply endures as a possible source of tension, even when not being observed.

In medieval China such ideas helped constitute the philosophical under-pinning of the special cultural characteristics of Chinese education: there is a qualitative differerence between training that helps transform the social nature of people, and at the same time turns them into suitable candidates for official positions in the civil service, and other technologically oriented forms of state education. The former is superior to the latter. Also, where feasible, even the latter should contain as much moral training as possible. Thereby it too can attain some partial congruence with the legitimacy criterion.

The legitimacy criterion continued as a force even during the Republican period. From 1911 to 1922 many school texts still stressed Confucian values. The period from 1922 to 1928, when there was extensive copying of American practices in modern primary and middle schools, was the only time in which the principle was largely submerged.[14] The language of America's progressive movement shines through the official guidelines emanating from Peking in 1922, although it is doubtful how clearly they were understood or implemented. Teachers and administrators were en-joined to help develop the unique personality of each individual student, give special attention to the bright students (*t'ien ts'ai chiao-yü*), teach environ-mental adjustment and job-skill preparation because education is "prepara-tion for life," and universalize education.

Although many Western-educated teachers continued to revere these ideas derived from America's progressive education movement, the Nationalist government abolished the American style middle school and a number of its core principles in 1928. The authorities reinstated the emphasis on moral education. The officially stated purpose of education that directed school practice in the 1930s and 1940s was that education should support nationalism. A 1944 summary of the basic guidelines lists moral training (*te*), physical development (*t'i*), and intellectual and technical skill training in that order, with first place to moral education.[15] Many Chinese educators in the first part of this century, such as Ts'ai Yüan-p'ei, gave the appearance of seeking to establish a new educational philosophy and structure appro-priate to the modern world. Yet even they often reflected the Confucian principles that set the very concept of knowledge culturally apart from any European counterpart. Although condemning education as it was carried out in the Confucian school and advocating the importance of the individual's interests, Ts'ai ended by stressing the role of education in transforming "the myriad things into one harmonious family."[16]

The Soviet Experience

In spite of the legitimacy criterion's enduring strength, its appearance in contemporary China was by no means unopposed or easily worked out. Although Soviet educational guidelines gave the appearance of congeniality to the enduring assumptions, in the end they were found both confusing and in many ways uncongenial. In order to understand why the contemporary Chinese in the end returned to many theories and practices that were distinctively Chinese, we must first take note of those Soviet experiences.

In terms of basic orientation, Lenin was compatible in spirit with the Chinese legitimacy criterion. We need only take note of these remarks:

> The entire purpose of training, educating and teaching the youth of today should be to imbue them with communist ethics.[17]

> The contents of education . . . and, in particular, instruction in philosophy, the social sciences, and communist moral education, must be determined solely by the Communist Party.[18]

However, the vagueness with which Lenin used the term "education" (*obrazovanie* or institutional education, as opposed to *vospitanie* or morally oriented upbringing) accustomed his audience to associate with the term all possible directed forms of training. The same fuzziness is evident in his interchangeable use of the terms education and propaganda, so that the line between teaching Marxist philosophical truths to the masses and manipulating them through passion arousing slogans was blurred.

If one separates out from moral education those teachings that pertain to *vospitanie*, much that is left is rather abstract.[19] It does not clearly indicate to the learner the nature of social goals and how academic material is to be integrated with articulated social duties to produce concrete acts to further those goals. The Soviets stress that academic knowledge should be presented so as to help the student develop a "Communist world view." I. A. Kairov, who became Minister of Education, spelled out the principle in 1943, when he said that "every school subject must contribute to the development in the pupils of a materialistic conception of the phenomena of nature, social life, and the mind of man."[20] The official encyclopedia made a similar point about textbooks in 1956: "the textbook [*uchebnik*] covers the scope and content of ideas in the curriculum program, assists in the elaboration of the bases of a world-view [*mirovozzrenie*] for pupils and in developing their thought, memory, and speech.''[21] About the subject of world view, the 1964 edition of the Soviet *Encyclopedia of Philosophy* states, "In our time, the properly revolutionary working class and its Communist Party, i.e. Marxism-Leninism, and dialectical and historical materialism constitute the philosophical worldview.''[22] Creating a materialist world view is a very different goal from the Chinese one of conditioning students to relate their factual knowledge to personal, social obligations or current official policies. This factor in the Soviet approach was regarded as a defect by the Chinese.

There is a further point specifically on the matter of mathematics and the sciences. Mr. Kairov did state that mathematics develops the method of "dialectical thinking in pupils" and "at each step confronts the pupil with the manifestation of such laws as the conversion of quantity into quality and the unity of opposites.''[23] Chemistry reveals "the unity of the structure of the material world" and contributes to the "formation of a dialectical-materialistic world outlook," while physics teaches the students "that the material world exists objectively, outside and independently of our consciousness.''[24] However, it is far easier to make these claims than it is to prepare useful textbooks that convey them on every page. The very vagueness of a "world outlook" in contrast to the specificity of scientific and mathematical information militated against any significant saturation of these materials so as to accord with Leninism and the Kairov guideline for all subjects.

If the Chinese could find in Leninist pronouncements a statement of educational principles quite congenial in form to those that had such a long history in their own culture, they could find no support from Marx. At the General Council of the First International, Marx said,

> Political economy and religion ought not to be taught in the lower grade schools or even in the high schools; adults should be left to form their opinions on these matters, about which instruction should be given in the lecture hall, not in the school. Only the natural sciences, only truths, which are independent of party prejudices, should be taught in the schools.[25]

The spirit of these words is opposed to moralistic saturation of academic study.

On the other hand, one Marxist educational notion that was not at all congenial to anything in China's past did have a profound effect on both

Soviet and Chinese education. This was that some production experience should be combined with academic instruction. The purpose was to break down the distinction between mental and manual labor, in line with progress toward eliminating the division of labor; and to ensure that students learn to combine theory and practice.

In the Soviet Union, the concept of polytechnical education was introduced in order to implement Marx's principle. Through exposure to many types of productive labor (*poly*technical), the many facets of Marx's all-round ideal person could be cultivated. During the 1920s a system called the "unified labor schools" made some progress in this connection. However, from the 1930s on into the 1950s, there was a return in fact to nearly complete formal academic education. The term polytechnical did not drop out, but, as Nicholas De Witt has concluded, almost anything except reading a textbook or listening to a lecture was passed off as polytechnical: work in the school workshop, laboratory work in natural science courses, the use of visual aids in instruction, and visits to factories.[26]

In 1958, though not without forewarning, Khrushchev and some other Soviet officials publicly and passionately took note of the deficiencies in Soviet education that were impeding the New Man ideal.[27] Essentially, the criticisms state that previous school policies had tended to create habits of thinking abstractly instead of concretely, and about issues that are separated from real social life.[28] Concurrently, it had promoted snobbism. Khrushchev stated:

> "We still have a sharp distinction between mental and manual work. . . . This is fundamentally wrong and runs counter to our teaching and aspirations. As a rule, boys and girls who have finished secondary school consider that the only acceptable path in life for them is to continue their education at higher schools. . . . Some of them even consider [work] beneath their dignity."[29]

Speaking of new changes in the wind, Pravda said that now, in contrast, "a genuine cultural revolution is being achieved."[30] Manual labor was ordered back into the formal curriculum.[31]

For many reasons, the reforms were abrogated by Khrushchev's successors in 1964. But the discontinuities between the educational products of the previous Soviet approach and the New Man ideal were already obvious to the Chinese from the Soviet's own self-criticisms, if not from their Chinese vantage point. There were compelling reasons to look elsewhere for guidance concerning ways to combine facts and values in the schools.

Chinese Theory and Practice

Beginning in Yenan, Chinese Marxists gradually developed educational guidelines that were distinctively Chinese. These principles were submerged temporarily during the period of Soviet influence from 1953 to 1958. But they reemerged under Mao's direction in 1958, waned briefly, and then rose once more in 1964 to endure until the present. By the 1970s, the guidelines were not in all ways identical with those first appearing in Yenan. But, as in the earlier years, they have remained consistent with the spirit of the age-old legitimacy criterion. We will begin by examining the theoretical core of these principles, and then illustrate their role in practice since the 1940s.

The Social Utility Criterion
In its application to contemporary Chinese education, the legitimacy criterion has two dimensions. Both are routinely quoted in policy documents and the prefaces of textbooks, published in 1972 and 1973, and they are prominently displayed on school walls and classroom blackboards. First, any material that is presented to a student should in some way reinforce his awareness of rules of conduct or social goals, or contain indications as to how the material, when used by the student, is conducive to the realization of social goals. This aspect is conveyed in Mao's statement: "All of the work of schools must be for the purpose of transforming the students' thought."[32]

The second dimension delineates the content of the rules and goals, conveying some sense of their ultimate purpose. This dimension is described in two different statements by Mao. One lays out the all-round development ideal: "Our educational policy [or "guideline," *fang-chen*] must enable everyone who receives an education to develop morally, intellectually, and physically and become a well-educated worker imbued with socialist consciousness."[33] This guideline has served functionally as an argument to reduce the amount of regular academic material covered in courses in order to make room for more directly moral and political studies and for sports and physical labor. The other statement addressed to the content of the rules and goals is: "education must be in the service of proletarian politics, and it must be combined with productive labor."[34] This guideline has played the primary role in determining the content of courses per se. It is the justification for including a labor requirement for all students from primary school up. That portion that refers to being "in the service of proletarian politics," or "in the service of the people," a widely used equivalent, has had the most effect on the content of all textbooks, teaching outlines for instructors, and curriculum design (remember the interchangeability of ethics and politics).[35] In short, it is the key to the legitimacy criterion operative in contemporary China, and the subject of our discussion in this section.

Thus in order to meet the legitimacy criterion today, academic material and teaching methods must convey some indication to the student of the duties through which he can serve the people, or contribute to his ability to make proper moral judgments as he uses the material, or contain suggestions as to how the facts when employed by the student are conducive to the realization of the goal of serving the people. Productive labor meets the conditions by creating a positive attitude toward manual work and a sympathy with those who do it. Other subjects must rely on the weaving of moral messages into the texts as examples, prefatory notes, story problem topics, and so forth.

The most intelligible and readable English equivalent for the guideline on serving the people is "social utility criterion." This is not a literal rendering of the Chinese ("criterion" instead of "guideline," *fang-chen*), but it is less cumbersome than the literal and accurately conveys the meaning of the Chinese expression as it is used in practice. Thus, when referring to this key dimension of the contemporary Chinese legitimacy standard, I will use the term "social utility criterion."

When is education socially useful? A case can be made that all theories that can be taught have some utilitarian value. This requires expanding the kinds of usefulness to include even such matters as promotion of psychic tranquility by facilitating the order of one's experience. And it leaves open the question of the beneficiaries, who could include people in future centuries. Normally, however, in contemporary China matters are socially useful or in the service to the people when they pertain to norms or goals that will have to be observed in concrete situations in the immediate present or near future.

Minimal mention is made in official sources of the individual's interests. Maximum mention is made of his responsibilities. In traditional China, the social whole always came first. This weighty legacy was underscored by Hegelian doctrine. But in addition this is a function of the conceptions of schools as an agency of state fosterage and of the malleability of man. Promotion of the growth of individual interests is not included among the forms of utility in China, and so developing free, creative individuality is minimally important. In America, Freudian influence on educators beginning after World War I caused them to condemn attempts to mold the character of the child to the neglect of the individual's interests and unique qualities. It was labeled a form of repression and was expected to produce permanent psychic scars in the student. This position is derided in China as "mother-love education."[36]

There is a problem with the criterion in the case of the sciences. In part they are regarded as inherently meeting the conditions of social utility because science is said to be relevant to the production process. It is certainly good Marxism to treat science as part of the "forces of production." In the Preface to his *A Contribution to the Critique of Political Economy,* Marx distinguished the forms of social consciousness (such as law and government) from the economic foundation of society or the process of production. Science must belong to the latter. Thus to the degree that the Chinese insist on production-oriented scientific study, they are being good Marxists. The problem is, however, that they really cannot and do not want to restrict their scientists to working exclusively on problems that satisfy material needs. The most that they can do is momentarily stress more than other societies the applied sciences and momentarily impede more advanced theoretical research; they cannot eliminate the study of the higher level theoretical subjects. Such studies, which Westerners categorize as belonging to the "pursuit of knowledge," have difficulty meeting the condition of the social utility criterion. The texts and scholarly articles in which such matters are discussed end up with a jerry-built appearance of snatches of dialectical materialism or Mao thought at the beginning and end, inadequately related to the body of the work itself. The paradigm cases of the criterion's applicability will be at the primary and secondary level of formal schooling and in on-the-job training; here we can expect to find the most politicization of materials. But at the advanced level there is a built-in conflict between the presupposition that all education is a form of moral education and subjects which are not easily amenable to this presupposition. Over the long run, this conflict will continue to breed hostility between those who pursue the sophisticated theory and those charged with ensuring that educational reality conforms to the assumption that all education is moral education.

The social utility criterion is often discussed in terms of "the unity of redness and expertize." The meaning of this commonly encountered phrase must be understood as describing the desirable operation of the legitimacy criterion. An explanation in the *Journal of Peking University* during the Great Leap is helpful:

> The relation between "red and expert" is the unity of opposites; they are intimately connected and indivisible; they are not mutually repellant. "Red" is politics; it is the leader and spirit of all undertakings; "expertise" is professional work; it is a tool and weapon in the service of the people; the two must be intimately combined, for only then do they develop their greatest usefulness. . . . This is the standard of combining virtue and talent that working class intellectuals must develop.[37]

In this statement, the necessity for a fusion of redness and expertise comes across, as opposed to their independent coexistence as attributes of any person. A similar discussion of the meanings of "politics" and "profession" makes the same point:

> There are people who believe that holding meetings and participating in social activities constitute "politics," whereas working at one's job in isolation from cares about surrounding matters constitutes one's "profession." They further maintain that if one is enthusiastic in attending meetings and participating in activities, while being responsible on the job, then that constitutes "combining profession and politics." But this is incorrect. The important thing is clearly to understand one's political direction and ensure that one's professional activities advance that political goal.[38]

These statements are probably inspired by the Maoist statement in 1958 that "It is beyond any doubt that politics and economy, politics and technology must be unified."[39]

Mindful of the disappearance in China of any sharp barrier between the zones of fact and value, we should not be surprised that "to unify red and expert" does not mean that a person should only study certain courses on politics or ethics and then study certain courses of a technical or academic nature. Rather, like the social utility criterion that it reflects, it introduces a question of legitimacy into all subject matter studied. This standard of legitimacy ensures that moral or political criteria determine what academic material is worth absorbing and therefore legitimate to include in the curriculum.

More specifically, the application of the social utility standard affects both the content of standard textbooks in all subjects and the responsibilities of the instructors. Regarding textbooks, it acts: (1) to determine how facts are presented; (2) to encourage the inclusion or exclusion of certain information; (3) to determine the topics that will receive the greater stress. Regarding instructors, it imposes an obligation for them consistently to point out to the students the social significance of what they learn.

From the Chinese perspective, there is one fact about the possible treatment of most material studied that lends itself to meeting the social utility criterion. This is that a subject matter is "redified" or made legitimate when the student studies it with the proper attitude. This attitude is a commitment to make all information "serve the people" or to discard it. Thus the proper attitude can transform a subject into something that satisfied the legitimacy criterion even when to the outside observer there is no visible evidence of political content to the text or technique. At other times, acts of study or use of academic knowledge are regarded as transformed into moral acts when done with an awareness of their "meaning" (*i-i*) or significance. Meaning is defined functionally, in terms of the services the knowledge can perform for certain people or how it relates to the realization of social goals.

The most dramatic way to show the social utility criterion in operation is to look at examples from textbooks and labor experiences. For reasons just discussed, the works will be drawn from primary or middle schools rather than from institutions of higher learning. Since we would expect texts dealing with history or literature to have political content, most of our examples will be drawn from mathematics and the sciences, which intuitively would seem to the Westerner to be relatively value free.

The nature of the moral infusion in the texts varies greatly at different times. One cause of the variation is whether or not the guidelines of "serving proletarian politics" and "serving the people" are actually operative. When they are not, the moral infusion is haphazard and theoretical; when they are, the infusion is more comprehensive and concrete. Over the years, the presence, degree, and nature of the moral infusion have also varied as a function of whether the texts or principles guiding their preparation were primarily indigenous or based on foreign models. We begin with the indigenous.

The Yenan Period

The first texts we will examine are those used in the Shen-kan-ning Border Region (encompassing parts of Shensi, Kansu, and Ninghsia provinces) and in the Su-Wan Border Region during the 1940s. These are selected for three reasons. First, they are Chinese products. They give no overt evidence of being copied from Anglo-American examples or of being produced under the guidance of Soviet advisers. Second, materials are available from comparable texts used in schools in Nationalist controlled areas. These were based on Anglo-American prototypes and highlight the distinctiveness of the indigenous works by their comparison. Third, the Yenan texts are cited as models to be imitated during the 1958 Maoist educational reorientation that followed the rejection of the Soviet approach, and again in the educational changes that accompanied the Cultural Revolution beginning in 1966.

In 1944 there were some eight hundred primary schools in the Shen-kan-ning Border Region. In course terms, the curriculum was fairly typical of what one might find in any primary schools in a developed country.[40] It was the content and manner of presentation in those courses that set China apart. Three other distinctive characteristics of those schools were described in the Border Region Report: (1) Linking academic study with productive labor. All staff and students over twelve years of age participated (spinning thread, planting vegetables, cutting wood). (2) Linking the school to "society." Students from brigades were expected to help spread the government's policies, teach characters to the illiterate, and so forth. (3) Linking the school to the family. Students helped their parents with family chores (balancing accounts, manual tasks), with the obligation to perform the jobs laid out in the school.[41]

The Border Region science and arithmetic texts at the primary level used two methods to conform to the social utility criterion. One was to conclude each section (especially in the science works) with a part entitled "To Investigate and Act," which constituted the homework. This section directed the student to use his newly acquired knowledge in a certain way. For example, the *Applied Nature Science* text in the Su-Wan Border Region contains eighteen lessons, of which the following are typical: Raising Pigs, Growing Vegetables, Addiction, Colds and Influenza, Itches and Boils, Small Pox and Diptheria, Corn and Soy Beans, Growing Rice. The "To Investigate and Act" section of the fifth lesson is: "(1) Eliminate to the best of your ability itches and boils affecting fellow students. (2) Tell family and friends the methods for curing itches and boils." The rest are of a similar nature. The most common "act" required in the homework is teaching villagers what the student has learned about something and persuading the neighbors to change previous habits.[42]

The story problem is the other vehicle through which students are conditioned to think of academic information in the context of its social uses and their personal duties. For example, a host of arithmetic problems deals with various ways in which students should "comfort" either the soldiers at the front or their dependents at home: "181 letters carrying warm regards were sent to the soldiers at the front by students from the Po Sui School, and 109 letters were sent by those from the Yu-an School. Altogether, how many letters were sent to the front?"[43] The desirability of the students being as self-sufficient as possible is a constant theme: "Pei Village Primary School planned to make their own ink. By so doing, each student can save 350 yüan. How many yüan can three students save?"[44] Finally, students learned not only their own responsibilities but also those that are incumbent on every adult living at that time: "The Chang family donated seven *tou* of 'Save the Country' public grain, and the Pei family donated 8 *tou*. What is the total amount of public grain sent in?"[45]

Those story problems that do not relate directly to some individual responsibility often pertain to general governmental policies. Examples would be the new work style of cadres in which they labor with the rural masses, the elimination of vagabonds, and the periodic establishment of model soldiers, workers, and students.

In sum, these books reflect well the actual life conditions of the students who used them. The students can recognize themselves or their families in them and learn something about the functions of knowledge acquired in school for coping with those conditions. The small amount of evidence that we have uncovered for Yenan period middle schools indicates that they were characterized by similar conditions (see note 56 to this chapter).

In contrast, the comparable science and arithmetic texts from the occupied areas (Peking) and the Kuomintang (KMT) areas were generally based on foreign models, although there was some rewriting for the Chinese audience. For example, compare the Border Region text section on "Corn and Beans" with the Peking area text's section on "Grains and Beans." In the Border Region text the homework is: Observe how the local people grow corn and soy beans and discuss with them the advantages and disadvantages of the different methods; then, utilize a small piece of land around the school or at home to grow some.[46] In the Peking text it is: Observe the different parts of the rice, wheat, and soybean plants; compare the morphological differences between them.[47] Or compare the respective sections on health and hygiene. The homework in the Border Region text: Investigate the most hygenic house in the locality and try to keep your house and the school similarly hygenic; after investigating the situation in public hygiene in the area, spread the word about being more hygenic, starting with your own house, and persuade people to change bad habits.[48] In the Peking text: Using charts and models, study the microbes that cause epidemics; collect samples of tape worms and string worms and study their morphology; visit a hospital.[49] In content, the Border Region text studies the pigsty and privy, the disposal of dead animals, the causes of the spread of parasites through excretia in the privy, and local disease prevention precautions. The text published in Peking examines theoretically how germs and parasites cause disease, associates different germs with different epidemics, and names the types of parasites.

A comparison of Border Region arithmetic texts with those published by the Nationalists in Chungking also reveals major differences. The KMT texts do contain a few story problems with political content, such as those dealing with army recruits, the distribution of bullets, or the curing of wounded soldiers, but the overwhelming number of problems relate to school life, school supplies, and the family. And in the entire series of eight texts there are only two problems remotely suggestive of the social utility criterion; one concerns students raising funds to pay for airplanes and refugee relief, and the other is about students helping farmers get rid of harmful insects.[50] The general impression with which one is left is that a KMT pupil is being taught the following chain: Wars can be won by sufficient money, and so fund drives are the clues to victory. But he will have a minimal sense of his own obligations, and that includes his obligations to advance the military victory. In contrast, on this single issue of the war, the pupil completing the Border Region texts will be taught about the moral and political significance of the war, his own duties to further its victory as well as those of his family and neighbors, the kinds of cooperative efforts required, and the kind of better life possible after the victory.

The Period of Borrowing (1953–58)

During the period of borrowing from the Soviet Union, residual practices from the Yenan era remained quantitatively strong, particularly in the primary school texts, although there was no conscious attempt to imitate the Yenan texts.[51] Both the science and the mathematics texts contained a substantial amount of moral and political indoctrination, some (not all) of which was similar to that used during the 1940s.[52] The homework in the 1955 upper primary science text is "Investigate . . ." rather than "Investigate and Act," but the impetus was still there for students to get out into their local communities to study local irrigation facilities or fertilizers.[53]

In spite of this quantitatively similar infusion of moral education, how-ever, there was still an important difference. There was a decided decrease in examples that conditioned the student to think of his concrete, personal responsibilities. The entire upper primary abacus text contained only two such problems; the science text had only one. Instead, the overall stress was on establishing confidence in the new regime and admiration for Russian achievements.[54] Thus the Soviet influence does not seem to have affected the quantity of moral education in the primary texts, but it definitely affected some of its content.

In the Soviet Union, although the sciences and mathematics have been fairly free from political content, geography is saturated. It is not surprising, then, to find Chinese middle school geography texts in the 1950s pervaded by such themes as: defending the coastline, liberating Taiwan, and pre- and postliberation conditions in forestry, river dredging, population distribution, weather stations, and minority group livelihood.[55] However, the departure from Yenan period principles was striking in middle school mathematics and science texts. The political information conveyed was consistent in content with that in the primary texts, intended to enhance pride in industrial achievement, forest conservation, changes in livelihood, and so forth. But how little it was! The three-hundred-page upper middle school physics text contained only two such examples (learning from the Russian successes in the expansion of the use of electricity, and the abuse of atomic power by imperialists). A similar situation characterizes the chemistry, botany, and algebra texts.[56]

Both the Soviets and the Chinese in the 1950s were living up to the letter of the Leninist view of education, except in the middle school sciences and mathematics. There was considerable exposure in middle school to the principles of dialectical materialism, to the differences between capitalist and socialist economies, and to patriotism. But there was far less that sensitized the individual to his social obligations, as the Chinese legitimacy criterion traditionally has demanded.

In 1956 many quarters advocated that all university professors learn to implement the policy of "combining education and cultivation" (*chiao-hsüeh yü chiao-yang hsiang chieh-ho*). They were told that it is best not to spend ten or twenty minutes in a class dealing with political matters but to unite the teaching of any scientific subject matter with politics. "Any course that is not a combination of instruction in scientific knowledge and politics is a course that is lost. Not paying attention to political thought education is neglecting the political meaning of one's speciality," it was said.[57] Yet the political information that was to be disseminated was primarily theoretical, pertinent more to what the Soviets call the proletarian "world view" than to enabling the students to relate their studies to their social responsibilities. Those professors who had made the fusion in their lectures reported good results in cultivating the students' dialectical materialist world view, criticizing idealism, advancing patriotism and love of science, and inculcating Communist morality.[58]

At the university level, confusion over how to apply the legitimacy criterion was poignantly noted by the secretaries of the party committees of all of the nation's institutions of higher agricultural education (in which it should have been easiest to accomplish) in a complaint at a meeting in 1960 that integration of academic and political education had still not been accomplished in many courses.[59] It did not help to have the Soviets claim that the natural sciences (including medicine), language, and mathematics are devoid of class character. This position, which was picked up by Lu Ting-i in an important May, 1956, speech and by others, was good Marxism and Stalinism, but its implications were inconsistent with the legitimacy criterion.[60] It served only to justify the actions of those who were refusing to attempt the fusion.

Soviet practices themselves were a prime cause of Chinese confusion. On the one hand there were Leninist observations that seemed to square with Chinese assumptions about the fosterage role of education, such as Lenin's claim that "the entire purpose of training, educating, and teaching the youth of today should be to imbue them with Communist ethics."[61] On the other hand, Soviet advisers in China inconsistently pressed the Chinese educators to minimize political and moral incursions into the curriculum. And in many instances the Soviet texts did not seem to meet what the Chinese could understand as a moral legitimacy standard.

There is a last basic split between the doctrines of the period of borrowing and those of the Yenan period. This has to do with the interpretation of the term "practice" in the principle that school materials should combine theory and practice. In China, practice had been associated with acquiring knowledge or attitudes that may be of use to the nation's production or political efforts. In the Soviet Union, in contrast, it is sufficient that academic work "introduces a student to life" in order to be considered linked with practice. This means that brief and generalized exposure to what happens on farms or in factories or other arenas of Soviet society can be offered as practice. A related issue concerns the definition of "productive labor." The Soviet eventually referred to almost anything other than textbook teaching or the teacher's oral instruction as "polytechnical." In China the directives of the period of borrowing accepted labor as an intrinsic value and also as a means toward developing the all-round man. Yet they also claimed that the act of studying and learning in itself constituted labor. With this definition, it could be argued that any teacher who ensured that his students worked hard in a course was satisfying the necessary conditions of the fact-value fusion, because the students were developing a proper attitude toward a value (labor) at the same time that they were absorbing facts.[62] This was consistent with the Soviet position that studying and learning are the students' unique brands of labor.

The available evidence points to one conclusion. In spite of the contrasts noted between primary and middle school science and mathematic texts, Soviet influence did qualitatively affect the content of moral education in the texts and in the schools in general at all levels. There was minimal attempt to condition the student to associate an awareness of potential personal duties with the factual material being learned. At the same time, there was a minimal attempt to perpetuate the spirit of the labor component of education of the Yenan period that also was an instrument for transformation of the social nature.

Reappearance of the Criterion
The slogan "Take the textbooks of the old liberated areas as models" first appeared in 1958 and then reappeared during the second half of the 1960s.[63] It was inspired by Mao, as was the call to take the Chinese People's Resist Japan Military and Political University (*K'ang ta*) of Yenan days as the exemplary university. By the late 1970s, China's schools had undergone a twisting course of evolution, and they by no means resembled closely those of the guerrilla days. But the social utility criterion once more became the keynote and was primarily responsible for the most distinctive characteristics of the formal educational system.

In 1958, the prototype of the new school that would embody the Maoist principle was said to be the half-work, half-study school. The labor dimension and the production oriented shortened curriculum were built into the very nature of the school, and the close link between academic material and the learning of social duties would be enforced by local authorities, who had a vested interest in graduating students who were aware of their obligations to the commune. Regular schools would continue to exist, but they would gradually incorporate the principles already operative in the half-and-half schools.

In the educational sector, high level opposition to Mao's policies may have emerged well before the failure of the Great Leap had become obvious. Lu Ting-i, Lin Feng, Ch'en Tseng-ku, and others are now reported to have criticized many aspects of the educational reforms during 1958 and 1959.[64] In any case, between July, 1961, and August, 1962, the Ministry of Education took formal steps to return to the pre-1958 educational system, eliminating the labor requirement. Many alliances between factories and schools were terminated, as were large numbers of the 1958 work-study schools.

In spite of attempts to abort the 1958–60 reforms and to return to a quasi-Soviet style educational model, the Maoist pressure to incorporate principles exemplified by the half-work, half-study system in all schools emerged strong again in 1964 and culminated during the Cultural Revolution. Within a few years, however, the attempt to universalize the half-and-half system was dropped. The disillusionment with the straight half-and-half model was a result of the attempt by certain educational officers to incorporate it as a kind of vocational, lower status track while concurrently maintaining a regular system devoid of any significant modifications from the mid-1950s.[65] In addition, China was at a different level of economic development with different skill needs from that of the Yenan period. These needs could not be met with a curriculum as drastically truncated as the Yenan approach or the true half-and-half style required.

An additional constraint on full realization of the Maoist approach was caused by the need to bring all subjects, including mathematics and the sciences, within the scope of the social utility criterion. The upper levels of instruction in these fields presented problems which are described earlier.

As the education system at the primary and middle school level began to stabilize in the early 1970s, certain basic principles became manifest. Most of them have their historic roots in the half-and-half concept, even though universalizing that specific system was no longer being advocated. First, changes in teaching techniques and materials were expected to sensitize a student to his duties, to official policies, or to local needs in his community, and to show him how his knowledge relates to these. Some changes had been tried out shortly before the Cultural Revolution. For example, teachers in a village school in Kiangsi described how they would teach mathematics by taking the children to a production unit where they would help calculate work points. In the process of learning the calculations, they would also be taught the significance or value of the work point system and that if the calculator does an accurate job, it will help stimulate the activism of the farmers.[66] Because texts used in rural areas often reflected an urban orientation, some variation (in accordance with regional particularities) from otherwise uniform materials was permitted in order to meet this problem.

In 1970, after several years spent revising teaching materials, provincial Education Bureaus and Science and Education Groups issued textbooks that had been prepared by the faculty of normal colleges in consultation with teachers and students. There was considerable resemblance in spirit to the 1940s Border Region approach. In primary school mathematics texts, the pictures showed children doing good deeds rather than playing games. The themes of class struggle and patriotism were most common. Government airplanes were counted rather than bananas. The story problems sensitized the student to his social duties and to general government policies. Some examples have even appeared in the press; for example, *Survey of China Mainland Press* (*SCMP*) 4631, April 8, 1970, p. 63.

Middle school science and mathematics texts usually had several pages at the beginning laying forth the legitimacy criterion or various other educational guidelines that must govern the teaching and learning of the material within. Much of the burden for relating the material to social obligations fell on teachers. Their comments in class were on the themes of the duty students have to use the knowledge of science to serve the people: that they must never take joy in science for its own sake or as their own private possession to do with as they like; how science can be used when paired with a proper analytical approach to solve practical problems; and examples of such benefits that can be explicitly studied in the class. Because much of the content of middle school and university science and mathematics texts does not easily lend itself to direct practical study problems, some of the teachers were retrained at May Seventh Schools (in orally sensitizing students to the usefulness of factual material in "serving the people") to help them deal with the problem. Much was made of the supposed transformation of attitudes that this sensitization produces, enabling the student to "redify" whatever technical facts are being studied. Obviously, the weakness in the approach is that teachers may not in fact make the running moral or political comments in class that they are supposed to make.

The second principle was popularized with the slogan (once associated with Lin Piao and the PLA) "Less but finer" (*shao erh ching*). It means to teach less but make what is taught more substantial. The "less" referred especially to theoretical information of the kind that is most difficult to justify with the social utility criterion. The reduction in amount of material covered also released more time for actual productive labor.[67] Although many Chinese officials have formulated their own attacks on excessive academic work, they took their inspiration from Mao's critiques, made strongly in 1958 and repeated thereafter.[68] Accordingly, some theoretical aspects of the natural sciences were dropped, as were much factual detail in history courses, study of formal grammar in foreign languages (moral examples are rife in the language texts), and so forth.

Third, a labor experience was required for all students. This experience met the legitimacy criterion because its aim was not primarily to make a monetary profit for the school out of the students' labor but rather to facilitate thought transformation. As of 1970, the labor began in the second grade (one hour per week average); middle school students spent three to four weeks per semester at labor, but half of that time is spent in classes that, where possible, introduce science theory relevant to the work being done. Much of the work in urban primary and middle schools was done in workshops on the school grounds that make items like thumbtacks, ball-point pens, and transistor diodes. Farm experience could be gained in suburban rural communes. The labor situation for university students was highly fluid; in the first years of the 1970s, theoretically all students were expected to spend one-third of the calendar year doing labor. However, the actual expectation usually was that half of that time would be spent in class (the faint echo of the once powerful half-half idea). Factories existed on many university campuses, but they were adjuncts of mathematics, physics, and chemistry departments. Their purpose was to serve research and teaching (illustrating how theory is combined with practice), not production.

Fourth, political education outside of ordinary academic classes was reoriented from being a largely theoretical introduction to dialectical materialism to being more concrete. This involved exposure to model figures who conveyed to the students a sense of the kinds of situations they might find themselves in and their duties in them. Thus at all levels of schools one found a few "selfless cadres" (in the late 1950s), People's Liberation Army (PLA) men and old workers or peasants (in the 1960s) doing token instruction along with academicians. However, there was increased agitation to employ in political education courses the works of Mao. These were said to be more useful guides to action than were the works of German Marxists or Russian Communists.[69]

We can be a bit more specific about the way in which some of the theoretical information was presented, in order to differentiate it from its place in Soviet education, where it is intended to enhance the learner's materialist world view. These remarks pertain to teaching about such matters across the board and not simply in the school.

Only certain types of "political" teachings can satisfy the social utility criterion. Those that pertain to speculative metaphysics or to cosmology are incomplete by themselves. This means that the doctrines making up the Marxist world view which are stressed in Soviet pedagogy do not satisfy the criterion when taught in their usual manner. Even statements that originated in Marxist-Leninist cosmological or epistemological writings often have taken on meanings in Maoist political education very different from that which they have in the Soviet Union, although the cosmological or epistemological meanings are not absent. We have here an interesting residue of the antimetaphysical strand in Chinese thought dating from the seventeenth century. In order to satisfy the criterion, a set of statements must indicate to the student something about duties or the method of dealing with practical production problems.

Many such statements are interpreted as guidelines for breaking out of archaic intellectual habits that retard scientific problem solving. They are simple lessons in embryonic scientific investigation for people who have no experience with such methods. Students might study the following statement: "The analytical method is dialectical. By analysis we mean analysing the contradictions in things."[70] The message that is conveyed has far more to do with scientific problem solving than with the dialectical materialist point of view. It is: When faced with a problem, do not rely solely on solutions handed down in the oral tradition by grandparents or in classical texts or foreign books. Examine the problem objectively yourself, slowly isolating the variables and working out a solution.

In an often-quoted passage, Lenin had remarked that "The Unity of opposites is conditional, temporary, transitory, relative. The struggle of mutually exclusive opposites is absolute."[71] In something of a commentary on this passage, Mao had written that the most accurate account of the relations of opposites is "one divides into two" (*i fen wei erh*) rather than "two combine into one (*erh ho wei i*). Such claims insist that struggle is a more fundamental characteristic of things than is harmony, and they imply that people should avoid sham reconciliations of opposites (as in Marxist humanism, which purportedly attempts to reconcile antagonistic classes). But *"i fen wei erh"* is also treated as "to split one into two." In this connection it means nothing more esoteric than that there is good and bad in every person or situation, and that a person making a proper analysis should always seek to uncover both. This is a far cry from cosmological inquiry.

This manner of using ideas associated with Marxist cosmology is consistent with the enduring Chinese preoccupation with the behavioral implications of theories. When such behavioral implications can be made evident and are acceptable, study of the theories successfully satisfies the conditions of the legitimacy criterion. Such has been the treatment of ideas associated with the dialectical materialist world view since the birth of Chinese Marxism. Maurice Meisner has said of Li Ta-chao:

> . . . he was continually preoccupied with the questions of the psychological impact of the Marxist view of history. Time and again he felt compelled to repeat that it would encourage "self consciousness" and human activity and not lead to quietism.[72]

Fifth, after 1970 added safeguards against university students having improper moral perspectives were instituted in two forms. One was the labor requirement after middle school graduation for all students except for a few in foreign languages, mathematics, and certain performing arts. This was supposed to reinforce correct attitudes toward manual work and those who do it. The other was the character recommendation from co-workers that was an integral part of the four-step entry procedure. The student was to apply to his work organization to enter an institution of higher learning. Co-workers would make recommendations based on the individual's attitude toward work, quality of work, class background (variously defined), and, occasionally, practical or written tests. Commune authorities would make an actual selection of candidates. These were interviewed and tested (for academic level and competence) by recruiting teams from the universities; this was called a reexamination. Thus a strong showing on a written examination by itself was not a necessary sign that a student's political virtues are in order, as some Soviet influenced Chinese had maintained.

Given the ideal fusion of academic and moral education, it was not surprising to find strong advocacy of entrance via recommendation as a supplement to examinations, which measure only the academic aspect. This entry device was expected both to encourage students to integrate the two subject matters in their adolescent years and also to reward those who gave evidence of being able to apply what they learned in a socially approved way. Hence the method called "combining recommendation and selection" (*t'ui-chien ho hsüan-pa hsiang chieh-ho*) developed. However, as in Confucian China, there is a history of conflict between those who want to use a method of recommendation and those who prefer to rely on formal, usually written, examinations. In contemporary China, those who prefer the latter course argue that it is a better gauge of the kinds of upper-level skills required by China's manpower needs. Those officials who treat the existence of certain character traits as top priority favor the former approach. There is enduring tension between these two positions that manifests itself in policy fluctuation in the educational sector. The issue is ready-made for factional dispute; the next swing would be toward much stronger reliance on written examinations.

In sum, the social utility criterion reappeared in the form of educational principles that owed their spiritual roots to Yenan practices and to the half-and-half schools, but that had to be substantially modified because of the differing level of China's development in the 1960s from that of the 1940s. However, the essential characteristics remain that mark it as consistent with the enduring legitimacy criterion of Confucian thought.

The principles discussed in this chapter have their roots in the phenomena of clustering and malleability. The legitimacy criterion is supposed to ensure that the student exposed to Marxist-Maoist principles absorbs a sense of social duties and commitment to them (promptings) rather than simply a theoretical knowledge of Marxist cosmology. Malleability provides the confidence that school policies employed to do these things can be effective in character transformation and the skill acquisition that builds on it. The strength of the principles we have examined here produced school guidelines that departed from the Soviet experience.

We should note that one can never expect to achieve total consensus on the goals and values that are to be promoted by education. For example, generational differences remain strong, even in China. Beginning in the 1960s there was a growing divergence between older Chinese veterans of the Long March era and younger individuals in the party hierarchy. The former were tied by shared experiences that transcended regional barriers, whereas the influence of regional variables in determining interests was stronger in the younger generation. However, agreement on goals is possible to the degree that there is overlap of some values, notwithstanding significant divergences in others. One of the major functions of fosterage is to promote political unity through value consensus: ''We must use the thought of Mao Tse-tung to unify the thinking of the entire party and the entire nation, to further promote the revolutionization of people's thoughts, to dig out capitalism, and to prevent revisionism.''[73] The importance of the unity of thought that can be achieved should not be underestimated, but the possibility of achieving complete uniformity is simple illusion.

Chapter 6

The Use of Models

Models are a teaching device that runs like a thread through education inside and outside the schoolhouse in every occupation. Thus government foster-age and its associated legitimacy criterion are at work in working, living, and recreational units as well as in schools. From the time of the establishment of the People's Republic, it was customary to invite model workers to speak at the school, to incorporate their deeds in texts, to take children to farms or factories to meet exemplars, to choose students as models of loving labor and honor them accordingly, and to insist that teachers be models (using old expressions, like *piao shuai* and *i-shen tso-tzu*). Beyond the classroom, writers and artists were enjoined to learn from advanced persons and to illustrate them in their works. The agricultural sector has had its ''advanced agricultural workers'' and ''Lei Feng types''; department stores have had their counterparts. All of these, in addition to the frequently encountered army heroes and industrial models.

The theory of model emulation has strong roots in traditional Chinese philosophy. It is also congenial with Marxist epistemology, which, in its Chinese interpretation, claims that people understand matters best by being exposed to examples of them in practice. Obviously, the Chinese are not unique in using models. However, there is something special in the degree to which Chinese believe that people of *all ages* learn by imitation and in the ways in which they apply that belief. There is a unique character to the functions that models serve in their society, to the status they receive, to the number chosen, and the seriousness with which they are regarded.

The Confucian Heritage

In the Confucian tradition, beliefs about how to transform the mind and thereby perfect man's character were intimately linked to assumptions about

135

how people learn. It was assumed that people learn primarily through the imitation of models. The learning can occur unintentionally, through the unconscious imitation of those around one, or it can occur intentionally, through the purposive attempt to duplicate the attitude and conduct of a virtuous model. Although the behavior of a negative model may be absorbed, most people are positively attracted to and consciously seek to imitate virtuous models.

It follows from this assumption that the most effective way to teach or to inculcate any attitude or regular conduct is to introduce a model for people to imitate. In the classical formulation, "teaching by example surpasses teaching by words" (*shen-chiao sheng yü yen-chiao*), a maxim that is still used in China today.[1] Sometimes models were exemplary people from the past, such as ancestors or sages whose exploits are recorded in writing. Sometimes the model was a living person, such as a father, teacher, official, or ruler. The Master remarked, "When one sees a worthy, one should think of equaling him."[2]

This assumption lies behind much of the political writing in Confucian China, which often describes the responsibility of the cultivated person to serve as a model for others to emulate, and praises the efficacy of virtuous models in changing the behavior of large numbers of people. According to the *Analects,* if the person in power leads the people with rectitude, no one will dare to act otherwise. Confucius said, "When those who are in high stations perform well all their duties to their relations, the people are aroused to virtue."[3] *The Great Learning* states: "When the ruler, as a father, a son, and a brother is a model, then the people imitate him. This is what is meant by saying, 'The government of his kingdom depends on his regulation of the family.' "[4] Much of the historical scholarship for which the Chinese are famous was concerned with unearthing models from the past for the education of the people, from exalted men of the past such as Kuan Yü (model of loyalty) and Shun (model of filial piety), to more local figures.[5]

The Confucians also taught that man's legitimate goal is to seek to be a model. In other words, respect, which comes from being imitated, is preferable to material reward. In concrete terms, this meant that Confucians acted as though respected position was the legitimate and natural aspiration of men, even though honor was, to Confucius, no more important than "a floating cloud." The opportunity to influence others, not material advantage, was supposed to be the goal of those who sought official position; thus political office was a natural aspiration of the virtuous. Officials who appeared unmindful of personal gain while in office came to be known as "pure officials" (*ch'ing kuan*). In this easy transition from being a moral exemplar to occupying an official position which affords greater opportunity for being imitated as a model, we encounter a fusion of ethics and politics: The virtuous model should be given political position.

Additional arguments beyond those based on man's innate tendency to imitate were advanced by Confucians to justify using models to transform the people. As early as the Chou period model emulation was one of two contending methods of social control, whose relative merits were heatedly discussed. On one side were the Confucians, advocating control by the presentation of virtuous models, whose attitudes and behaviors would be emulated by the people and made habitual. On the other side were the statesmen who advocated universally applicable penal laws, which controlled people primarily through fear of punishment. This was a debate about the best method of inducing *compliance* with rules; conditioning, or fear. It was not, as so many commentators have thought, a debate simply between proponents of rites ᵃ(*li*) and penal law ᵃ(*hsing*).

On the question of inducing compliance with rules, the Confucian argument was that law controls through fear of punishment; it does not change people's attitudes or habits. As a result, in the words of an ancient treatise, the people "come to have a contentious spirit, and make their appeal to the express words of the law, hoping peradventure to be successful in their argument."[6] That is to say, people will do everything they can to get around the wording of the law rather than submit to its spirit. Furthermore, since people's attitudes and habits are not changed, they will disobey the law whenever the policeman is not around. (A critic might argue that people often obey a law both because they fear punishment and also because they agree with its thrust.) For this reason and others, Confucian thought prefers to transform or control by the presentation of virtuous models. People will emulate them and develop a constant attitude toward the norms, which will ensure proper conduct even when no one is around. Of course, people may still internally accept a given rule as good even when subject to coercion or punishment for breaking it.

It should be noted that Chou Confucians did not totally reject penal law and punishments, but sometimes acknowledged their supplementary role as a control technique. By Han times, with a vast empire to govern and a complex governmental machinery to do the job, Confucian officials recognized the need to regularize people's duties. Therefore, law existed, although it was infused with a Confucian spirit. The ᵃ*li* were used as a basis for the law, and penal law was used to enforce the ᵃ*li*. But in the last analysis, the

Confucians placed far more confidence in control by model emulation, and it always occupied first place.

We must pass beyond an account of why models were believed to be useful to consider how they were expected to help foster the development of the social nature. In essence, models are concrete, in contrast to abstract moral principles. Thus their acts and attitudes (revealed in regularly appearing acts) are the objects of learning by others. Such learning need not be through words, though it often is verbal when the model is deceased. But even those written accounts lean to the concrete, with vivid description of acts and the evidence for virtuous attitudes. Models manifest the link between knowledge of principles and action in accordance with them and help to make this link habitual in the learner. They stand for principle in action. They promote the clustering of proper promptings to act with knowledge and the transition of the covert beginnings of action into actual social conduct. By being "watchful" over their own inner lives, models remind the learner of the need for proper clustering, and of impediments to it and to the inner-outer transition. This is a conditioning process.

Much of the historical writing depicts positive and negative models. Others contain descriptions of typical social or political problems, the solution to which could serve as models to the reader. People during the Sung and Ming periods were taught that institutions depicted in the *Rites of Chou* (*Chou li*) provided appropriate patterns for subsequent societies. Of course, it was also believed that people learn by imitating live examples, with whom they can compare themselves. But words occupied a special place in this learning, such that the following assumptions seem to underlie many of the discussions of moral education. Knowing verbal descriptions of exemplary things is almost the same as knowing the actualities. Verbal formulations by models are sacrosanct and not in need of constant revision (being legitimately subject only to reinterpretation or addendum through the attachment of commentaries). Not only were the words of models sacred, but also the models themselves were so revered that it would have been unpardonable arrogance to attempt to surpass one in the performance of relevant deeds.

Contemporary Theory and Practice

The principles associated with model emulation in the past are still operative. And as before, the presentation of models is juxtaposed to the use of force. In the language of China today, using models is a form of "persuasion" (education) as opposed to "coercion."

Mao's formulation of contemporary model theory is contained in his often quoted thesis that "it is only through repeated education by positive and negative examples and through comparisons and contrasts that revolutionary parties and revolutionary people can temper themselves, become mature and make sure of victory."[7] References to the utility of setting up models are frequent enough in Mao's writings to suggest the presence of assumptions about the best way to motivate people. Other Chinese presumably will comprehend the references without reading a treatise on the matter. For example, "All Ministries must encourage achievement, set up model workers for emulation, praise them extensively, and at the same time criticize mistakes. Praise should be the main thing and criticism should be supplementary."[8]

A precondition of personality transformation is honing the mind's capacity for self-evaluation. Imitating models is a means of making habitual the practice of this self-analysis. Chinese writings convey a belief that people tend to evaluate by thinking in terms of comparisons between two poles. We have already learned that "without comparison, men cannot think correctly, nor can they comprehend things correctly."[9] Marxian dialectics has reinforced the enduring Chinese penchant for classifying things in the world in terms of complementary or contradictory pairs (*tui,* in Confucian thought). Comparison with one pole in a set of polarities is an element in evaluation. Those who concentrate on models will learn to see the imbalances between their own virtues or work capacity and those of the models (in both quality and quantity). Mao described the awareness of this disequilibrium between the model and the emulator in dialectical terms, pointing out the subsequent redress, that is in turn followed by a new disequilibrium:

> The method to be used is comparison. Compare the advanced with the backward under identical conditions and encourage the backward to catch up with the advanced. They are the two extremes of a contradiction and comparison is the unification of them. Disequilibria exist between enterprises, machine shops, teams, and individuals. Disequilibrium is a general, objective rule. The cycle, which is endless, evolves from disequilibrium to equilibrium and then to disequilibrium again. Each cycle, however, brings us to a higher level of development. Disequilibrium is normal and absolute while equilibrium is temporary and relative.[10]

Self-criticism cannot proceed without some external standard for comparison.[11] The presentation of a model is believed to cause people to desire to be like the model. Emulation then introduces an internal contradiction between the individual's own values and those with which he is comparing himself. A struggle between the two differing sets of values follows, as a result of which the new norms are understood and accepted.

Mindful of this theoretical basis for the use of models, we now shift to an examination of its operational dimensions. Let us deal in turn with questions of the function of models, the incentive system of which they are a part, their selection, and their cultivation.

Function of Models

Models serve five main functions. The first is served by persons who are presented almost exclusively as examples of certain virtues or attitudes that the rulers wish the masses to learn. This function has been filled primarily by deceased individuals, who are propagandized throughout the nation:

> We must create new men, men with the communist spirit to build the new society. What kind of men possess the communist spirit? They are similar to those commended by Chairman Mao, such as Chang Szu-te, Norman Bethune, Liu Hu-lan, and Lei Feng, or those like Ou-yang Hai, Chiao Yu-lu, Wang Chieh, and Liu Ying-chun. They were new men with the communist spirit.[12]

Not all of the national models are deceased, of course. At various times after 1949, Chairman Mao himself was explicitly treated as such an example, whose words and deeds were to be studied (in imperial China the chief model was Confucius):

> Whether in practical experience, or in the Marxist-Leninist theory, or in individual talent, Chairman Mao is not only our superior, but also the greatest Marxist-Leninist in the world today. We must use his example to measure ourselves against him. We must closely follow him, imitate him, and emulate him.[13]

Furthermore, during an emulation campaign, most organizations will have their own living models described as most proficient at emulating one of the national models, "so that there is a heroic figure afar to emulate and a model and sample close by to catch up with."[14]

Conversely, negative models are established as examples of erroneous thinking. People can compare themselves with the negative model and be alert to thoughts needing correction. One of the first was Li Li-san; one of the most recent was Lin Piao.

The second function is to set an example of technical skills and innovative ability. Collectively these models are called "advanced people" (*hsien-chin jen-wu*). At times, these same models fill the third function, one based on the legitimacy criterion. They serve both to pass on a technical skill and also to help people to integrate that skill with value-laden feelings and with promptings to act in accordance with some enduring norm or recently promulgated rule. In no case, except in 1953–58 when Soviet practices were copied, should respect or status be possessed by a model simply because of production skill or inventiveness; a properly cultivated social nature is a precondition. In or out of the schoolhouse, knowledge is never to be separated from proper evaluations and promptings.

Among the ways in which a model demonstrates the integration of skills and values, one is especially worthy of note. This is the model's understanding of the "meaning" of his work.[15] In other words, it is his understanding of how performing that work is consistent with specific values he holds and how it can help to realize them. This understanding will enable him to see links between a task and others that could be more effectively related to it. This leads the model to acquire new knowledge and apply it to the earlier task. Perceiving interconnectedness also entails perceiving heightened value in the work at hand. For example, workers in a shop that filled bottles of medicine tended to look down on their work as trivial. A model in the unit was singled out for taking advantage of an occasion when one worker could not find a substance because it had a chemical name on it rather than its popular appelation. He drew attention to the increased efficiency that would occur if all of the workers learned some technology, and he called in a technician to teach them. In addition, the model was able to make the bottle fillers see the relation between their work and agricultural production. Achievements in the latter were shown to be intimately associated with the furtherance of their own values.[16] Learning the meaning is supposed to have a positive impact on morale. It is the Chinese answer to the alienation problem.

In 1920, Lenin made a speech in which he outlined a role for the trade unions as "transmission belts" for passing the ideology of the Party to the backward masses, including some of the workers.[17] Mao seems to have drawn on the imagery, but he applied it to model soldiers and workers, and added the idea central to the mass line, that there must be an institutionalized channel for opinions of the masses to reach the leadership. Models also perform this fourth function. In his first speech to labor models in 1945 in one of the border regions, Mao said, "You are the bridge between the leader and the masses. The opinions of the masses go through you to the top, and the opinions of the top go through you to the masses."[18] Models are spoken of as the "nucleus of the state," meaning that they cannot be isolated from the masses, and the "vanguard," meaning that they take the lead in supporting an official political policy.[19] For example, a thirty-one-year-old model heard at a National People's Congress meeting that the country would need more steel to make agricultural machinery. On returning to his commune his first task was to spread this information and explain its significance to other commune members. In addition, he stands as a model of trust in the government through his acceptance of the new policy and, thereby, as a vehicle for encouraging peasant trust for the government.[20]

The primary reward that the model receives is group respect (from being imitated). This respect is believed to enhance the model's efficacy as an instrument of state fosterage. From another standpoint, the hope of becoming a model acts as an incentive to spur people to greater effort. Hence model presentation is an incentive device, and this is the fifth function that models serve. But it is not possible to understand this last function without placing it in the context of the enduring tension in contemporary China between the advocacy of peer respect and of material rewards as appropriate incentives.

Peer Respect as Incentive

The Maoist position on incentives is complex and has varied somewhat at different times. Writing in 1961–62 ("Reading Notes on the Soviet Union's 'Political Economy' "), Mao said:

> Even if one acknowledges that the use of material incentives is an important principle, it still does not constitute the only principle. There still must be another principle, and this is the principle of spiritual encouragement from the perspective of political thought. At the same time, material incentives cannot be discussed solely from the standpoint of the individual's interests, but should be discussed from the standpoint of the collective interest, and in terms of making the individual's interests submit to those of the collective.[21]

This indicates that both material and nonmaterial incentives are acceptable. But material rewards must be sought with the proper attitude, and because they normally are pursued for personal gain, the long-term Maoist trend has been to downgrade them. Thus in 1975, there was widespread attack on them. Such incentives are said to hamper unity among workers by making them seek their own profit; they promote status inequality; and they foster capitalist thoughts.[22] Yet they continue to exist, because wage differentials cannot be abolished, only minimized. Once again, there is tension in a Chinese philosophical concept, between toleration for a psychologically dangerous incentive that accompanies wage differentials, and a preference for other incentives (like peer respect) that are less automatically associated with a self-regarding orientation.

We now know that there was a high-level dispute that began to emerge at the famous "7000 cadres conference" in 1962 concerning the degree to which material incentives should be used. Liu Shao-ch'i, leaning toward the Soviet pattern of socialist development, apparently favored their emphasis, a position that Mao opposed.[23] Thus there was by no means total consensus on the desirability of alternatives to the profit motive.

The Chinese have no intention of eliminating inequalities in the distribution of income.[24] But their attempt to minimize status differentials based on distributive variations stands out among socialist societies. Models have high status, but it is not based on their cash income. They receive primarily honor, and others are believed to be motivated by a desire to obtain it too. Thus even when models serve as part of an incentive system, they receive objects or appointments intended to bolster their prestige, rather than receiving money. In the Soviet Union, where the attempts of the early 1920s to avoid using monetary incentives to increase worker output are denounced as "Menshevism," model workers can receive, in addition to large piece-rate wages, huge cash awards of from fifty thousand to one-hundred thousand rubles.[25]

In the Soviet Union the primacy of material incentives is conveyed to individuals not simply in the reward system found in work units, but also in the very educational materials to which they are exposed from early childhood. A study of Russian textbooks used in grades five to ten of the Soviet ten-year school from 1917 to 1957 analyzed the explanations given in the texts as to why large segments of the population have worked hard to advance socialism (table 1). The study suggests both the high level with which material rewards are actually used as incentives in the USSR and also the absence of significant official disapproval of their use.

At the height of China's "learn from the Soviet Union" period in the mid-1950s, production models normally received both honors and material

TABLE 1

Motivation of Majority Support of Socialism in the Soviet Union

Years	Material	Political	Status	Ideological	Soviet Patriotism	Other
1917	41.0%	34.0%	0.0%	23.0%	0.0%	2.0%
1918–20	38.0	40.0	0.0	22.0	0.0	0.0
1921–25	53.5	24.0	4.5	16.5	0.0	1.5
1926–32	58.0	7.5	28.5	2.0	0.0	4.0
1933–37	54.0	4.0	34.0	2.0	2.0	4.0
1938–41	57.5	2.5	28.5	0.0	6.5	5.0
1941–45	27.0	9.0	16.0	3.0	37.0	8.0
1945–57	50.0	1.0	35.0	0.0	7.0	7.0

N.B.: Total classifiable statements in each time period range from 25 to 97. It should be remembered that 1941–45 were war years. Definitions of the motivations: *Material*—desire for or acquisition of means for an economically better life (e.g., payment according to quantity and quality of work done is often given as a cause of increased production). *Political*—desire for or acquisition of freedom, the right to participate in self government, etc. *Status*—desire for or acquisition of power, rank, or privilege in some institutional hierarchy (e.g., acceptance into party, medals, titles, promotion in rank, etc.). *Ideological*—recognition of the validity of Marxism-Leninism or of party policy. *Soviet Patriotism*—love of socialist) fatherland. *Other*—various infrequently mentioned motives such as desire for peace, cultural opportunities, etc.

Source: W. K. Medlin, "Analyses of Soviet History Textbooks Used in the Ten-Year School," *Studies in Comparative Education: Teaching in the Social Sciences and the Humanities in the U.S.S.R.* (Washington, D.C.: Office of Education, Division of International Education, U.S. Department of Health, Education, and Welfare, December, 1959), p. 26.

rewards. For example, during the Szechuan labor competition in 1956, according to the official directives, models were to receive honors in several forms (a title, certificate, name on the honor board, or a banner) and material rewards.[26] The general trend has been for both the amount of monetary reward and its prominence to diminish substantially beginning in 1958 and lasting to the present time. For example, references from the late 1950s onward state that model innovators are not concerned about monetary rewards, and that they are not motivated by the desire for a bonus.[27] There is evidence from both interviews and the media that monetary rewards, in the form of bonuses, were given to model workers until 1966, although they were never publicized, as they had been during the mid-1950s. The following example is rather typical. The inventor of a special drill, a factory engineer of working class background, was reported to have been asked by a fellow worker how much of a reward he had received for his invention. He did not answer directly but replied, "The highest award I received was the honor and praise of the Party."[28] In some regions, the practice was to ensure a substantial time gap between an individual's elevation to model status and his receipt of a bonus, strengthening the pretense that there was no causal relationship between the two. Furthermore, there was a decrease in the amount of monetary reward after 1958.

Material rewards have crept in the back door in other forms. Preferential consideration has been given to applications from models' children to enter the institutions of higher learning that pave the way for entry into a privileged stratum. For example, the eldest son of a labor model, a representative to the National People's Congress, entered an industrial research institute in Harbin; the other children were described as a doctor and an upper middle school student. The message that none of these children was working down on the farm would not have been lost on readers. Models themselves could be selected for a part-time or half-work, half-study university, and it is not unusual to find model teachers at the primary and lower middle school level being sent to a regular university. There are also references to special medical care. Model workers generally receive preferential consideration for apartments in factory-owned buildings and are also tapped to be sent to workers' resorts.[29]

Increasingly, however, the age-old Confucian theoretical aversion to profit (*ᶜli*) as an incentive has widened the gap with Soviet practices. The primary form of honor (which takes the place of *ᶜli*) comes from being emulated by others, but the range of techniques used to enhance the stature of the model is very wide. He may be given a political post or membership; his name may be attached to a technical method; or, especially in the case of the deceased, a brigade may be named after him. Honorific titles are frequently assigned to both individuals and groups. For example, an individual may receive the title of "a three-good student," "a five-good youth," or "National March Eighth Red Flag Holder," in addition to the common titles of advanced producers listed in table 2. A four-year old selected for his adeptness at gathering cow and pig droppings for use as fertilizer was awarded the title "droppings-collecting model," a red flower, and a rubber ball. Groups may be entitled "Tough Bones Sixth Company," "a five-good organization," or "Exemplary Red Ninth Company in the Study of Chairman Mao's Works." Certificates, likewise, are issued to both individuals and organizations. Banners to hang in work areas may be awarded, and names may be registered on honor boards. Various other honorific mechanisms include being sent abroad, being sent to Peking to participate in

TABLE 2

Titles of Models

I. Production models
  A. Labor heroes (*lao-tung ying-hsiung*)
  B. Model workers (*mo-fan kung-tso che*)
    1. Top grade labor model (*chia-teng lao-tung mo-fan*)
    2. Special grade labor model (*t'e-teng lao-tung mo-fan*)
    3. Advanced producer/worker (*hsien-chin kung-tso che*)
      a) First class
      b) Second class
      c) Third class
    4. *a*) Commune labor model (*kung-szu lao-tung mo-fan*)
      b) Factory labor model (*ch'ang lao-tung mo-fan*)
    5. City, country, regional, and provincial labor models.

II. Cultural models
  A. Heroes in culture and education (*wen-chiao ying*)
  B. Model educators
    1. Excellent teachers (*yu-hsiu chiao-shih*)
    2. Advanced teachers (*hsien-chin chiao-shih*)
    3. Advanced educational worker (*hsien-chin chiao-yü kung-tso che*)
    4. Advanced worker (*hsien-chin kung-tso che*)
    5. Model teacher from the masses (*mo-fan min shih*)
    6. Specially cited excellent teacher (*yu-hsiu chiao-shih t'e-teng chiang*)

III. General terms
  A. Pacesetter (*piao-ping*)
  B. Typical model (*tien-hsing*)

ceremonies, which might include dining with a high party official or having one's photograph taken with the mayor (or head of the Revolutionary Committee) of Peking, being given membership in various scientific and technical societies, and having one's innovations displayed in public exhibits. Posthumous rewards include elevation to Party status and publicly financed funerals. The use of the reward of honor has an added significance in China in that groups tend to regard themselves as sharing in the honor of one of their members. This strengthens the importance of the incentive.

Of course, this incentive is not used simply to increase the quantity and quality of production in a manner consistent with state values or policies. It is also used to stimulate people to follow any course of action that may currently be required by official policy. Thus faced with the need to have large numbers of young people move to the countryside, officials have relied, among various positive and negative inducements, on selecting certain individuals who had already made the move successfully. They were made delegates to the National People's Congress and labeled as "New-Type Farmer Heroes" (*hsin-hsing nung-min ying-hsiung*).[30]

How Models Are Selected

The Chinese have been selecting labor heroes and model villages and propagating their deeds since guerrilla days. Newspapers throughout the border regions carried the accounts, and the literate related them to residents of remote villages. Exemplary teachers were also chosen then, and other teachers brought in to learn from them.[31] One of the most striking phenomena about exemplars in China today is the pervasiveness of model selection throughout all organizations right up the chain of command and the quantity of exemplars chosen. In 1959, in the country as a whole, some 3,000,000 "advanced producers" and over 300,000 "advanced units" were selected. In Tientsin city the following numbers of models were selected in various grades in 1963.

66 "special grade models"

33 "special model groups/teams"

568 "labor models"

290 "model groups/teams"

38 "advanced enterprise units"

Seven-thousand model teachers were selected in Heilungkiang Province in 1956, and in 1957 Tientsin city held a meeting for 255 model teachers, while over 1,000 attended a similar gathering in Shanghai. The Cultural Revolution did not, by any means, decrease the use of models.[32]

Two rather different processes of selection and propagation of models have been implemented in China, one somewhat imitative of Soviet "socialist emulation" (*sotsialisticheskoe sorevnovanie*) campaigns and one indigenous, which eventually took front stage from the other after incorporating some of its features.

In the Soviet Union, socialist emulation was first adopted on a mass scale in the late 1920s.[33] It was conducted either between work units or between individual workers and usually involved a challenge to compete for some given economic goal. Its major purpose was to increase production by stimulating the less productive to reach the level of their leaders. Eventually, there was a shift in emphasis from individual physical effort to improved cooperation and technical leaps. Until the mid-1950s, then, the purpose of socialist emulation was to increase worker output; this later shifted to increasing innovation.

Following in the Soviet path, labor competition campaigns involving the use of models were first held throughout China on a wide scale in 1956. The use of campaigns to establish models has generally been directed at a specific kind of work organization. For example, in Szechuan province the most widely publicized campaign affected organizations in commerce and foodstuffs, marketing and supply cooperatives, organizations concerned with the purchasing of agricultural products and salt, and those having some link with foreign trade. The purpose of the campaign was said to be to improve the transportation flow of products, reduce damage to goods, raise the quality of service, and increase worker activism. One of the most famous campaigns was the "compare, learn from, surpass, assist" (*pi-hsüeh-ch'ao-pang*) (hereafter, CLSA) campaign that began in the spring of 1963 in eastern China, primarily in Shanghai, and was directed at light industry, textiles, and communications. Gradually this campaign converged with a nationwide movement which itself imitated an emulation campaign begun in the People's Liberation Army in 1960.[34] Inspired by the PLA ideal of the "five-good soldier" (*wu-hao chan-shih*) and the "four-good company," these industrial organizations sought to discover "five-good workers" and "five-good enterprises."[35] By 1964, in some areas the established label "advanced producer" had given way to the label "five-good advanced producer." Besides drawing on the experience of the PLA campaign, the leaders of the "five-good" campaign drew upon knowledge gained in all previous socialist emulation practices since 1956. Eventually, this campaign took on nationwide characteristics. In addition to the major campaigns there were routine quarterly and annual procedures for the selection of models in factories, which also drew some inspiration from Soviet socialist emulation campaigns.

Sometimes paralleling the "labor competition campaign" method for the selection of models, but gradually superseding it in degree of official approbation, is a method derived from guerrilla warfare strategy. This method is characterized in the phrase "from point to surface" (*ts'ung tien tao mien*).[36] During the anti-Japanese and civil wars, guerrillas were supposed to occupy the *mien*, or rural areas, which they would use to attack the *tien*, or cities, controlled by the enemy. At the same time, Mao used these two terms, *tien* and *mien*, to describe the need for leaders first to link themselves closely with the masses in a given area and then return to their leadership responsibilities for a larger area more knowledgeable than before. In *Some Questions Concerning Methods of Leadership* (1943), Mao stated that leaders should "squat on a point (*tun-tien*), gain experience, expand the experience from the point in order to lead the whole surface, and unite point and surface.[37] After the establishment of the People's Republic, the term "from point to surface" continued to indicate this obligation of leaders to spend time at the local area, and, in fact, a "three-thirds" system was established, in which one-third of the provincial cadres were sent to "squat on a point" for a given period, while another third toured the entire large area (*mien*).

Elements of this doctrine were extrapolated and reformed into a new style of model selection and propagandization. Cadres were instructed to "squat on a point," uncover a potential model, cultivate him, and then spread knowledge about him to the larger area. The inspiration of guerrilla warfare practices is still evident in the new model theory. For example, cadres are advised not to set up too many models, because this would be like extending one's front line too far, thereby dispersing strength. In other words, the primary qualities of the models will tend to blur as more models are selected, and, also, the masses will not be sure which models to follow. Guerrilla tactics were used by small forces against larger forces. Similarly, the method of selecting specific points for concentrated effort is justified in the name of the contrast between a limited number of officials and the large mass of workers who need to be educated. Use is also made of a principle derived from Marxist epistemology, i.e., "any particular is included in the general, and one must proceed from the particular to the general and from the general to the particular."[38]

The point-to-surface model theory differs fundamentally from Soviet social-ist emulation theory even though it continues some practices derived from Soviet theory. The first major difference is the partially decentralized character of the point-to-surface theory. Central authorities do not always give the signal for workers or work organizations to compete in making innovations or increasing output. County or commune cadres can identify and propagandize models on their own initiative. A general spirit of infor-mality and local initiative characterizes the point-to-surface technique. Offi-cial guidelines pressure for a grass roots character to the selection. Cadres are encouraged not to sit at the top and judge, but to make the selections while themselves temporarily working on a problem with individuals at the point.[39] In contrast, the absence of mass participation at any state in the Soviet approach is revealed in official criticisms by Soviet officials them-selves. An analysis of a one of these critiques states it this way:

Instead of encouraging the "initiative of the masses," emulation is often launched from above. Managers draw up workers' pledges to overfulfill the norms and issue them in the name of the workers, without previous discussion and oftein without their knowledge.[40]

Theoretically, in China the selection of candidates for model status is supposed to entail "free discussion and democratic election"; in other words, it should reflect the application of the mass line.[41] Needless to say, as with all attempts to stimulate decentralized management in China, there have been strong countertrends toward retention of certain key controls at the center. Some units have been criticized for adopting a method of "nomination by the leadership and approval by the masses."[42] But the grass roots orientation is not a sham.

The local input is significant because co-workers are often said to be best able to judge the character of the candidates. Production output and quality, in contrast, can be easily judged by central authorities without taking the trouble to consider the moral excellence of the workers. It is felt that the danger of ignoring the local voice is that technical skill alone may be judged by those at the top.

A second difference between the Chinese and Soviet practices is that in the Chinese format, in order to be selected, an individual or group does not need to meet a technical standard above the norm for a given production task in the country as a whole. This is based on a dialectical principle, similar to that discussed in the chapter on malleability with regard to the perfectibility of individuals. All units and places contain within themselves elements that are advanced, middle, and backward. No unit lacks a potential model, and a spirit of intense relativism should characterize the standard used for judging models.

The informal point-to-surface method of selecting models was used in rural areas periodically during the 1950s. It was first integrated with nationwide mass movements in 1963, consummating the marriage of elements from Soviet socialist emulation with the indigenous methodology. Since 1960, model selection has been accomplished either through campaigns that incorporate elements of the point-to-surface method, or, locally and informally, by that method alone. Both of these approaches provide vehicles for the identification of individuals who combine a knowledge of technical facts with the proper values. Common to both has been the expectation that the prospective candidates will satisfy certain political or ethical conditions:

perhaps good family background, activism in political meetings, and aiding less advanced workers. These elements have always appeared stronger in the Chinese selection procedures than in those in the Soviet Union. Still, there is a qualitative difference between the criteria used after 1958 and those used during the period of borrowing, 1953–1958. This difference tells us something of importance about the enduring function of models in China.

During the period 1953–58 model campaigns were used primarily, though not exclusively, to raise the quantitative output or to improve the technical qualifications of industrial, commercial, or agricultural workers. In the guidelines concerning rewards to be given to models of innovation that were promulgated in Szechwan in 1956 it is explicitly stated that the model's attitude toward labor is not to be considered. This fact reflects fairly accurately the spirit of the period in the country as a whole. Although moral and political factors were elsewhere taken into account, they were not treated as central. After 1958, models were used as an incentive to raise output or increase skills, and also as a vehicle for facilitating the mental transformation of all workers, both during the campaigns and afterward. Those selected as models were those who had excelled at teaching others, and they were expected to continue to do so. Enthusiasm (''socialist activism and creativity'') and understanding of the ''meaning'' of their work are expected to become permanent personality features of those who participate.

How Models are Cultivated

The cultivation of a model is conceived simply as a special mode of fosterage. Even the langauge is reminiscent of the image of nurturance we have encountered since the beginning of this study. It is said that ''the model is like a tender seedling, and the leader like a laborious gardener.''[43] The potential model's social nature must be properly molded, as must the natures of those to whom he is presented as a learning object.

Theoretical studies speak of three phases in the process: ''uncovering,'' ''cultivating'' per se, and ''summarizing.''[44]

Formal campaigns have begun with what is called ''a period of fermentation'' (*yün-niang*). This period gives officials the opportunity to observe ''sprouts of goodness'' and to identify defects in all workers, including prospective models. The way is thereby paved for the cultivation phase when such sprouts and defects become the objects of the cadres' attention. During this phase officials take pains to explain the relationship between professional excellence and conformance with officially sanctioned norms. As observers, they are in a position to note which individuals are making acceptable progress in this connection. The whole process might be capped by a rally (*tung-yüan hui*).[45]

There are less formalized methods of uncovering potential models. In the point-to-surface technique, the decision is usually made by a county official who has "squatted on a point," observing for himself and consulting with workers in a given brigade. Then, after a cadre squatting on a point has identified a potential model (or after the quarterly selection in a factory), the future model is subjected to an intensive cultivation program.

The primary purpose of this cultivation is to ensure that, in addition to learning the "meaning" of his work, the model correctly relates the technical skills that he develops to both proper evaluative feelings toward state political policies and also to a sense of his own duties to further them. Prior to 1966, the primary responsibility for this cultivation would be assumed by either the Youth League or Party representatives in the work organization.[46] In this connection, political readings are assigned to the candidate, and home visits are made in the evening, both for further directed instruction and to involve family members in the cultivation process. In addition, the worker will probably be sent to meetings in which established models discuss their experiences. Occasionally, the individual may be sent part-time to special classes in a formal school or, in even rarer instances, he may attend school full time. Finally, the individual's responsibilities will usually be increased.[47] These phases of the cultivation process continue, at a lower pace, even after the individual is given formal "model" status.

The principle of the existence of positive and negative points in all individuals was discussed in the chapter on malleability. The purpose of this ongoing cultivation is to continue aiding the individual in the proper resolution of his thought contradictions, thereby impeding backsliding.[48] The following statement illustrates the seriousness with which this continuing education is taken:

> We must strengthen the education, training, and management of advanced figures. We must not let them float or sink by themselves. In the past, some municipalities and *hsien* relaxed their control over education. As a result, a handful of advanced producers lagged behind, and some individuals even changed in nature for the worse. This should have provided us with a profound lesson. . . . We must adopt the "divide-one-into two" approach, toward advanced figures. We should avoid "booting them out" on finding the least fault. Yet we should not be too lenient or too ready to make concessions. We

must constantly exhort and guide them to study and apply Chairman Mao's works in a flexible way. We must educate them so that they can have a correct attitude toward achievements and honors, and refrain from being arrogant and self complacent by steering away from the masses. In strengthening the education and management of advanced figures, some localities from the municipal to the basic level call for graded management, for pledges to complete a job at every level, for constant contact, for strengthened leadership, and for continuous help. Some localities and enterprises hold regular forums. At such get-togethers, they study production tasks with the advanced figures, listen humbly to their suggestions, exchange ideas with them, and give them education. All these measures have been tested and found effective. They are worth being popularized.[49]

The final aspect of the process is "summarization." In this phase the model publicly explains his "advanced experience" so that others may imitate them. There is a variety of forums for summarization. The model may travel to other work units to spread his advanced experience, people may be brought to visit him, or the media may carry interviews. However, the primary forum is the selection meeting, at which the formal status of model is confirmed. The meetings serve a variety of purposes. They are the occasion for public reward to the model in the form of honors or certificates. They serve to spur other workers who are under social pressure to take an oath at the meeting to try to emulate the model just selected.[50] Most important, though, is the summarization itself.

In his summarization, the model assumes his role as educator. He will relate his technical skill and problem-solving ability to state guidelines (*fang-chen*) and values. For example, he might explain that his new machine design was developed in harmony with the following policies, of which he approves: (1) emphasizing agriculture, rather than heavy industry, as the base; (2) adapting that which is "foreign" to China's actual situation (the original machines being of foreign origin); (3) self-reliance, manifested in using old parts and thus avoiding requests to higher levels for new ones; and (4) reducing the number of technicians which the central government must provide to the factory.

A model teacher summarizing his teaching innovation (perhaps a new textbook design) would explain how his product reflects consultation with peasantry regarding content to be taught in a given area. The point would be that his innovation conforms to the Party's policy of "ending the domination of the schools by mental aristocrats aloof from the masses."

Once again, we find confirmation of the principle that the content of all education is dictated by the legitimacy criterion and the fosterage function of government. This holds true in the obvious case of models when they are serving exclusively as moral exemplars and also in the case of models who facilitate the transference of technical skills.

The most distinctively Chinese characteristics of model utilization are direct consequences of the concept of man in Chinese Marxism. The ramifications of these are enormous, affecting both the selection criteria and the process of cultivation of models after they have been tapped as potential exemplars. The operative principle is the same as that found in formal schools: Education and moral education are fused. The legitimacy criterion must be operative. Thus, a model must be able to link technical and value considerations.

The refusal sharply to bifurcate the realms of fact and value remains intact, even when the facts to be purveyed are technical skills displayed in the handling of machinery, use of the plow, or application of independent judgment to invent a better spindle. In addition to standing as an instance of the operation of general principles developed in the earlier chapters, model theory reveals further dimensions to the Chinese concept of man. These include the beliefs that people learn primarily through imitating models and that peer respect is a powerful human need that can be successfully used as an incentive.

The Chinese theory of model emulation reveals an awareness of psychologically valid principles of human behavior that are seldom given their due in liberal democracies. The need for recognition is a primary need, and the establishment of models caters directly to that need. Liberal democratic societies, in contrast, have traditionally relied largely on monetary rewards or other material privileges of office rather than on devices of minimal financial value that symbolize group honor or respect. In doing so, they have neglected to tap a source of human motivation that the Chinese have understood so well and embodied in their selection of models.[51] In addition, there is considerable Western research that gives support to the Chinese claims about the efficacious nature of learning through imitation. We simply point here to the work done by American psychologists such as Albert Bandura, who have been working on the principles of ''observational learning'' since the 1960s.[52]

On the negative side, one might expect that the use of models would impede creativity in the technical sphere, through encouraging people to think of an antecedent approach to a problem (how the model would solve it) rather than to examine the objective dimensions of the problem themselves. Theoretically, the solution is to insist that each model be an exemplar of independent judgment and flexibility. A manual directed to university teachers addresses itself to the link between moral development and the ability to think for oneself:

> Cultivating independent thought and independent work abilities are not only questions of method, but first of all they reflect people's attitudes towards learning. Only if you establish the correct attitude towards learning can you then speak about self consciously and actively cultivating the abilities of thinking and working independently.[53]

Models are frequently said to achieve their "advanced experiences" (often, making innovations) as a result of the exercise of independent judgment. However, on normative matters, the use of models does support and perpetuate authoritarian tendencies. Models do not exercise independent judgment on such issues.

In addition, there is still some muddy thinking in the Chinese view of models as an incentive device. Why is the pursuit of honor any less "selfish" than the pursuit of material rewards? The Chinese themselves seem aware of the problem. Occasionally, it is mitigated by the primacy given to the selection of advanced units as opposed to advanced individuals, but the singling out of individuals has continued. Periodic attempts to cope with the matter by combining anonymity with rewards have taken on almost farcical, detective-like aspects. The following announcement is typical.

> However, several blisters caused by the boiling oil on the young man's face betrayed his identity. He was Chang Nien-i, a second-year student at the university. When he was asked why he kept his action secret, he said, "It was nothing to shout about. It was only natural for a Communist Youth Leaguer to lend a hand in such an emergency. Why should I tell anybody about it?"[54]

Actively seeking honor and being blatant about it might lead to the charge of "individualistic heroism" (*ko-jen ying-hsiung chu-i*).

On the other hand, other works openly treat respect by the group as a natural goal that individuals seek, and humiliation by the group (the dunce cap is the usual symbol) as the punishment most naturally to be feared. In these contexts, because money alone is associated with profit and selfishness, it is assumed that there is nothing wrong with motivating people by offering the possibility of peer respect or honor. In this curious view, there is nothing self-regarding about pursuing peer respect.

An adequate answer to our critique would require the Chinese to cease using the concept of material incentives to describe the negative kind of motivational devices and to substitute a term broad enough to comprehend a whole range of other rewards, including being a model, when those rewards are pursued for primarily private, egotistical reasons. Thus, the emphasis, quite consistent with their general orientation, would be more on the recipient's attitude toward the reward than on the nature of the reward itself. Conversely, material incentives, when sought on behalf of some group good, could be legitimized. This seems consistent with Mao's 1961–62 discussion of material incentives: "material incentives cannot be discussed solely from the standpoint of the individual's interests . . . but should be discussed in terms of making the individual's interests submit to those of the collective."[55] Perhaps new terms such as "selfless or selfish incentives" are needed, instead of "moral or material incentives."[56]

Chinese analyses of human motivation often ignore the fact that the people's motives are complex and varied. A person can both act on behalf of a group in a manner that most objective observers would describe as selfless, yet also be selfishly concerned to receive that approbation of the group. Even though the pursuit of personal gain is praised in a capitalist society, this does not mean that it alone is sought by those who apparently most actively relish it. They may also enjoy the group respect that is an indirect consequence of wealth.

Another theoretical difficulty with model emulation lies in the idea that they should be typical. One of the most commonly encountered terms for models is *tien-hsing,* which has precisely the meaning of typical and is often used in the sense of the typical character that socialist realism requires writers to depict. Providing a typical model assumes that there is potentially a reasonable overlap in the significant descriptive comments one could make about the model (class, personality traits, interests) and about the people to be influenced by him. This convergence may occur in many cases, but it is also true that certain workers can never expect to meet the qualifications of a model, perhaps because of class background. Thus, for them the ideal will have little incentive power.[57] Furthermore, the virtues of some models may be so exalted as to appear an unrealistic goal to attain.

As a practical difficulty, some individuals regard the status of model as undesirable, in that it is burdensome. They do not relish constantly having to be like Caesar's wife. And continual shifts in policy sometimes cause situations in which principles identified with models at one moment become obsolete the next. At the least this confusion can cause apathy toward the models who locally stand for the obsolete principles; at worst, it creates an unwillingness to go out on a limb and become actively associated with any policy guidelines.[58]

In addition, the Chinese themselves often maintain that certain segments of society labeled ''reactionaries'' cannot be transformed by the presentation of models alone. They must undergo other forms of struggle as well. This is patently inconsistent with the general assumptions that all people are attracted to and seek to imitate virtuous models. Thus there is something fuzzy in claims about the conditions under which model presentation will and will not be effective. Most likely the conditions under which it will and will not work are far more difficult to unravel than the Chinese have been willing to consider.

Some Western social scientists have proposed the existence of a tripartite set of incentives to explain the varying control techniques emphasized by the Chinese leadership at different times, namely: coercive (fear of physical punishment), remunerative (opportunity for increase in money or goods), and normative. Our study of models helps to show the inadequacy of the third category. ''Normative'' hides at least two distinct sources of successful control, both of which may be facilitated by the presentation of a model. One occurs when a person is taught to know the meaning of his work. The other is peer respect. These are completely different causes of desired behavior. The distinction between them is simply obscured by the single term ''normative.''

It is commonplace to find the adjective ''egalitarian'' applied to contemporary Chinese society and to the core values promoted by state sponsored thought reform. Yet the very existence of models suggests practices inconsistent with some egalitarian principles, because models have a status superior to other people. On the other hand, models are not supposed to receive monetary rewards that would set them off from fellow workers. All of this indicates that the idea of equality in China is a complex one, and that models help both to realize it in their teachings and to complicate it by their existence. The topic of equality, to which we turn in chapter 7, caps our previous investigations because it deals specifically with the content as opposed to the means of state fosterage.

Chapter 7

Equality and the Content of Fosterage

It is not enough simply to speak of fosterage without supplying it with content. In what direction are the social natures of men to be cultivated: What is the ideal personality? We single out equality for special consideration in answer to these questions, first, because it is central among Maoist values, affecting by its realization or abuse all of the other ideals to be possessed by the new man as a result of nurturance. "Democratic" attitudes between the leaders and the led require it. Nonmaterial incentives work best where distributional inequalities are minimal. All-round development involves the elimination of status differences between mental and manual work. In addition, status equality is associated with political unity. Such unity (with equality) is an ultimate goal. It also is a means for achieving the more immediate national, economic, and social goals spelled out in the policy statements of the first years of the People's Republic. The reasoning is: How can one appeal to the people for unified efforts to protect the country against the foreigner, to create an industrial society, or to establish socialism, when social unity is not a fact? The appeals cannot succeed without the unity, and the unity is approached as the social divisions diminish. Political unity is the oldest and foremost ideal in Chinese political philosophy. In the past, it was quite compatible with a harmoniously integrated set of social hierarchies. Characteristically, in the world of the latter half of the twentieth century, it is not. Indeed, in the past political order was believed positively to require status inequalities, whereas in contemporary China it requires their minimization.

A distinctive characteristic of the current era is that for the first time in history in most political systems, officials feel a need to defend unequal treatment of people. In other words, treating people equally today generally requires no justification. In past ages, treating people equally required the defense; there were more cases in which equal treatment would have encountered popular disapproval. Some of the objections to equal treatment were that it: (1)

158

violated religious claims which demand a hierarchical society (the Platonic and Aristotelian influences in Christianity) and comparable variations in treatment before the law; (2) inhibited artistic creation or scientific advance, which necessitates concentration of wealth and leisure in certain hands; (3) it was intrinsically valuable to have variety in society (including in life conditions). The current trend is for societies to eliminate many of the social arrangements and laws that, along with public opinion, helped to perpetuate inequalities of treatment in accordance with justifications which are no longer accepted.

In China, this trend takes the form of an advocacy of minimizing the division of labor; the fosterage process is a key means of accomplishing the task. The ideal that Americans and many Europeans would be most likely to describe with the term "equality" is discussed by the Chinese in terms of "eliminating the division of labor" and turning all people into "all-round persons."

Marx had noted two kinds of evil effects of the division of labor. One of these pertains to its crippling effect on the psyches of individuals. The manufacturing division of labor "converts the labourer into a crippled monstrosity, by forcing his detail dexterity at the expense of a world of productive capabilities and instincts."[1] The Marxian goal is the Leonardo da Vinci style of comprehensive blossoming of each individual psyche. In the long run, all-round development is an ideal for all people. The other evil caused by the division of labor pertains to society in the aggregate, and derivatively to its effect on individuals. Mental labor (decision making) is the preserve of one group. In capitalism, it is the nonproducing property owners, as well as the priests and intellectuals allied with them. A deep antagonism exists between this class and the nonowning producers, which takes the concrete form of class conflict. Ending the division of labor is one way to terminate exploitation and class conflict.

In this chapter, we will focus on the kinds of divisions among people that the Chinese can theoretically and practically hope to minimize through their fosterage efforts, and on the corresponding kinds of equal and unequal treatment that may be expected. Simply put, the aim of this chapter is to clarify what foreigners are describing when they speak of the "egalitarian ideal" in China.[2]

When we talk about egalitarianism in contemporary China, we are not talking about official acceptance of the proposition that all people share to a similar degree important endowments from birth, such as intelligence. We are talking rather about official acceptance of the principle that all people should be treated in certain ways. In the West, arguments for equal treatment usually were supported by appeals to the equal worth of all people. The equal worth came from the fact that God loves all of his creatures equally, and in His eyes they are of equal value. The link between equality of worth and equality of treatment is supported by people's psychological tendency to shift from acceptance of the one to acceptance of the other; but there is no logical connection. In Confucianism, utopian thinkers could have argued for equal treatment on the grounds that all men receive the same benevolent nature from Heaven, or that *^bli* (principle, present in man as the "four minds" described by Mencius) is present to the same degree in all men. In fact, however, they did not. The closest they came was in describing the utopian society of Grand Unity (*ta t'ung*) wherein "they did not treat only their own sons as sons."[3] Parents were still to be treated differently from sons. Most Confucians argued for differential treatment of adults based on their degree of virtue and education. In contemporary China, equality of treatment is based on an individual's membership in that sacred body called "The People," whose value comes not from God's concern but from their role as an instrument of History in remaking China. This membership provides the equal worth.

Compete egalitarianism in any society is theoretically undesirable and realistically impossible. It is morally blind, because it does not take into account differences in people's needs, merit, work, or prior agreements.[4] These should lead to differences in the way people are treated. It is impossible in practice for several reasons. Societies require various functions to be performed for their own maintenance and survival; the number of such functions increases enormously with industrialization. The occupants of the different positions will receive treatment based on their social roles. Related to this is the usefulness to the group as a whole of providing some individuals with privileges others do not receive. Such an argument was used by Mao to justify better rations for officers during the Long March:

> At one point, absolute egalitarianism in the Red Army developed to a very serious extent. It is true that after numerous struggles it has been greatly reduced, but traces of it still exist. For example . . . denying the necessity for officers to ride horses in the performance of their duties and to regard horseback riding as a sign of inequality. To demand absolutely equal distribution of supplies and to object to larger allotments in special cases. . . .[5]

When, then can we say that a society is tending in an egalitarian direction? When three conditions are being satisfied. First, it must be committed to eliminating inequalities or differences in treatment based on grounds which most people feel are not justifiable. Many American observers would include among the unjustifiable bases sex, age, accumulated wealth, race, religion, native region, and social class. Chinese discrimination in school admissions and elsewhere against children of "exploiting class" families means that on that particular point there would not be agreement between American and Chinese views. But there is sufficient agreement on the other points for China to satisfy the first condition. Second, the society must show a need to justify those inequalities that do exist, utilizing arguments with which we would agree. Examples in the Chinese case would include: a person's having been convicted of a crime, his needs (state of health, size of family, etc.), the importance of his work to the society or his level of skill, and his merit. Third, treating people equally would normally require no justification in the society.

But having laid out the circumstances in which we can claim that a society is tending in an egalitarian direction, we have still to discriminate among the differing possible kinds of direction. This is a matter of "treatment," and that idea in itself is in need of analysis. There are four ways in which we can speak of equality of treatment: that based on equality of rights, equality of opportunity, equality of distribution of goods, and equality of status. We shall discuss them in that order, from the least important to the most important, as seen by the Chinese.

Equality of Rights

The kind of treatment associated with equality of rights is protection against government interference with whatever rights are claimed to exist. In liberal democracies, this has been the most important kind of equal treatment, and the right of freedom of conscience has been first among the set of rights.[6] In chapter 1 we noted that the notion of equal rights owes a considerable debt to the struggles of religious minorities in Europe to preserve "liberty of conscience" or the freedom to hold their unorthodox religious convictions. Traditional China had no such background.

Contemporary China could have copied the Soviet Constitution of 1936, which guarantees to each citizen various rights: free speech, free assembly, freedom from arrest (except in accordance with a court's decision or with the agreement of a procurator), freedom from search, etc. Most such statements represent legacies of earlier Russian Marxists who were enamored of Western "rights of man" theory. Their actual implementation in the USSR has been something of a farce.[7] This is not to deny, however, that these notions have had some social impact in the USSR. For example, the Twenty-Second Party Congress of 1962 and the program of the Communist Party of the Soviet Union (CPSU) adopted by it focused attention on the "fundamental rights of citizens" and on the "unfolding of personality" within the realm of human rights. If nothing else, this caused a flurry of philosophical discussions of rights in Eastern Europe. Perhaps the most that can be said is that Russian intellectuals have continued to accept the principle of human rights, to draw spiritual strength from it, and to feel they are not using an unintelligible concept to criticize government restrictions on freedom of expression.

The Chinese Communists never bothered much about equal rights, no matter what the Soviet Constitution said. The concept is simply alien to the Chinese. In its classical formulation, it is almost unintelligible to those who have an organicistic conception of society. How can people exist and have rights prior to joining society by consent (a society that then has an obligation to protect those rights that existed before it)? People are not conceivable apart from society in the organicistic view. To make a claim for such rights is likely to subject one to the charge of "selfishness." (I am referring specifically to the idea of natural rights that constitute part of the human endowment. Obviously, there is an awareness of the legitimate expectations that, along with particular duties, are associated with typical social roles.)

"Selfishness" and "egotism" meant very different things in traditional Chinese philosophy from the meanings associated with the terms in English. They had nothing to do with avariciousness in Chinese. The phrases used to refer to selfishness or its opposite, selflessness, often employ one word used in the polarity "self" (ᵃ*szu*) and "public" (*kung*).[8] Selfishness had different meanings in Confucian philosophy, but the common elements in all were a failure to perceive oneself in terms of a more comprehensive entity to which one belongs and a futile attempt to isolate oneself from it. Thus in the writings of Chu Hsi one finds the statement that "selfish intentions separate, causing a polarity between the self and things" [*kai szu-i hsien ko erh wu wo tui-li*].[9]

None of this is to deny that words like "the right to freedom of speech and expression" may be included in the Chinese constitution or other state documents. Russian influences on these formalities may still endure. But such guarantees are even more hollow than those in the Soviet Union. There they are at least backed up by some comprehension and some acceptance of human rights. In China, when criticism of officials is tolerated, it is justified in terms of the mass line, not the "rights of man."

Equality of Opportunity

Most liberal democratic thinkers today believe that the exercise of individual rights must be curtailed somewhat to permit equality of opportunity also to flourish. Otherwise, some people in the exercise of their rights will acquire sufficient riches and power to provide their kin with far greater opportunities than others can provide their own. Thus any adequate definition of political freedom in liberal democracies will include reference to both equality of rights and equality of opportunity.[10] People have equality of opportunity when they can in fact exercise nontrivial rights.

We must begin by making a distinction between an active and a passive sense of this equality. A contemporary political theorist was describing what we call the active sense when he wrote:

> Man . . . has equality of opportunity with other men when he is free to choose any occupation he is fit for, and when his chance of acquiring that fitness is limited only by defects of nature or morals and not by lack of education or wealth or social prestige.[11]

Furthermore, equality in the active sense requires the presence (or provision by others) of conditions in which people can discover something about the various occupations available and whether or not they have any interest in or aptitude for them. Opportunities in any positive sense are not present when the possibility that one might enter a certain range of occupations never enters a person's head as something within his reasonable expectations.[12] Can one have an equal opportunity of becoming a doctor if no one in one's geographical area or community racial grouping has ever done so and the option is never presented as a live one by teachers, preachers, or mayors?

Equal opportunity in the passive sense occurs when there is a minimum of legal or social restraints on an individual's entering the occupation of his choice. It is found in some agricultural communities when there is substantial license to open up new lands, as was true in America in the eighteenth and nineteenth centuries.

Opportunities for education play an important role in what people have in mind when they speak of equality of opportunity. Equal opportunities in this sense exist in part when inherited wealth, family status, or geographical region have little or no influence on movement up the educational ladder. Thus in the Soviet Union, the better quality of urban schools and the higher percentage of children of ranking intellectuals and cadres in the better schools indicates from one perspective an abuse of equality of opportunity.[13] China's Cultural Revolution was intended to help ameliorate a similar situation; whether it can in fact do so is another question. But in terms of rules issued and actual changes implemented, China has in recent years done much to meet the conditions of active equality of opportunity in education. These include efforts to raise the quantity and quality of rural schools, to bring qualified peasants and workers into regular institutions of higher learning, to provide levels of remedial study for them, and generally to be flexible enough to accommodate those who must work during normal school hours.

Preferential treatment based on natural and moral supremacy is also apparent in China. Although the principle of the malleability of man does not permit talents to be identified as innate, individuals with special ability in the abstract sciences, mathematics, foreign languages, and some performing arts are singled out; a decree of 1972 waived the two year labor requirement between middle school and higher institute for some of them. As for merit, one of the most common rewards for model workers is preferential consideration for more advanced education, either in a regular or in a part-time school.

Part of the definition of equality of opportunity in the active sense referred to all persons being free to choose any occupation for which they are fit. But there is no society in which this can be absolutely true; it will always be limited by the society's need for certain services. (The most obvious example in a liberal democracy is the military draft.) Thus we can with additional precision conclude that any society fulfills the conditions for equality in the active sense when: (1) it permits only defects of nature or morals to serve as justifiable barriers to educational access; (2) its limitations on the selection of occupations affects only some of the people some of the time; and (3) its people are able to discover the nature of a range of occupations and their potential interest or talent for them.

It may be that only prosperous liberal democracies can meet the second condition. Shortages of basic skills in developing countries may require the governments to control strictly the course selection open to any student, and to require graduates to enter specific fields for varying durations. In some African countries, the "tied bourse" is used to enforce the control.

In China, access to education is not as a matter of policy foreclosed to individuals because of lack of wealth (although those from "culturally low" families in rural areas have less chance of rising into upper middle schools than do offspring of more educated parents). But there are definite limitations imposed on the individual's choice of academic program and adult occupation. Students have a very limited range of elective courses. They have little role deciding whether they will go into upper middle school or university. And, although they may indicate a choice of occupation, the final decision is made by others. China is a society in which, one could claim, active equality opportunity exists only in some quite limited respects. But, to the degree that it does exist, it helps establish certain material or objective conditions conducive to status equality.

Equality of Distribution

Striking contrasts between America, the Soviet Union, and China emerge when one considers equality of distribution. The facts relevant to distribution in the United States are so well known that it hardly comes as a surprise to encounter de Tocqueville's remark that "I know of no country . . . where a profounder contempt is expressed for the theory of the permanent equality of property."[14] The legitimacy of the significant property gap was institutionalized in the late eighteenth century in the distinction between Persons, represented by the House of Representatives, and Property, represented by the Senate. One historian described the significance of this 1780 act in Massachusetts as follows:

> For such a division between Persons and Property, as many soon pointed out, was a clear violation of republican equality and homogeneity . . . the Americans in a fashion had solved the nagging problem constituting their bicameral legislatures; but in so doing, they have perverted the classic meaning of mixed government, which had placed honor and wisdom, not wealth and property, in the middle branch of the legislature, and had explicitly violated the homogeneity of interests on which republicanism was based.[15]

This tended, as Madison said, to "offend the sense of equality which reigns in a free Country."[16]

A historian searching for the postrevolutionary moment when the precedent of offering special privileges to certain strata of the USSR was established might fix on that day in 1918 when a delegation of Petrograd Communists went to Lenin to ask if Communists, who had special political duties, could set up a closed restaurant, exclusively for themselves, that would serve better food than was generally available to workers. Lenin replied, "The working class cannot march in the vanguard of the revolution without its activists, its organizers. The activists have to be cared for, and at the present time, within the limits of existing possibilities, must be supported physically. A closed restaurant should be organized. The workers will understand the necessity of it."[17] Inequalities of distribution have not required much justification in the Soviet Union, although one can point to some qualitative changes from the Czarist distribution of wealth. With respect to income during the period of socialism, "to each according to his work."[18]

Distributional equality, like equality of opportunity, derives its importance in China from its role as a means of approaching the paramount ideal of status equality. Yet it is both theoretically troublesome (conflicting with the Marxist principle of payment according to labor, in socialism), and practically impossible (every society will reward differently those who obey its rules more or less than others). The result is one more instance of an ideal existing in a state of tension, lurking in the shadows to create problems even when the usual practice is to have policies inconsistent with it.

There have been many indications of limiting distributional inequalities as an ideal worth approaching when it does not conflict with other official principles. A recent example is contained in the following statement of Mao that was made public on February 22, 1975, in *Jen-min jih-pao* and given wide coverage thereafter:

> In sum, China belongs to the socialist nations. Before liberation she was not far removed from capitalism. Even now she employs an eight grade wage system, distributing to each according to his work, and using money exchange. These policies are little different from those used in the old society. The difference lies in the fact that the ownership system has changed. . . . Presently our country practices a commodity system. The wage system is also unequal, there being an eight grade wage system, etc. Under proletarian dictatorship, this can only be limited.[19]

This statement is often quoted in comments on Marx's *Critique of the Gotha Program,* in which the authors draw on Marxist justifications for distributional inequalities. But the language of those discussions of wage disparities suggest strong tensions between the recognized unavoidability of the disparities, and the power of the ideal. One problem is that wage disparities detract from status equality, which is the most important equality. ("This principle of distribution, applied in the form of wages, divides people into different grades and inevitably causes some people to seek fame, higher position and better treatment.")[20] In addition, the theory behind wage differentials conflicts with the motivational assumptions about men discussed in chapter 6. ("This runs counter to the attitude of communist labor which is voluntary, without quotas and in disregard of pay.")[21] With these tensions, wage egalitarianism is ready-made for factional dispute (Yao Wen-yüan was accused in 1977 of wrongly opposing differentials).

Complete equality in distribution is indefensible for reasons previously given. Practical difficulties from society's standpoint are the importance of given skills to the society and their degree of sophistication. Within these constraints, one could say that a society is approaching realistic conditions of distributive equality when several conditions, pertaining to both wealth and income, occur. The wealth condition is met when the extremes of property possession are eliminated, and when people have only minimal rights to pass property on to their heirs. This condition has been met in China. The holdings of the wealthy were expropriated; state funds are used to ensure a floor under the poorest, to guarantee them funds even in times of drought, and also to provide them with medical services; and there are no significant rights of property inheritance (bicycles, tools, and private plots can be passed on). This does not mean that there are no variations in wealth in China. Some people have bicycles and watches, whereas others do not. But the amount of wealth involved is small.

The income question is more complex. There are significant variations in income, measured in several different ways. Within a factory, the salary range from the highest to lowest of the eight grades of workers may be three to one (excluding apprentices), and reach four to one if one includes engineers. In the society as a whole, the spread among technicians may be seven to one. A few university professors may earn as much as 350 yen per month, perhaps two hundred more than many factory engineers and vastly more than a primary school teacher. The urban-rural income difference may be around two to one. In the rural areas, income differences between individuals on the same production team may be two to one or three to one.[22] But the major variation in the rural areas is between average incomes of agricultural workers in rich and poor communes, perhaps four to one. This prosperity factor is a product of climate, soil, water resources, and so forth.

The state has taken a few steps to minimize the disadvantages that come from membership in a poor commune—for example, providing a larger subsidy from state funds for its primary schools—but the differences between residents of the rich and poor communes remain. In fact, two other current values of the society, self-reliance and decentralization, impede distributional equality in this case. Self-reliance encourages communes to make do with what they have and not to expect too much infusion from outside sources. The fact that self-reliance is often inconsistent with distributive equality enhances the importance of the floor on individual incomes. The decentralization policy favors the smaller organizational or accounting unit. Yet, the smaller the accounting unit or the unit that is expected to be fairly self-sufficient, the more distributional inequality there will be.[23]

Thus one cannot say that distributive equality is being sought in the matter of formal income. However, in terms of real income, the trend has been to narrow the gap, while not seeking to close it. This is done by establishing a minimum wage (eliminating destitution), periodically raising the income of the lowest paid and giving them access to jobs in new factories, and providing many free welfare services. These facts, coupled with minimizing income fluctuation due to illness or natural calamity, constitute the major accomplishments of the Chinese with respect to egalitarian distribution.

With the measures discussed in this section, the Chinese are establishing economic conditions that help reinforce the kind of equality in which they are most interested, equality of status. As we have noted so often before, one of the most significant Chinese insights is that one must make a multi-pronged effort to change a social fact. Educational programs may play a crucial role in achieving equality of status, but they are insufficient without economic bolsters.

Equality of Status

Egalitarianism in Maoist thought refers most properly to the teaching and enforcement by official rules of status equality. Stated in the form of an ethical principle, this claims that, except on justifiable grounds, no person in the performance of his daily life activities should be regularly regarded by others with an attitude of respect or disrespect, conveying a sense of superior or inferior status. The emphasis is on *attitudes*. Attitudes of respect or disrespect may not be based on an individual's type of occupation (in a generic sense, not in terms of a job classification within a type) or geographical region of work or origin, or the life-style associated with either (clothing, speech, hobbies, and so forth). It is legitimate to respect properly appointed supervisory personnel and others selected for particular excellence of performance or to frown on those who deviate from officially sanctioned rules.

In America; status equality has been less important than protection of rights or license to pursue opportunity. This does not mean that opposition to making judgments about superiority or inferiority has been unimportant; it is just that the lesser interest in this form of equality has tended historically to create a mixed situation. In the eighteenth century, southern areas like Virginia were extremely fragmented along social caste lines, with landed aristocracy at the top of the heap. In Massachusetts on the other hand, the situation was completely different. Although favored church and meetinghouse pews were assigned according to social distinction, there was a changeover every three or four years, and the children "huddled together into a common pew without regard at all for differentiation according to parental status."[24] Manual labor in the form of public service (such as road maintenance) fell to everyone. Thus one historian wrote:

> Oligarchy, then, was a virtual impossibility in provincial Massachusetts because there were virtually no oligarchs . . . none whose scale of living or style of life set them off at a secure distance from their neighbors, none whose civic and economic and intellectual superiorities were known and acknowledged by all. . . . If political and economic inequality existed, definitive social distance did not. Deference in such a society was just a dimly remembered dream from the mother country.[25]

Everyone can think of commonplace symbols of enduring egalitarian tendencies in America, such as the need felt by politicians to claim humble origins, the dislike of cultivated English accents, and the avoidance of situations in which one must "pull rank." Yet it is also true that after the industrial revolution, it became popular among the newly wealthy to ape the British aristocracy, and best of all, to marry their daughters into it.

Although status equality has never been a central Soviet ideal, there have been moments when the highest Russian leaders have emphasized it. At one time Lenin found status differences between bureaucrats and ordinary workmen unsupportable:

> the great majority of the functions of the old "state power" have become so
> simplified and can be reduced to such exceedingly simple operations of

> registration, filing, and checking that they can quite easily be performed for ordinary "workmen's wages," and that these functions can (and must) be stripped of every shadow of privileges, of every semblance of "official grandeur."[26]

Obviously, semblance of "official grandeur" can exist in strata other than the bureaucracy. In any case, the clearest evidence that the status distinction does exist is the language of the people themselves. The existence of a distinction between the types of occupation so central to Marx's theory of the division of labor is reflected in the terms *rabochi* (manual workers) and *sluzhashchii* (office workers). The popular press condemns a situation in which parents terrify their children into studying hard, lest they end up doing *chornaya rabota* or "black work," meaning manual labor.

Contrary to the spirit of Lenin's disdain for airs of official grandeur, status differentials are manifested in medals, honorary titles, grants of special apartments, free railway passes, access to stores carrying scarce goods unavailable elsewhere, and uniforms. In the coal industry's engineering and technical staff, for example, nineteen different grades distinguished by prestige and authority were identified in 1947.[27] Each had a distinctive uniform.

There have been two key attempts to utilize the educational system to achieve status equality. The aim was to create the New Soviet Man fashioned in the image of Marx's ideal of all-round development (beneficial to the individual psyche) and to destroy social inequalities (beneficial to society in the aggregate). The first attempt, in the late 1920s, centered on the "unified labor school," a true *poly*technical school. It was aborted in the early 1930s. The second was suggested by Stalin in 1952, implemented by Khrushchev in 1958, and aborted by 1964. In Khrushchev's plan, all students were to be exposed to the various branches of production and science in an eight-year combined primary-secondary school. Though polytechnical in name, many of the schools in fact rapidly became monotechnical, training single labor skills so that they could feed predictable talents into a planned economy. In both the 1920s and 1950s it was assumed that the achievement of status egalitarianism would result both from the fact that all students would be exposed to mental as well as manual labor (bridging the status gap) and also from the fact that they would be exposed to the full range of production occupations found in Soviet society. With exposure would come acceptance of the equal importance of each occupation.

Status equality, especially in practice, strikingly sets the Chinese apart from Americans and Russians. Confucian society was highly stratified, with the major social split being between scholar-officials (mind workers) and peasants (hand workers). Confucian ethics sanctioned special reverence for the cultivated scholar. The trend in contemporary China is dramatically the reverse. Status equality, rather than having an uncertain position in the row of normative icons, has become a central idea. And, in some ways, the Chinese are establishing a society partially conducive to satisfaction of the conditions for status equality. Cadres and model workers are examples of the few justifiable recipients of superior respect, and so-called bad elements of disrespect. As a rule, however, equalities of status need no justification.[28]

The Maoist idea of being a ''servant of the people'' suggests that there are no status distinctions in work done with that intent and result. In commenting on a statement of Mao that ''All our cadres, whatever their rank, are servants of the people,'' *Liberation Army Daily* said in 1967:

> Among the different kinds of revolutionary work, there is only the division of labor; there are no differences such as high or low, lofty or humble. The work in every trade and profession is an indispensable part of the revolutionary cause. . . . He who does whatever work the Party gives him and does it gladly and with a will, without considering rank, burdens or conditions as long as the work is needed by the Party and the people, is a good comrade.[29]

When Mao talked about treating people as equals, as in the statement, ''Marxism-Leninism looks at everyone on equal terms, and all people should be treated as equals,'' he normally was referring to status equality.[30]

The Chinese Marxists have shown very little interest in the crippling effect on the individual's capacities that stems from the division of labor. Their primary concern is with the evil consequences for society in the aggregate. In their view, it perpetuates status inequalities. From their perspective, status inequality, sustained by the division of labor, is intrinsically bad, because it denies the kind of relations between peoples that are always associated with the utopian vision. In Mao's words, ''We must adopt an attitude of genuine equality towards cadres and the masses and make people feel that relationships among men are truly equal.''[31] In addition, the division of labor impedes national unity by perpetuating a gulf between officials and masses, making the latter more difficult to govern and to nurture. It does this by reinforcing status distinctions, based on educational differences, between (to use the expression from the Chou period) ''those who work with their minds and rule and those who work with their hands and are ruled." Unjustifiable status differences, the origins of which are traced to the division of labor, also impede modernization, to everyone's detriment. They do this by inhibiting managers from mingling with workers, thus preventing each from learning from the other. The Chinese conclusion is that the division of labor is wrong because it causes status inequalities, and the status inequalities erode the political and economic processes. To put this instrumental defect once more in terms of equality, we can quote the remark that Mao made in an interview with Andrew Malraux, "Equality is not important in itself; it is important because it is nature to those who have not lost contact with the masses."[32]

In the writings of Marx, as the division of labor ends, the fully developed human emerges. Although the ideal of an individual's Leonardo da Vinci style of full development is almost unacknowledged in China, this does not mean that the phrase "all-round development" is not used. On the contrary, it is widely employed, the Chinese expression being *ch'üan-mien fa-chan*. During the 1950s, there were some people who spoke of all-round development in a manner quite consistent with the da Vinci style. It was said to encompass "broad interests, boundless knowledge, and surpassing talents."[33] Many were Western-educated teachers who advocated the positions summed up under the slogan "teach according to the students' abilities" that were discussed in previous chapters. But one hears almost nothing more of this un-Chinese ideal after 1958. Instead, most writers refer to Mao's statement in "On the Correct Handling of Contradictions Among the People" that repeats the three items in the standard Soviet description of the well-rounded student, advanced in "knowledge, morality, and health." The usual shorthand subsequent description for all-round development in China is "fully developed human capacities in the various spheres of virtue, knowledge, and physical fitness" (*te chih t'i chu fang-mien ch'üan-mien fa-chan ti jen'ts'ai*).

Four basic measures have been taken to ensure status egalitarianism. First, there is a productive labor component in formal schools and an obligation for office workers to go to the farm or factory for varying periods each year. This guarantees a manual labor component in the lives of white-collar workers. The purpose is thought transformation rather than the learning of production skills. Second, literacy campaigns and other attempts to bring culture to peasants and workers through such devices as the part-time school and the increased educational possibilities for their children provide manual workers with some exposure to mental labor. Third, all people are trained in how to participate in discussions concerning group work and welfare, and there is strong pressure actually to do so. (There are constraints on the discussions, of which Marx would not approve; official guidelines set certain topics or points of view out of bounds.)

The educational institutions originally singled out as the best instrument for cultivating students in a manner consistent with Mao's guideline for the all-round person were the half-work, half-study schools. Today, their descendants are the regular schools in which academic material has been reduced and the practical content stressed. Most graduates at the middle school level are supposed to have a knowledge of how some sciences relate to production requirements, literacy, and culture, and a knowledge of state goals and their duties. As a result of both the cultural training, which creates an ability to articulate, and the moral training, which provides the interest, they are supposedly prepared to participate in discussions concerning production and personnel problems in their work units. This provides the possibility of indulging in one of the forms of mental labor, thus helping to bridge the mental-manual gap. As Maoist-style, all-round people are created by educational means, the division of labor gradually evaporates. With it go status barriers that impede unity.

The final set of activities that reinforce approaches to status equality fit under the umbrella of the mass line:

> Treating others as equals means that our cadres must not think that they stand head and shoulders above the masses; they must not issue orders like leaders; they must not take the duties of cadres as a special capital; they must not show conceit and arbitrariness and force their views on others without consulting the masses, while they themselves do not accept mass criticism and supervision. Treating others as equals requires our cadres to concern themselves with the weal and woe of the masses, to know the aim of the masses, and to form a compact whole with the masses. It requires our cadres to consult the masses over problems, to seek their advice and to arouse them to criticize and supervise our work. . . . In the final analysis, the question of assuming a genuinely equal attitude towards the masses is a question of the mass viewpoint and the mass line method of work.[34]

The mass line, one of the important topics in state fosterage efforts, is supposed to instill a sense of specific obligations among officials or supervisors and to create corresponding expectations among the people. These obligations and expectations have resulted in periodic officially sanctioned attacks on and reeducation of members of the bureaucracy tainted with "official grandeur," which demonstrates that the Chinese have not been content simply to tamper occasionally with the school system, as is the case in the USSR.[35]

"From the masses to the masses" does not mean that the center does not make the major decisions. But officials are obligated to mix with the people and ask for their proposals on specific production, planning, or welfare matters. There is no need to romanticize the process. The officials who go to lower levels often give advice about what they consider to be an appropriate proposal. But the proposals can be modified as a result of input from the lower levels. Proposals formulated exclusively by the center and those that are filtered through mass discussion are different commodities. People have a sense of participation in policy formulation, and probably do from time to time in certain places, even if only to modify decisions made above. And those making decisions at the center or giving "advice" are different people because of their rotation to the farm or factory from their counterparts in other societies who do not have that obligation; it would be absurd to think the experience did not affect their work-style or way of perceiving problems. In sum, the people have a minimum mental labor experience (as defined by Marx) to the degree that they discuss under official auspices production and planning problems relevant to their work. This is a nonschoolhouse device for bridging the mental-manual gap that the Soviets have not tried since the demise of worker-controlled factory soviets in 1918. Whether or not the mass line is ever implemented as it is idealized, it is always present to create tensions when the leaders ignore it. It is a constant reminder of the unacceptability of status inequality based solely on occupational positions held by officials, technicians, and managers.

In the pursuit of the utopian goal of status equality, there remains one status barrier to be overcome after those of occupation and region are vanquished. This is the special status that individuals ordinarily attribute to themselves in distinction to other people. As long as this barrier remains, people will not automatically think of the interest of the largest relevant unit in their actions, but will favor themselves. Thus there is a voluminous literature in contemporary China on the topic of "destroying the 'I'," noted in the section on equality of rights.

There is a curious paradox about the ideal of status equality in China, and it pertains to another social value of similar strength: order. In some ways status equality is conducive to order. By decreasing tensions between supervisors or officials and those for whom they have responsibility, it solidifies their relations and promotes order. Communication lines are more open. On the other hand, at times order requires some sharp differentiations between those who give instructions and those who take them. The former may ride in limousines or cars and the latter in buses or on bicycles. In spite of the inconsistent consequences, both values continue to exist in the same society.

Other Values

A positive attitude toward status equality is by no means the only trait to emerge in the new Maoist man as a result of state fosterage. In addition to egalitarianism, the ideal person has positive attitudes toward other characteristics of society in the aggregate. He accepts the need for a proper balance between democracy and centralism. He will be an activist in class struggle and an enemy of humanism. Actually, his greatest efforts may have to be channeled in this direction, because the avoidance of conflict was strongly prized in Confucianism and Taoism for so long in his nation's past. This traditional ethical principle even had cosmological support in the reduction of all phenomena to the status of modes of the action of *complementary* opposites. (China has not had a Heraclitean strand, which spoke of strife between opposites as essential to the creation of things and to ordered change.) His attitudes toward material incentives will be consistent with those of the models described in chapter 6.

The ideal person will also embody certain traits that can more properly be described as belonging to individuals. Selflessness is one of these, and we have already spoken of it in the context of utopian status equality. The selfless person submerges his own immediately experienced interests or wishes to those of a larger unit of which he is a part (in Confucianism, a network of social relations). It is an old value in China, closely associated with mystical currents in Taoism, Confucianism, and Buddhism that proclaim the essential unity of individuals by virtue of their possession of some universal attribute, like Tao, the Buddha nature, or Principle. In its Confucian and Communist form, it derives from the moral intuition that fulfillment of one's role in a social system takes precedence over all other ethical considerations. This produces the ethical stance that duties are a function of that role rather than of more basic properties which a person possesses independently of any social system—needs, interests, or rights. Because selflessness is an ideal supported by a moral intuition and because its fate was not tied to any particular school, it survived the death blows to Confucianism levied in the first part of this century.

All-round development is another individual trait to be fostered, both in the sense of being willing to do mental and manual labor and in the sense of being able to go from book knowledge (theory, mental labor) to problem solving in the field (practice, manual labor). So is knowing the meaning of one's work.

There is something additional of importance that we can say about all of these values. Since people have both long-term aspirations or ideals as well as more concrete, immediate, or self-serving goals, we may regard each of these values promoted by fosterage as doubly prized by Maoists. That is, they are viewed as noble ideals for a future society. They also are prized for helping to attain China's developmental targets, which concurrently pay off in the political loyalty of people whose livelihood interests are satisfied by meeting those targets.[36] Political and social unity in the twentieth century require minimizing social barriers. Accelerated development is the bounty of such unity.

Because the existence of model persons was always so important to educated Chinese (stability and peace depending on their influence), the nature and function of such sages are central in Confucian ethics. They embodied all the traits of the ideal man, such as filial piety, loyalty to prince, reverence for elders, benevolence, and sincerity. The May Fourth Movement (a series of cultural, economic, and political events over a period of several years that were stimulated by anger at the perceived sell-out of Chinese interests by the Great Powers at Versailles, 1919) violently attacked many of the sagely virtues, such as filial piety and loyalty, as ways of keeping China hopelessly backward and in the clutches of an old order. The May Fourth Movement was successful in discrediting the sage. We can view the new man as idealized by Mao as an attempt to fill the void by creating a replacement exemplar, who has characteristics that are understandable and acceptable to many Chinese. By pointing to all these societal and individual traits, we have painted in the final strokes of our portrait of man in contemporary China, before stepping outside it for a critical overview of the next chapter.

Chapter 8

The Chinese Concept of Man

One of the many motives that led me to write this book was the desire to find an answer to this question: What is the source of the extraordinary self-discipline of the Chinese people? Three pieces of this puzzle have emerged in our study. The first is the omnipresent state fosterage or educational activities in which all subject matter ideally should conform to a legitimacy criterion, to ensure that factual information reinforces the learner's awareness of his concrete social duties. Another piece of the puzzle includes conditioning people to be on the lookout for internal ''springs of action'' so as to inhibit the manifestation of the undesirable ones and to promote the implementation of the good. From their earliest years, Chinese children inside and outside the school are surrounded by numerous watchful educators, ready to praise or criticize their fulfillment of those duties and exercise of that self-control. Finally, the attempt to teach people the ''meaning'' (*i-i*) of the work they are required to do is a successful control device, I believe, because it leads to a reduction in the deviant conduct through which alienation is often expressed. Learning the meaning is learning how doing a certain task is consistent with the furtherance of goals and values already accepted. It is one of the motivational approaches that can be unpacked from that muddy phrase ''normative incentives.''

This has been primarily a study of Chinese theories. There has never been a society in which social practices are completely consistent with the theories accepted in that society. The fact that most Americans have accepted the position that ''all men are created equal'' does not mean that political and social institutions have ever been completely harmonious with that claim. In China, the existence of the legitimacy criterion did not mean that Confucian poetry or paintings always conveyed a didactic message. Nevertheless cultural differences between societies caused by their acceptance of certain theories or values, are real and important. The theories and values lurk in the background, ever ready to cause tensions when they are not observed. Thus

177

in future Chinese schools, the sciences may for periods be value neutral, but there will remain strong pressures to bring them back into line with the legitimacy criterion. Purely academic criteria for entry into universities may again be in the ascendency; however, the pressure for weighting heavily the personal character of the candidate will remain latent. The concern for some overt demarcations between chiefs and followers may perpetuate the simultaneous existence of limousines and buses, but the values of distributive and status egalitarianism will endure to generate policy conflict and changes.

Most Americans or Englishmen would find two dimensions to the Maoist concept of man quite striking. One is the minimizing of any distinction between a private and a public domain. The Westerner is accustomed to thinking of a private realm of consciousness or beliefs that normally is no business of anyone except the individual himself; officials may justifiably concern themselves only with the externals of behavior. The other dimension is the commitment to the plasticity of the human mind. This may jolt the American, whose forefathers were brought up on the doctrine that man is born with self-regarding tendencies that cannot be eliminated. He himself is accustomed to thinking in terms of unalterable I.Q. differences or instinctive aggressive tendencies or Oedipus complexes that inhibit personality change or skill acquisition. Moreover, he has probably assumed the truth of the principle that each individual is the best judge of what is in his interest. Therefore, he will probably react with distaste to Chinese assertions that this is not completely true, and that there are a few people in the state apparatus who, drawing wisdom from the masses, become better judges. Finally, though he may not be so startled by two other aspects of the Chinese concept of man, he may not take them seriously. These are the beliefs that emerged in our study of models: people learn through imitation and peer respect is a powerful human need that can be effectively used as an incentive.

In view of the fact that the Chinese and liberal democratic concepts of man differ so radically, it is not surprising that their beliefs about the proper role of the state and of people within it also diverge. To explain why these latter matters vary as a function of the former in itself carries no presumption in favor of either approach. Each can still be examined and evaluated on its own merits. Criticisms of the Chinese positions, to which we now turn, can be made without presupposing that the liberal democratic views are the correct ones. They may be based on a consideration of the way in which Chinese theoreticians use certain terms, the soundness of their reasoning, and consistencies or inconsistencies between various positions they wish simultaneously to hold. Nor does identifying the strengths of the Chinese view commit one to accept it as a whole. Potential support for some of the Chinese doctrines may be suggested by empirical evidence that tilts favorably in its direction, or that undercuts the validity of factual criticisms against them. And yet some of these items may also be found compatible with numerous other liberal democratic themes.

Weaknesses of the Concept

In previous chapters we have noted a variety of weaknesses in the Chinese concept of man and the fosterage principles to which it gives rise. But there are additional defects to which we have not yet referred. These defects concern the nature of the manipulative process directed by some people to others. Specifically, they include the presence of coercion and the fallacious assumption that private and public interests are identical.

The transformation of the people's social natures produced by fosterage is said to manifest itself as an awakening or self-awareness, accompanied by an acceptance of the rules and values of which the rulers approve:

> Purity of thought consciousness is a matter of inserting proletarian thought-consciousness with self-awareness into the brain and continually overcoming and cleaning up all nonproletarian thought consciousness in the brain. This kind of purity amounts to being in an awakened state.[1]

According to the Chinese theory, the awakened person then acts, without visible compulsion, in a manner consistent with official rules and values. Somehow, however, Chinese fosterage seems more like control to the Westerner. There is reasonable cause for this uneasiness, and it is produced in part by confusions in the Chinese discussions of fosterage.

The best way to begin analyzing these confusions is to introduce the Chinese distinction between "persuasion" (*shuo-fu*) and "suppression" (*chen-ya*), because the word "persuasion" is often used to describe the process leading to transformation of the social nature. Chinese commentators have tried to maintain a distinction between persuasion and suppression based on the presence or absence of coercion or compulsion (*ya-li* or *ch'iang-p'o*). ("Communists must use the democratic method of persuasion and education when working among the laboring people and must on no account resort to commandism or coercion."')[2] Persuasion characterizes the activities carried out in regular schools, in study sessions, in presenting models for emulation, and in managing recurrent movements such as those in which people are sent to farms or factories (*hsia-fang*). Thus, its range is commensurate with that of education. It involves reasoning as a means of getting rid of bad ideas and habits and substituting good ones.

Because persuasion employs reasoning, it is distinguished from techniques that use force and praised as superior to them. Chinese today continue to use a Confucian maxim to state this point: "Through the use of force one causes men's mouths to submit; through reasoning one causes their minds to submit" (*i li fu jen-k'ou, i li fu jen-hsin*).[3] Although stated as a general principle, in practice this maxim is not believed to be applicable to all people under all conditions; for example, it does not apply to "nonpeople" and "counterrevolutionaries."

The Chinese term for "to persuade" literally means "to bring into submission by spoken means." And the same character contained in "bring into submission" (the *fu* part of the "persuade" compound) is also used in the phrase, "through reasoning one causes their minds to submit [*fu*]." The Westerner who encounters this fact may become suspicious that there is more to Chinese persuasion than is contained in the English equivalent. Most likely, as a first step, he will think that if minds are being caused to submit, some manipulation of the autonomous man is occurring, and that is bad. This is a concern that will not be shared by a Chinese, for whom the concept of the autonomous man has little meaning. But there may still be a problem with the concept of persuasion itself that does not beg an acceptance of the ideal of autonomy.

B. F. Skinner has described persuasion as follows:

> We *persuade* people . . . by pointing to stimuli associated with positive consequences. Etymologically, the word is related to sweeten. We persuade someone by making a situation more favorable for action, as by describing likely reinforcing consequences.[4]

In contrast, the Chinese conception of *shuo-fu* actually involves verbally linking certain acts with both positive *and* negative consequences. One of the most common techniques in this connection is the study of "negative examples." The state periodically puts forth nationwide negative examples. Mass criticism of them sensitizes everyone to the possible consequences of taking unorthodox positions on a vast range of issues. Other negative examples are rife in the pages of primary school illustrated readers and adult newspapers. For example, an account of work points may refer to the benefits that have come to model workers who were always honest about work points and to the severe criticism and other sanctions leveled against negative examples. Or, people may observe direct verbal attacks on those who utter the wrong views. Because exposure to negative consequences is so intense during the periodic movements in the ideological sector, it is less necessary to stress them when positive models are front-stage in more routine times.

The sweetening that Skinner called persuasion might better be called "making offers."[5] Chinese *shuo-fu* includes both offers and threats (*wei hsieh*). Threats point to consequences that a person finds aversive and are therefore a form of coercion. Threats do not need to be explicitly stated. They can be evident from hints and clues in people's facial expressions or indirect word choices. Our conclusion is that coercion comes in both subtle and blatant forms. It does not consist only of pistols and prison cells.

The distinction between persuasion and compulsion thus breaks down. In China persuasion involves conditioning people to associate both carrot and stick with kinds of behavior they may be called upon in the future to perform. Because coercion is involved in both cases, the distinction between persuasion or education and suppression cannot be made in terms of its absence or presence. Suppression can only be defined as the highly visible, immediate, presence of undesirable controls, such as prison walls, the surveillance of guards, or the firing squad. Obviously all societies use so-called positive and negative reinforcement. We are concerned here more specifically with examining the claim that the persuasion used in Chinese personality transformation does not involve coercion.

At the end of the process of education or persuasion, a person may have new needs and new values. This is part of the "awakening" that phenomenologically characterizes how it feels to be transformed. The Chinese justification of the persuasion of the individual by offers and threats generally is twofold: first, the end result is good for the individual; and second, the small group has every right to bring people around by coercion or any other officially approved means to get them to work for the group interest and the country's and to prevent their working against it.

Let us examine these claims. First, is the person who is "awakened" the same person who was the subject of the lengthy process of transformation?

Before transformation he did not have certain needs or certain values that he now has and that now can be satisfied. But the needs and values of the pretransformation person may still not be satisfied. Is it that one is uncovering "real human needs" that were lying dormant and unnoticed? But, if so, how does one justify the claim that they are more important than other needs?

The other justification is that the group is entitled to control the individual for the sake of the larger, group interest. Workers are told that they must accept temporary sacrifice in order to achieve a utopia that will satisfy the interests of their own working class. But that is a future event. The argument obscures the fact that the present interests of those workers have as great a claim within the meaning of the generalized phrase "interest of the working class" as do those who may live in the golden industrial, classless society of the future. Their present interests must be taken into account too.[6]

There is another criticism that can be levied against elements in the Chinese theory that derive most directly from the principles of malleability and fosterage. In a sense, it is an expansion of the problem just mentioned of equating the interest of a worker today with the interest of the working class collectively. Although Mao himself states in "On the Correct Handling of Contradictions among the People" (1957) that today there may be conflicts between the interests of the state, collective interests, and individual interests, he also concludes that underlying them there is a "basic identity of interests" of the people.[7] Other writers regularly assert the ultimate identity of individual and public interest. The difficulty lies in the fallacious assumption that long-term private and public interests are identical. This assumption affects the kind of education people receive and the careers they enter, as well as what personality traits they assume. The individual's personally, perceived abilities, interests, and needs are in fact of minimal importance.

Chinese theoreticians have made strong, though not original, arguments for the state having some claim over what the individual studies. Since the cost of education is borne by the people, the people therefore have some legitimate voice in what subjects persons study. Students are constantly reminded of how many bushels of grain produced by peasants are required to maintain them in school. The social utility criterion serves as another argument—one should study a subject that will be of most service to the people, and the decision as to what is of most service will be made by officials, not the individual. The first of these arguments is one that is not inconsistent with other norms that Americans accept.

Sometimes the Chinese argument is based on the assumption that abilities, interests, and needs are malleable. Therefore, the authorities are not under as strong an obligation to fulfill them as they would be if those attributes were permanent. But just as often, the Chinese position rests on a misplaced analogy involved in the claim of identity between interests of the individual and those of his party or state. This claim permits rulers or officials, who speak for the party or state, to manipulate people whose stated interests do not meet official approval, on the grounds that those citizens do not understand what their "true interests" are. But claiming this identity of individual and party or state interests is to pretend that political parties and states are like individual organisms. The latter do indeed have identities that are fairly stable and that cover a definable life span. But parties and states do not. They span many generations, during which time their members change and so do the interests that are common to the members. On the one hand there is interaction between an individual's biological nature and social influences leading to his awareness of his own distinctive interests; these normally retain a certain stability over a definable period. On the other hand there is a class, party, or society that never undergoes regular, predictable, kinds of changes as a result of predictable internal and external causes. Individual identity and state identity are not a lion and a pride of lions. They are a lion and the history of many prides.[8]

We can conclude by flagging another problem, one that highlights potential inconsistencies between several Chinese positions. It stems from a few leaders' deciding not only what the people's true interests are but also what values they should adopt. A state needs to have some consensus of values, both to ensure a degree of national unity and agreement over goal priorities, and also to provide some psychic tranquility to the people. In China, the consensus is achieved through the fosterage activities of government. We do not question the need for some qualified consensus. Accepting this position, however, requires us to raise an important question in political philosophy: Who decides what values will be incorporated within the consensus?

Simply to raise this key question is to illuminate a difficulty inherent in one dimension of the twentieth-century egalitarian trend. In China, those who make the decisions are a few leaders who have a practical background of involvement with the masses in solving problems, along with a theoretical background necessary to interpret, articulate, and apply to future problems those practical experiences. The ability to formulate the constituents of a value consensus and then to serve as supreme teachers gives to those leaders a special social position. And this special position is inconsistent with the spirit of the very status egalitarianism that the leaders also choose to foster.

Strengths of the Concept

A number of the strongest points in the Chinese concept have been noted in the earlier chapters. We noted such insights as the following: the fact that the doctrines of "nurture" as well as "nature" have behavioral implications and can serve as self-fulfilling prophecies; that peer respect is a basic human need and appeal to it a powerful incentive; that understanding the meaning or purpose of work is a means for minimizing what we call alienation; that people can learn effectively through imitating models; and that there is a great diversity in the natures of people even within the same social class. There remain several positive points that have not yet been the subject of any specific discussion. These pertain to the Chinese belief in the socially plastic characteristic of human nature and to the refusal to bifurcate the person into a private and a public domain (psychologically).

Without accepting the extreme repudiation of innate ability differentials or character predispositions contained in the Chinese position, one can still find evidence to support their recognition of the significant social influences in the formation of some skills and personality traits. The legacy of belief in prenatal or early childhood impediments (innate depravity, self-seeking tendencies, aggressive instincts, Oedipus complex, and I.Q.) to any alteration of these matters has been powerful in the United States. But the American who is aware of the views of his own leading twentieth-century philosopher, John Dewey, may be more inclined to look with an open mind on the Chinese views. Dewey's position, inspired by the German philosopher Hegel, but supported by his own psychological studies and those of others, is similar to those we have been applauding in China. It departs from that of classical liberalism and Calvinism. He said that human traits are not innate, as the psychological egoist would have us believe, but learned. Social arrangements replicating those in life situations can be built into the schools. Such arrangements "are not means for obtaining something for individuals, not even happiness. They are means of creating individuals."[9] Another fallacy he noted in classical liberalism lies in its view of human nature:

[It] lies in the notion that individuals have such nature and original endowments or rights, powers, and wants that all that is required on the side of institutions and laws is to eliminate the obstructions they offer to the free play of the natural equipment of individuals.[10]

To some degree, the American educational system that Dewey helped to inspire shared with the one in contemporary China the aim of molding personalities. Specifically, it served to turn immigrants of diverse cultural backgrounds into citizens who would accept the predominant nineteenth-century doctrines of liberal Protestantism, progress, and capitalist psychology and ethics. If we accept the fact that some degree of cultural unity is necessary for political stability, the need to create through the schools a certain cultural homogeneity out of perhaps an Irish-Polish-Italian set of immigrants becomes understandable. But there remains a difference. The American educational philosophy remained in principle less committed to this kind of specific personality transformation than did the Chinese. The goal was more present in the reality of the United States schools than in the theory that guided it. The theory was more vague about what values were to be inculcated. Hence the efforts were erratic and the results uneven, causing some to question how much melting actually went on in the melting pot. In China, this transformation is central to the theory and to the reality.

Dewey's obsession with "interaction," both between humans and between people and their environment, is evidence of the residual effect of his original Hegelian orientation:

But only intellectual laziness leads us to conclude that since the form of thought and decision is individual, their content, their subject matter, is also something purely personal.... Association in the sense of connection and combination is a "law" of everything known to exist. Singular things act, but they act together. Nothing has been discovered which acts in entire isolation. The action of everything is along with the action of other things. The "along with" is of such a kind that the behavior of each is modified by its connection with others.[11]

The congeniality of this view of individual entities with the Marxist one that has flourished in China should be clear. Mao reflected a similar orientation:

"the vulgar evolutionist world outlook... regards all things in the universe, their forms and their species, as eternally isolated from one another and immutable . . . the development of things should be seen as their internal and necessary self improvement, while each thing in its movement is interrelated with and interacts on the things around it."[12]

Dewey's position shares important assumptions with the Chinese views discussed in our account of the idea of malleability. These assumptions are summarized in the titles of two sections of his *Human Nature and Conduct*, "Plasticity of Impulse" and "Changing Human Nature." Although the job of transforming the schools as he wished is not complete, Dewey's new view of man did have a powerful and positive impact on American schools. In sum, many Americans have found his position and the evidence supporting it compelling. At the least, this calls for serious attention to the Chinese doctrines that are in spirit compatible with his.

On the subject of the public versus the private domain, most Americans would find repugnant the Chinese violations of privacy or of what Justice Brandeis referred to as "the right to be let alone."[13] Yet they may also find some factual base to the Chinese insistence that it is impossible to draw as fine a line between all private and public events as liberal-democratic theory has been accustomed to draw. Even the nineteenth century's staunchest advocates of the distinction, J. S. Mill, ended by admitting there were problems with it, at least as far as "private" conduct is concerned: "No person is an entirely isolated being; it is impossible for a person to do anything seriously or permanently hurtful to himself without mischief reaching at least to his near connections, and often far beyond them."[14]

Robert Paul Wolff, one of Mill's most articulate critics, asks us to ponder whether or not the beliefs (and practices to which they surely lead) of the meat eater do not cause vegetarians as much pain as blows on the face. Beliefs in class, national, or sexual stereotypes almost always manifest themselves in actions that may lower the self-esteem of people. Psychological impediments to achievement may result, even where formal barriers to career opportunities are outlawed. These matters are open to empirical verification. As Wolff accurately says, "The root of the problem is that Mill treats the distinction between the inner and outer spheres as a matter of fact whereas actually it is a matter of *rights* or *norms*."[15] It is not difficult to find concrete examples to support the Chinese position that many beliefs have a high probability of eventuating in actions that affect others. This leads the Chinese to conclude that these beliefs thereby become the legitimate business of those other people. The private-public distinction indeed is not based on fact.

We end by noting two paradoxes that have emerged from our study. First, although China is the largest Communist society of our era and identifies itself as in part Marxist, it does not accept one of Marx's paramount ideals: the all-round development of the individual who "needs a complex of human manifestations of life."[16] In fact, the society most likely to come closest to reaching Marx's goal may well be a liberal democracy.

We must remember that both Marx and Mill were drawn to the nineteenth-century German Romantic idea expressed, among others, by Wilhelm von Humboldt, for whom "the true end of man" was "the highest and most harmonious development of his powers to a complete and consistent whole."[17] For those Romantics, the artist was regarded as the quintessential self-fulfilling person. Marx accepted the symbol: The free and self-directed man "constructs also in accordance with the laws of beauty,"[18] and such a wealthy man is one "whose own self-realization exists as an inner necessity, a need."[19] *Capital* speaks of "fully developed human beings." Similarly, after praising von Humboldt in *On Liberty,* Mill spoke of human nature as "a tree, which requires to grow and develop itself on all sides, according to the tendency of the inward forces which makes it a living thing," and he spoke of "the importance of genius, and the necessity of allowing it to unfold itself freely both in thought and in practice."[20] The difference between the liberal and the Communist view concerns whether or not that full development is most likely to be attained in a highly directed social situation and integrated community, or in a looser association of persons with a limited range of permissible state or community attempts to control choice making in the realm of life-plans and life-styles. Our supposition would be that it is more plausible in a liberal democracy. And American and British educational institutions, with their legacy of the "child-centered curriculum," are more favorable environments for its nourishment than is the Chinese school that is an instrument of state fosterage.

The other paradox is that the liberal democratic society that enshrined the phrase "all men are created equal" in its founding document is less likely than is China to achieve status egalitarianism. Though not the primary kind of equal treatment implied by the similar worth of all people claimed in this maxim, it was certainly one of the kinds of treatment taken seriously by some Americans, such as the good people of Massachusetts whose favored church pews were forever changing occupants.

Writing in the latter part of the eighteenth century, Edmund Burke put forth arguments against the social mobility that characterizes any society in which the ideals of equality of opportunity, distribution, or status have had a significant impact. Essentially, he argued that people who move from one sector of society to another will become alienated. As children they learned the values of one part of society; when they move into another, they encounter values that are different, and they then feel estranged from the new group. Thus mobility causes unhappiness.

In utopian communism, of course, no such problem would arise because there would be general agreement as to what values are most consistent with man's real nature. In actual societies, however, the argument is plausible enough to consider. One can imagine that in China, which has not yet reached the golden age, a youth of peasant origin who achieved appointment to Peking University might experience differences in life-style and some values between his city-raised colleagues and his home village folk. He might also experience some unhappiness as a result. But the answer that the Chinese would give to Burke's position is probably the most adequate critique of it: his argument does not take account of the fact that people's personalities can change, and with them their beliefs about what is good or right.[21] This is what state fosterage is all about. When properly carried out, it is intended to minimize the disparities between our peasant scholar and his city friends by introducing more convergence in their normative judgments. Fosterage is intended to create individuals who, in traditional terms, will realize the *Ta T'ung* (Grand Unity), in Marxist-Maoist terms will minimize the social division of labor in its mental-manual form, and in American terms will realize an egalitarian society.

Abbreviations

CB   *Current Background*, United States Consulate-General, Hong Kong
CFJP   *Chieh-fang jih-pao* [Liberation daily] Shanghai
CKCN   *Chung-kuo ch'ing-nien* [China youth]
CKCNP   *Chung-kuo ch'ing-nien pao* [China youth news]
CNA   *China News Analysis*, Hong Kong
ECMM   *Extracts from China Mainland Magazines*, United States Consulate-General, Hong Kong
FBIS   Foreign Broadcast Information Service, Hong Kong
HHPYK   *Hsin-hua pan-yüeh-k'an* [New China fortnightly]
JMJP   *Jen-min jih-pao* [People's daily]
JPRS   Joint Publications Research Service, United States Department of Commerce, Office of Technical Services
KMJP   *Kuang-ming jih-pao* [Brightness daily]
NCNA   New China News Agency
NFJP   *Nan-fang jih-pao* [Southern daily], Canton
SCMP   *Survey of China Mainland Press*
URI   Union Research Institute, Hong Kong

Notes

Preface

1. Mao Tse-tung, "Talk at an Enlarged Central Work Conference (January 30, 1962)," in Schram, *Chairman Mao Talks to the People*, p. 163.

Chapter 1

1. This tendency to accept or reject a position because it is expected to make other people's behavior more moral or less moral was not restricted to the Confucians. The general point I am making is a controversial one, and so it is useful to present a number of illustrations. Examples from a variety of thinkers representing different strands in Confucianism and different schools follow.

Mo Tzu: "In addition, the Confucians believe firmly in the existence of fate. . . . If the various officials believe such ideas, they will be lax in their duties; and if the common people believe them, they will neglect their tasks." (Watson, *Mo Tzu*, p. 126).

Mo Tzu: In Section 23, Mo Tzu mentions three tests by which to judge a theory. The one he uses most effectively is "applicability" ("whether, when the theory is put into practice in the administration, it brings benefit to the state and the people.") (Watson, *Mo Tzu*, p. 118).

Mencius: "Mo's principle is to 'love all equally,' which does not acknowledge the peculiar affection due to a father. But to acknowledge neither king nor father is to be in the state of a beast . . . If the principles of Yang and Mo be not stopped, and the principles of Confucius not set forth, then those perverse speakings will delude the people, and stop up the path of benevolence and righteousness." (Legge, *Mencius*, iii.B. 1x.9).

Hsün Tzu: He held that propounding a theory is an exercise in either rectifying names or abusing them. He regarded names as having the power to affect others to such an extent that they can change their behavior. This is a psychological assumption that has some merit. It lies behind the following discussion: "Therefore, the practice of splitting terms and arbitrarily creating names to confuse correct names, thus causing much doubt in people's minds and bringing about much ligitation, was called great wickedness." (Chan, *Source Book,* p. 124).

Lao Tzu: "When the great way falls into disuse/ There are benevolence and rectitude" (*Tao Te Ching,* 18, in Lau, p. 74) and "Exterminate benevolence, discard rectitude,/ And the people will again be filial;" (*Tao Te Ching,* 19, in Lau, p. 75). Reference is to the evils that flow from peoples' adherence to some principles in Confucian moral philosophy. One could also point to references in the same work to the relation between beliefs about names and having desires.

Tung Chung-shu: "Now to claim on the basis of the true character of the basic substance of man that man's nature is already good (at birth) is to lose sight of the will of Heaven and to forgo the duty of the king." (Chan, *Source Book,* p. 276). The king will not do his duty if he believes that men are already good. To reject the theory of the innate goodness of man is to rectify names and thus change the behavior of the rulers, according to Tung Chung-shu.

In "On the Correct Handling of Contradictions Among the People," Mao Tsetung lists six criteria applicable (along with others) to all activities in the arts and sciences, to distinguish right from wrong "in one's words and actions." They include: "(1) Words and actions should help to unite. . . . (2) They should be beneficial . . . to socialist transformation and socialist construction." Reference to the rightness of "words" is the significant point. (*Four Essays,* pp. 119–20).

2. Another way of putting the matter is to say that logical consistency among the ideas constituting a general philosophical position is much less important in China than are the behavioral implications of each individual idea, taken in isolation from the others. Western commentators have seen similar traits in European and Russian thinkers. For example, Barrington Moore, Jr., picks up this theme in referring to Soviet political doctrines: "Nor is it surprising that the Soviet political formula is immune to logical attacks upon it by intellectuals nourished in another tradition. It has long been recognized that the power of ideas does not depend upon their logical coherence alone, but also upon the social functions that they perform." (Moore, *Soviet Politics,* p. 224). Reference here is made to party doctrine rather than to the positions of philosophers, and to the concern of party leaders with what ideas do rather than with their consistency. In the Chinese case we are not witnessing a phenomenon without counterpart elsewhere, but rather one in which a larger segment of the population than just leaders is accustomed to retain or reject ideas on grounds other than those to which we are habituated. That segment includes most philosophers and other intellectuals.

3. Lukes, p. 73. I have learned much from Lukes's analysis of individualism.

4. For example, much of John Dewey's writings on the subject derive from Hegel. With its emphasis on the impossibility of considering a person psychologically or ethically apart from his social nexus, those Hegelian elements stand in contrast to other elements also present in Dewey that derive from the English liberals, such as the two Mills. John Stuart Mill rejected the desirability and, by inference, the necessity of accepting the egoistic portrait of human motivation

advocated by so many in the spirit of liberal democratic individualism. Mill also was not a believer in natural rights, though he did stress the importance of other elements that bring his portrait of man within the liberal fold, namely that of the private self.

5. B. Constant, *Mélanges de literature et de politique* (1829), *Préface*, in *Oeuvres*, Paris, 1957, p. 801. Quoted in Lukes, p. 64.

6. Mill, p. 16.

7. There is another assumption on which these beliefs are based, about the nonsocial source of knowledge, that is generally also accepted by advocates of the private self. This is epistemological individualism, which focuses on the individual, subjective experience of an individual mind and its sensations, ignoring or treating less importantly the shared public context in which experience occurs.

8. J. S. Mill spoke about the freedom from outside interference in both the individual's acts and his beliefs. He helped reinforce what has become a basic difference between liberal democrats and Chinese on the matter of the priority of liberty (freedom of conscience) over other values. But he did so with his position on beliefs, not on acts. His views on the control of acts by outside agents are less far from those of the Chinese than his view on beliefs. (Contrary to some interpretations, he was not a libertarian anarchist, and the best evidence is that he was sympathetic to the socialism of Saint-Simon.) The range of acts that are to be protected from societal constraints is limited: acts that may be dangerous to the performer and those that may conflict with the standards of the majority or with popular custom. The range of beliefs subject to liberty is unlimited. It includes all beliefs.

9. There is also a broader sense of the ''liberty'' which is a right with which we are all born. It refers to the power to exercise without restraint the other rights (self-preservation, acquisition of property, pursuit of happiness) so long as the same rights in others are not violated. Civil rights are those that help individuals achieve these ''natural rights'' (political participation and political association).

10. Quoted in Kenyon, p. 475.

11. Mill, *On Liberty*, chap. 3, p. 72. All social theorists have acknowledged the potential conflict between the goal of liberty and the general well-being of society that is achieved in part by citizen service to the state.

12. Kant, p. 59. Brought to my attention by Steven Lukes.

13. Kenyon, p. 40.

14. Lodge, *Works of Alexander Hamilton*, vol. 2, p. 51.

15. Hamilton, Jay, and Madison, *The Federalist*, p. 337.

16. Hobbes, pt. 1, chap. 13, p. 65.

17. Quoted in Roazen, p. 215.

18. Some recent writers have stressed that Freud also recognized the beneficial aspects of social limit setting, especially regarding the aggressive tendencies. Paul Roazen spoke of Freud's view of ''culture as a defense system against anxiety . . . the insatiability of man's drives produces insecurities so deep that only social coercions can provide relief.''

19. Such as Lionel Trilling, *Freud and the Crisis of Our Culture* (Boston: Beacon Press, 1955), and Paul Roazen. Compare Roazen, p. 276.
20. Cremin, pp. 186–91.
21. There was an unusual sense in which Marx sometimes used the terms "social" and "society." He refused to make any qualitative distinction between Nature and human society in the aggregate. As men try to know nature, they change objects in accordance with their own needs and actions, turning them into social phenomena. Thus everything that people normally include under the rubric "Nature" is a social or human object, and all of Nature is coextensive with Society.

    Marx was willing to speak of man's biological dimension as "human" only when it was treated in the context of his unique social activity. In other words, the biological needs must always be related to the cooperative, productive labor of which man alone is capable. Such labor aims at their satisfaction, and it takes place in a definite social nexus. Furthermore, the satisfaction must be characterized by conscious, rational planning.
22. *The Descent of Man*, quoted in Kautsky, p. 99.
23. Marx, "Theses on Feuerbach."
24. Marx, *Capital*, vol. 1, p. 198.
25. Marx, *The Poverty of Philosophy*, p. 124.
26. Marx, *Capital*, vol. 1, p. 668.
27. Frederick Engels, *Ludwig Feuerbach and the End of Classical German Philosophy* (1888), quoted in Passmore, pp. 235–36.
28. John Plamanetz has discussed this in his writings on Marx. See for example, *Man and Society*, vol. 2, p. 376.
29. Drawing on a Hegelian discussion of civil society in *The Philosophy of Right*, Marx identified needs that arise through the individual's attempt to adapt to his particular society; an example of such an acquired need would be that for money, which develops among members of bourgeois societies.
30. "Thus man constructs also in accordance with the laws of beauty," we are told. (Marx, "Alienated Labour," in Bottomore, trans., *Early Writings*, p. 128.) And, further, that "the wealthy man is at the same time one who *needs* a complex of human manifestations of life, and whose own self-realization exists as an inner necessity, a need." (Marx, "Private Property and Communism," in Bottomore, trans., *Early Writings*, p. 165.)
31. Human needs are static only in the sense that predictable, generic types of activity will satisfy them (mental and manual work; self-generated work; self-expressive work; and so forth). To call human needs static does not mean that a person's specific, particular needs never undergo change or that the same objects always satisfy them. Rather, with abundance and the continued exercise of one's capacities, one becomes able and desirous of either satisfying or expressing the needs in different forms.
32. For a discussion of Chinese comments on this passage see Fokkema, p. 238.
33. Bauer, p. 73.

34. Waley, *Analects,* xviii.6, p. 220.

35. *Mencius,* vi.A.14 and 15.

36. Fung Yu-lan, vol. 2, p. 569.

37. Liu Shao-ch'i, ''Jen ti chieh-chi-hsing'' in *Lun szu-hsiang,* p. 9.

38. *CFJP* (Shanghai), September 4, 1957. (URI, 710. 131215/57–58, chap. 2). A frequently encountered instance of Mao's own use of the term occurs at the beginning of his essay ''On Practice.''

39. Quoted in Dai, p. 150.

40. Talk on questions of philosophy (1964) in Schram, *Talks to the People,* p. 220.

41. This item appears in a 120-page monograph entitled, ''Chairman Mao's Selected Writings,'' publishing authority unknown, translated in *JPRS,* no. 49826 (February 12, 1970), p. 58.

42. See, for example, Wang T'ieh, *Ch'ing-nien ying-kai tsen-yang fa-chan ko-hsing?,* p. 29; Hsü Shu-lien, ''Ts'ung hsin-li-hsüeh kuan-tien k'an ko-hsing wen-t'i,'' pp. 5–6, and Fu Yung, ''Lun jen-hsing,'' p. 2.

43. As A. C. Graham notes, ''the general tendency of the Neo-Confucians, which Chu Hsi himself does not altogether escape, is to think of the nature as a substance present inside man from his birth, which is responsible for all that is not due to external influence.'' (Graham, p. 48). Chu Hsi described the dimension of human nature in which the unmanifested Heavenly principles exist as ''quiet'' and unmoving. Of course there are human attributes that do change and that vary from man to man. These are products of a person's material (*ch'i*) endowment; its purity or turbidity is subject to change. But these are always regarded as secondary attributes.

44. *Erh-Ch'eng ch'üan-shu, I-shu,* 18.17b. See also 19.4b.

45. Quoted in Graham, p. 50.

46. In talking about the sameness in the natures of all people, Neo-Confucian writers usually used the term *i* meaning ''one'': ''Thus from Yao and Shun down to the most humble person all are one;'' and ''the nature is the same in all'' (*hsing i yeh*). (*Erh Ch'eng ch'üan shu, I-shu,* 18.17b and 18.19b). There is apparently a metaphysical claim here that there is one nature that permeates all mankind. In China, ''selfishness'' means to attempt unnaturally to separate oneself from the total group of men that are thus linked. More recently, ''individualism'' and ''selfishness'' may have been associated. Arguments against individualism may derive as much strength from this underlying metaphysical view as from psychological and moral considerations.

47. Mao, ''Where do Correct Ideas Come From?,'' *Four Essays,* p. 134.

48. Mao, ''On Contradiction,'' *Four Essays,* p. 35.

49. Mao, ''Talks at the Yenan Forum,'' pp. 31–32.

50. Mao Tse-tung, speech in Hangchow on December 21, 1965, quoted in ''Mao Tse-tung tui wen-ko chih-shih hui-pien'' [Collection of Mao Tse-tung's Directives during the Cultural Revolution], pp. 41–46.

51. Ch'en Po-ta, p. 5. Other subsequent references to the same point include Wang T'ieh, p. 13, and *KMJP,* October 28, 1965.

Chapter 2

1. Munro, *Man in Early China,* p. 51.
2. Ibid., p. 134.
3. This is T'ang Chün-i's suggested interpretation.
4. Quoted in Fung Yu-lan, *History of Chinese Philosophy,* vol. 2, p. 405.
5. Chan, trans., *Practical Living* by Wang Yang-ming, p. 243.
6. Ibid., p. 150.
7. *Mencius,* vi.A.7.8. See the discussion in Munro, *Man in Early China,* pp. 67–68.
8. *Chu-tzu ch'üan-shu,* Hsing-li, 14.12.b.
9. The feeling that this is part of the act of knowing is strictly speaking not classifiable as one of the seven feelings frequently listed by Neo-Confucian thinkers: joy, anger, pity, fear, love, hate, and desire. (There are other listings. Some include respect, pleasure, and the sense of duty. Others attempt to associate feelings with the four minds described by *Mencius* [*jen,* ^{a}*li, chih*].) These would be subsumed under the rubric of the "human mind" (*jen hsin*), in opposition to the *Tao*-mind that is engaged in the pursuit of knowledge described in the paragraph quoted earlier. However, it is difficult to imagine how the humanheartedness with which one permeates his deeds differs fundamentally from "love." The split between the two kinds of mind is a muddle. They are both forms of mental activity. Indeed, Chu Hsi himself uses a single (though hardly informative) term to refer to the common mental process shared by both: "When the spirituality [*ling*] of the mind is consciously revealed in the ^{b}*li,* it is the Tao-mind, and when consciously revealed in the desires, it is the human mind." (Ibid., 44.20a.) The difficulty in substantiating such a split between two kinds of mind is especially keen in the case of Chu Hsi, who, unlike Ch'eng Yi, refused to identify the mind and the principles it knows. (Graham, p. 62.) Within the context of Chu Hsi's own language, we would be safe to say that the same "spirituality" concurrently intuits the ^{b}*li* in things and feels compassion for them.
10. One should not make too much of Chu Hsi's distinction between knowing the ^{b}*li* of something and knowing through the moral sense ^{a}*i* or ^{c}*chih.* Undeniably one loses something if one equates them. He who understands the ^{b}*li* grasps something that cannot be sensually perceived, and there may be an aesthetic experience that accompanies it. But there remains considerable overlap. When one grasps the ^{b}*li* one knows what is right or wrong in a given situation, and one knows the same thing through the moral sense ^{a}*i* on ^{c}*chih.*
11. The first four in the list are supposed to refer to the "four fonts" that Mencius stated were innate to man, and which are usually listed as commiseration, reverence, shame and dislike (associated with ^{a}*i*), approving and disapproving (associated with ^{c}*chih*).
12. Chan, trans., *Practical Living* by Wang Yang-ming, p. 228.
13. Ibid., p. 10.
14. Legge, *Great Learning,* vol. 2, p. 367.

15. Bruce, pp. 262–63. Textual reference 45.18b–19a. The language used to describe them reveals that this is the case. For example, Chu Hsi stated that [b]*i* is an "operation" (yün-yung) of the mind that "emerges" (*fa*) from it. [*Chu-tzu ch'üan-shu*, Hsing-li, 45.16a.] Also that "[b]*i* is the out-thrust of the mind" (*i che hsin chih so fa*). [Ibid., 45.17a.] He spoke of [a]*chih* spatially, as the straightforward emanation of the mind (*chih shih hsin chih so chih i chi ch'u ti*) [Ibid.]; [b]*i* is also spoken of as the activity of the [a]*chih*. Wang Yang-ming said that "[b]*I* is what brings knowledge into operation" (*chih chih fa-tung chih i*) [Wang Yang-ming, *Ch'üan-hsi lu*, 1.18a.], and "[b]*I* is what issues forth (*fa pien*) from the mind. Its original essence is knowledge. What it settles on is a thing." [Ibid., 1.14b.] The fact that [b]*i* was regarded by Wang Yang-ming like a prompting to act explains why he could say, "The mental phenomenon consisting of a desire to eat is [b]*i*; it is the beginning of action." [Ibid., 2.2a.]
16. *Chu-tzu ch'üan shu*, Hsing-li, 45.19b.
17. Mencius described the internalized ruler when he spoke of a Heavenly "nobility" (*t'ien chüeh*), referring to certain innate moral tendencies that should be valued above human nobility (*jen-chüeh*) or the actual occupation of a position of great rank. Hsün Tzu spoke of the mind as the Heavenly Ruler (*t'ien chün*), a label that had been used exclusively to designate the reigning king during the West Chou.
18. Munro, *Man in Early China*, p. 63. My interpretation of this matter was greatly aided by the work of T'ang Chün-yi of New Asia College, Hong Kong.
19. *Erh Ch'eng ch'üan shu, I-shu*, 18.19a.
20. Ibid., *I-shu*, 15.16b. My attention was drawn to these passages by the work of Ts'ai Yung-ch'un.
21. *Erh Ch'eng ch'üan-shu, I ch'üan wen chi*, 4.4a, quoted in Ts'ai, pp. 234–35.
22. *Chou i cheng i*, chap. 8, p. 76. An example of a Neo-Confucian reference would be *Erh Ch'eng ch'üan-shu, I-chüan*, 2.6a, where Ch'eng Yi refers to "flattery" and "rudeness" in their stage of being "minute beginnings." The early Taoist texts also refer to a related phenomenon. For example, the *Tao te ching* says:

> It is easy to maintain a situation while it is still secure;
> It is easy to deal with a situation before symptoms develop; . . .
> Deal with a thing while it is still nothing;
> Keep a thing in order before disorder sets in. . . . (*Tao te ching*, 64, in Lau, p. 125.)

23. Nivison, " 'Knowledge' and 'Action'," pp. 113–14.
24. Legge, *The Shoo King*, viii. 2.3, in vol. 4, p. 258.
25. Chan, trans., *Practical Living* by Wang Yang-ming, p. 201.
26. *Fundamentals of Marxism-Leninism*, pp. 115–16.
27. Lenin, *Materialism and Empiro-Criticism*, p. 133.
28. In all technical discussions of knowing that occur in philosophy and psychology, the term used to refer to knowing, understanding, recognizing, and knowledge is *jen shih*. In ordinary usage, there are a great many ways to speak about knowing, understanding, and knowledge in contemporary China. A child

may be said to understand things (*tung shih*) at a given age, meaning that he knows enough about his immediate world and how to manipulate it to be expected to perform acts previously done by parents. People are said to understand (*liao chieh*) the rules of something like language. Knowing in the sense of being aware of (*chih-tao*) is differentiated from knowing in the sense of having direct acquaintance with something such that one could recognize or identify it (*jen-shih*). Thus, referring to a certain person, one says "I know of him, but I do not know him personally" (*Wo chih-tao yu t'a che ke jen, k'o-shih wo ping pu jen-shih t'a.*) But the idea of some direct acquaintance leading to comprehension of how something works is not totally absent from *chih-tao;* for example, "the best method I know" (*wo so chih-tao ti tsui hao fang-fa*). The term *chih-shih* is often used to refer to knowledge in the sense of factual knowledge that comes from books (*shu-pen chih-shih*). And in the phrase "virtue, knowledge, and health," referring to the qualities that must be developed in students, the term "knowledge" (*chih*) carries the sense of the information conveyed in academic subjects.

29. *Mao Tse-tung hsüan-chi,* "Shih-chien lun," p. 273.
30. *Hsin-li hsüeh,* pp. 81–82.
31. Ibid., p. 25. See also Huang En-an, p. 61.
32. *Mao Tse-tung hsüan-chi,* "Shih chien lun," p. 280; see also Huang En-an, p. 100.
33. *JMJP,* February 24, 1964.
34. Ch'en Chan-ch'iao, "T'an pi-chiao," p. 28.
35. Hsien Ch'ien-ch'iu, p. 258.
36. *Hsin-li hsüeh,* pp. 81–82.
37. Mao Tse-tung, *Four Essays,* "On Practice," pp. 2–3.
38. Liu Shao-ch'i, pp. 9–10.
39. *KMJP,* June 23, 1959.
40. Wang T'ieh, *Ch'ing-nien ying-kai tsen-yang fa-chan ko-hsing?,* p. 29, and *KMJP,* June 23, 1959.
41. *CNA,* no. 260, p. 3; Ch'en Kuo-mei, pp. 16–17; also *KMJP,* August 15, 1958.
42. Yao Wen-yüan writing in *Wen-hui pao* (Shanghai), January 26, 1960.
43. See, for example, Kuan Feng, "On Human Nature and Class Nature," p. 15; Fokkema, p. 137; *KMJP,* June 23, 1959; article by Ch'en Kuo-mei in *KMJP,* August 15, 1958.
44. Kuan Feng, "On Human Nature and Class Nature," p. 15.
45. *KMJP,* October 28, 1965, trans. in *SCMP,* no. 3587, p. 10.
46. Interesting support for this position can be found in the most common critiques of the popular Soviet work on child psychology by H. D. Levitov, translated into Chinese in 1961. It is that the author frequently selects for analysis childhood feelings that are morally neutral. For instance, his examples of situations in which anger arises include wishing to ski and being prevented, and being erroneously blamed for something. The Chinese claim that only such feelings of anger as those experienced in response to someone acting contrary to the group are worth citing as examples. *Ni te lieh-wei-t'o-fu.* (H. D. Levitov,

Erh-t'ung chiao-yü hsin-li-hsüeh, p. 192 ff.) Ms. Tseng Mei-hsia described for me the response of educational circles to sections of this work.

47. *Hsin-li hsüeh,* p. 85.

48. Robert Chin and Ai-li S. Chin, p. 15. My interpretation differs somewhat from that of the Chins in being tripartite: knowing, feeling (approval or disapproval) and having a prompting to act in accordance with what is known and accepted.

49. An Tzu-wen, p. 9.

50. Wei Yu-p'ing, p. 149.

51. Chang Man-hua, p. 18.

52. " 'Hung-se hsüan-ch'uan-yüan,' " p. 6.

53. Chung Ching-wen, p. 8.

54. In contemporary Western philosophy, many philosophers influenced by spin-offs of the logical positivist school, make a distinction between cognitive and noncognitive meaning or factual and emotive meaning. Cognitive meaning is present only where verification or falsification are in fact possible, or, in the case of "operationalism," where the operations needed to confirm or deny can be set forth. Values are considered to be factually meaningless, in that they are not subject to any possible verification steps. Sentences referring to them do not describe a state of any object or subject or a relation. Statements of value are expressions of feelings of the speaker, and, therefore, called emotive statements. This theory makes a sharp differentiation between two senses of meaning that are absent in the Chinese case. When the Chinese speak of knowing (*jen-shih*) the meaning/significance (*i-i*) of something, they are speaking of factual, verifiable information that may be partially about values. Recently, some American philosophers have sharply rejected the strict separation of emotive and factual meaning. Examples would include Richard Brandt and William Frankena. The same could be said for most American pragmatists.

Occasionally, when we use the word "meaning" or "meaningful" in English, we are saying that something is valuable or significant, as in the statement, "He regards her as having made a meaningful contribution to the cause." But most often, the terms are value-neutral. Similarly, there are exceptions in the Chinese case. The Chinese term *i-szu* can denote "opinion" and "intention." In addition, the Chinese terms for meaning can be used in the sense of an "explanation," that may be provided by a list of various acts suggested by a word, by reference to the idea that produced the word or that it produces itself in hearers or readers, or to the use to which it is put. Thus both *i-szu* and *i-i* can be used in a request for the explanation of a word ("What is meant by this word?"—*Che-ko tz'u shemma i-i/i-szu?*).

55. *KMJP,* March 15, 1972.

56. Wu I-ling and Li Cho-min, p. 144.

57. Li Yu-ning, p. 105.

58. *Che-hsüeh hsiao tz'u-tien,* p. 26.

59. Li Po-shu and Chou Kuan-sheng, p. 31.

60. Wu I-ling and Li Cho-min, pp. 139, 140.

61. Shen Chih-yüan, p. 2.

62. Huang En-an, p. 80.
63. Shen Chih-yüan, p. 12; Li Pao-heng, p. 3.
64. *Wen Wei*, p. 14; *Kuo Hsing-fu chiao-hsüeh fang-fa*, p. 22.
65. *Che-hsüeh hsiao tz'u-tien*, p. 21.
66. An Tzu-wen, p. 6.
67. "Tsen-yang hsüeh ying-hsiung?" p. 27.
68. An Tzu-wen, p. 6.
69. Shen Chih-yüan, p. 2.
70. "Tsen-yang hsüeh ying-hsing?", p. 27.
71. Meyer, *Leninism*, p. 28.
72. See Bauer, p. 100.
73. Lenin, *Materialism and Empirio-Criticism*, p. 190.
74. Ibid., p. 193.
75. Marx did not reject the dichotomy of consciousness and body or of mind and the material objects. But, along with Feuerbach, he put forth a more fundamental category that includes both consciousness and material objects, calling it "material nature," "Nature," or "material." There was no insistence here that consciousness is the same as matter. The essential claim is that Nature is not external to man (Descartes). Rather, man's conceptual tools for understanding Nature are a function of his needs and activities, and he uses those tools to produce Nature. He produces it in the sense that he acts on objects in such a way as to relate them to his own needs and goals. As he acts on them, he alters them or turns them into social (human) phenomena. Through this process alone does he know them. *Praxis* (practice) is the name for this activity. (Grier, p. 159.) Discussions with Philip Grier were helpful to me in formulating the above criticism.
76. Beginning about 1948, under Stalin's personal pressure, a strict environmental determinism was reintroduced. Robert Tucker's explanation of the 1948 shift was that Stalin sought a basis for the claim that his own formulae for Russia were not arbitrary but unchallengeably congenial with natural laws themselves. Furthermore, he was dissatisfied with the rapidity with which Soviet citizens "of their own free choice" were adopting the goals appropriate to the new Soviet man and opted for more intensive environmental manipulation. The theoretical origins of the shift can be traced to Stalin's *Economic Problems of Socialism in the U.S.S.R.* (1952). Therein Stalin said that Soviet policy should conform to the "objective processes taking place independently of the will of human beings." (Tucker, *The Soviet Political Mind*, p. 96.) Natural laws are immutable, and all events are totally predictable if one grasps the laws. In the realm of human behavior, this orientation led him to champion Pavlovian theories of the conditioned reflex. The laws of conditioning are the counterparts of the inexorable laws in nature and society. The consciousness so important to discussions of autonomous man was minimized in analysis. A knowledge of the laws of conditioning coupled with a knowledge of what historical forces were operating through the minds of the rulers at any given time theoretically could

lead to predictability of behavior. The rulers' minds provide the signals for people to act.

Yet even with this return to a "reflexology" having certain echoes of the 1920s, there was still some hedging. Stalin himself spoke of individuals being able to "saddle the laws" of nature and make them serve the interests of the state when they understand the laws. Fair enough as a claim. But it makes nonsense of the other claims in Stalin's so-called "Michurinistic" determinism. And by the mid-1950s there began another swing back toward the propriety of allowing a place for free choice. In time it became permissible once more regularly to use terms referring to subjective consciousness such as "feelings," "will," and "imagination."

Commentators on Soviet criminal theory have noted the inconsistency between the Soviet desire concurrently to retain a doctrine of the social conditioning of mental events and also the idea of individual responsibility that owes so much to Russia's European heritage:

> Taken as a whole, Soviet theory can be designated primarily as "social-determinist." The data that Soviet researchers assemble refer predominantly to social factors— education, occupation, residence, family background, etc.—that "shape" or determine the individual. . . . But for practical purposes, in the Soviet Union as elsewhere, to "explain" (even in a determinist way) is not to excuse. This determinism is "soft" enough to accommodate a voluntarist view of each deviant individual. The criminal and delinquent, corrupted as they may be by unfortunate environments, decide to act—they need to act. Their deviant acts are acts of the "will," for which they bear responsibility. (Connor, pp. 244–45.)

77. Quoted in Bauer, p. 13.
78. Li Shih-sheng, p. 34.
79. This was confirmed for me in discussions with Chinese philosophers in the People's Republic of China in 1973.
80. This point was clarified in the course of a discussion meeting that took place in New York City in January, 1977, involving the following persons: Irene Bloom, Antonio Cua, Arthur Danto, W. T. de Bary, Sidney Greenblatt, Chad Hansen, Francis Hsü, Donald Munro, Benjamin Schwartz, Tu Wei-ming, and Pei-yi Wu.
81. The muddled understanding is evident in Chang Chun-mai's remarks: "Why do men possess a moral sense of right and wrong, and a sense of responsibility and sometimes wish to repent? The cause of a moral decision is to be found in the inner heart and not externally, and such a mental decision derives from free will and not determinism." Quoted in Charlotte Furth, *Ting Wen-chiang,* p. 103.

His colleague Fan Shou-kang, spoke of free will as subservient to an inner mind that can be described as a social conscience that intuits a priori moral principles. Fred Grunewald brought this passage to my attention.

For a good essay on the absence of a doctrine of strict moral responsibility in Confucianism, see Chad Hansen, "Freedom and Moral Responsibility in Confucian Ethics," *Philosophy East and West* 22, no. 2 (April, 1972): 169–86.

82. FBIS, February 5, 1974, p. 133.
83. *CNA,* no. 388, p. 4. In another instance, Soviet-oriented psychologists were criticized for using such terms as "enthusiasm," "strong-willed," and "brave" to describe traits applicable to any person. The reason given was that such terms "are not appropriate for enemies." (*KMJP,* August 15, 1958.) In other words, to apply such terms to enemies would be not only to describe their personality traits but also to approve morally of the acts being described by those terms.
84. Lenin, *Marx-Engels-Marxism,* p. 333.
85. Kuan Feng, "On Human Nature and Class Nature," p. 10.
86. Lindzey and Aronson, pp. 155–56.

Chapter 3

1. A conflict between proponents of a view of human nature that assumes innate impediments to change, and those emphasizing its malleability flourished from the mid-seventeenth century on between European individualists (Adam Smith, Locke, Kant, Rousseau, Mill) and advocates of a more sociologically oriented view of man (Saint-Simon, the French Positivists, F. H. Bradley, and Emil Durkheim).
2. The identification of the innate with the unchangeable informs the Mencius-Kao Tzu arguments. (Mencius, vi.A.2.) For example, the point is made that water can be dammed, but it still has the same natural endowment of nature, namely the tendency to flow downhill. An analogy is then made with humans. Hsün Tzu also suggests the converse, namely that whatever is changeable is not innate. This point emerges in sections 1 and 23 of the Hsün-tzu, in the discussions of *wei* or that which is a product of human artifice.
3. Ma Wen-ping, pp. 80–83.
4. A typical example of this position is contained in the works of Liu Chieh, who was on the faculty of Chung-shan University. (See the articles by Ma Wen-ping, and by Li Ch'ing-t'ien and Chao I-min.) Drawing his inspiration largely from the Ch'eng-Chu school of Neo-Confucianism and supplementing it with a dose of Hegel, he inferred from the fact that there is a "union between Heaven and man" that all people share a common innate endowment from Heaven (defined in a nontheistic nature). Human history is not a history of class struggle but the development of this human nature. (*KMJP,* November 10, 1963, and *Nan-fang jih-pao,* November 3, 1963.) He went on to treat the practice of *jen* (humanheartedness) toward all others as a universal human obligation. Sometimes the writers are less obvious, giving nominal assent to the Marxist authority figures and to man's class nature but still ending up with positions that their critics regard as "the humanism that emerges from human nature." Pa Jen spoke of common human sentiments and also that "a split class society still could produce democratic and humanistic ideas and sentiments." (Quoted in Fokkema, p. 239.) Through literature, he claimed, people can transcend their own

class. His leading ethical principle is said to be "one should love all people," and his theory of human nature is criticized as involving the claim that class-transcending love is possible. (Yao Wen-yüan, "P'i-p'an Pa Jen ti 'Jen-hsing lun'," pp. 31–34.)

5. *KMJP,* March 19, 1960, and Kuan Feng, "On Human Nature and Class Nature," p. 8.
6. Mao Tse-tung, "On People's Democratic Dictatorship," p. 11.
7. During the antirightist period in the 1950s, some intellectuals charged that the obligations entailed by Communist Party spirit (*tang-hsing,* Russian *partiinost*) "destroys human nature," especially the obligation that relatives inform on each other to the authorities.
8. Yao Wen-yüan, "P'i-p'an Pa Jen ti 'Jen-hsing lun'," p. 32.
9. P'eng I and Mu Huo, "The Theory of 'Drawing Close to Benefit and Avoiding Harm' is Bourgeois Egoist Philosophy," *JMJP,* March 19, 1965, in *SCMP,* no. 3432 (April 6, 1965), p. 1.
10. *CKCNP,* October 31, 1964.
11. Li Ch'ing-t'ien and Chao I-min, pp. 37–41, and Ma Wen-ping, pp. 62–83.
12. Chou Yang, "The Fighting Task," p. 30.
13. The New Program of the C.P.S.U. actually describes humanism as a goal to be achieved in communism:

> Joint planned labor by the members of society, their daily participation in the management of state and public affairs, and the development of Communist relations of comradely cooperation and mutual support recast the minds of people in a spirit of collectivism, industry, and humanism. (Mendel, p. 364.)

14. In September, 1968, the leading challenger to Wladyslaw Gomulka in Poland, Mieczyslaw Moczar, condemned the "perfidious call for humanization and democratization" in Czechoslovakia, begun by "imperialists, revisionists, and Zionists." In this denunciation, Moczar had the support of Gomulka. See *New York Times,* September 16, 1968.
15. *KMJP,* August 14, 1958.
16. In the summer of 1950, at the "Joint Session of the Academy of Sciences of the USSR and the Academy of Medical Sciences on Physiological Problems in the Theory of Academician I. P. Pavlov," Pavlov's theory of higher nervous activity was strongly endorsed. After 1950 Pavlovian principles began to be applied to the study of problems in the realm of both personality and learning theory. The change was seen as introducing a balance between ignoring the societal circumstances as was done by psychologists who identify physiology with psychology, and ignoring physiology (to which Pavlovianism belongs) entirely as is the wont of other psychologists.
17. Chao I-ping, "China's Achievements in Pavlov's Theory During the Past Decade."
18. Pavlov, *Selected Works,* pp. 446–47, quoted in Simon, ed., *Psychology,* p. 21.
19. G. S. Prozorov, "Heredity and Upbringing," in Redl, ed., p. 4.

20. Ibid.
21. Ibid., p. 7.
22. Ibid., p. 20.
23. "Personality" is the closest English rendering of the Chinese term *ko-hsing,* which includes disposition, abilities, interests, likes/dislikes. The Chinese, like the Soviets, also use the term "character" *(hsing-ko)* in a manner very close to our word "personality." Chang Chih-kuang, *Tsen-yang ch'ü liao-chieh hsüeh-sheng ti ko-hsing?,* p. 1, and Wang T'ieh, *Ch'ing-nien ying-kai tsen-yang fa-chan ko-hsing?,* pp. 1–5 and 101. See also Bauer, p. 166.
24. Chang, Chi-kuang, *Tsen-yang ch'ü liao-chieh,* pp. 14, 15, 32, 51.
25. I Fan, pp. 16–18.
26. Wang T'ien, *Ch'ing-nien ying-kai tsen-yang fa-chan ko-hsing?,* p. 24.
27. Ibid., pp. 15 and 24. See also the articles in *KMJP,* August 15, 1958.
28. Wang T'ieh, *Ch'ing-nien ying-kai tsen-yang fa-chan ko-hsing?,* p. 15.
29. "Revisionist Thinking of Class Reconciliation," trans. in JPRS, no. 16935 (January 4, 1963).
30. *KMJP,* August 15, 1958.
31. Ibid.; Wang T'ien, *Ch'ing-nien ying-kai tsen-yang fa-chan ko-hsing?,* p. 24.
32. In contrast to the Chinese case, whenever anyone in the Soviet Union is criticized for a lopsided attachment to biological or physiological variables (instinct, reflex, and so forth), the primary concern is that the person has not left room in his theory for man as a free agent, who can initiate action to change things in the world.
33. These include the doctrine that there are class differences in physiological laws, that psychologists should study only "working class psychology," that there are no developmental levels in the intellectual growth of children, and that all research topics that do not have some immediate practical application should be dropped (though the applied orientation of psychology in education, medicine, and industry remains). (Chu Chih-hsien in *JMJP,* March 13, 1962.)
34. The Chinese terms used to convey the idea of malleability include *k'o su-hsing* (man can be "molded" like clay), *tuan-lien* (abilities can be "forged" like molten iron, and one can forge oneself), *kai-tsao* (thoughts and selves can be "reconstituted"), and *su-tsao* (personalities can be "molded").
35. The first major public discussions took place in the pages of *KMJP,* August 15, 1958; see also *KMJP,* July 6, 1959. There was a period of liberalization in 1961–63 during which psychologists experienced a certain toleration for non-Maoist orientations. During the first half of the 1960s the new orientation focusing on the differing social environments of students and their effect on students' differing "thoughts" was not universal among professionals. Psychologists whose approach reflected a Western training continued to publish their views as late at 1965 but were clearly subject to attack from colleagues representing the new vision.
36. *KMJP,* June 23, 1959.
37. Chu Chih-hsien in *JMJP,* July 6, 1959.
38. Mao Tse-tung, "On Contradiction," in *Four Essays,* pp. 4, 6.

39. This expression was introduced by Chou Yang in September, 1963, before it became publicly associated with Maoist dialectics and opposed to that of Yang Hsien-chen. Chou Yang's context was the Sino-Soviet conflict and the problem of division and unity in world communism.

40. *CB,* no. 891 (October 8, 1969), p. 54. Back in 1942 Mao wrote that "The people, too, have their shortcomings. Among the Proletariat many retain petty-bourgeois ideas, while both peasants and the urban petty bourgeoisie have backward ideas; these are burdens hampering them in their struggle." (See Mao Tse-tung, "Talks at the Yenan Forum," in *Four Essays,* p. 3.)

41. *Pei-ching jih-pao,* January 8, 1959.

42. *Kung-jen jih-pao,* Peking, July 8, 1962.

43. Compare the discussion in Benjamin Schwartz, "China and the West in the 'Thought of Mao tse-tung'" in Ping-ti Ho and Tang Tsou (eds.).

44. Lin Chung-hsien, "Psychological Disposition Necessary for the Study of Flying," *Hang-K'ung chih-shih* [Aviation knowledge], no. 3 (March 8, 1960), pp. 24–25, in JPRS, no. 2973 (July 6, 1960), pp. 9–10.

45. Chen Ta-jou, "How Psychology Can be of Service to Socialist Construction," *Hsin-li hsüeh-pao* [Acta psychologica sinica], no. 3 (August 1959), pp. 142–45, in JPRS, no. 3424 (June 21, 1960), p. 5.

46. *JMJP,* February 20, 1966; see also *JMJP,* November 9, 1959.

47. Quotations from *Labour Laws and Regulations* and *Provisional Regulations Governing Science Awards* quoted in Charles Hoffmann, pp. 31, 32.

48. *New York Times,* June 17, 1972.

49. Plamenatz, *Man and Society,* vol. 2, pp. 377, 344.

50. Cf. ibid., p. 404.

51. Increasingly, this assumption has been given the practical lie in the emergence of special schools for the mathematically talented. A major inspiration for this phenomenon was the theory of the mathematician Andrei Kulmagorov that unique mathematical aptitudes manifest themselves very early.

52. A. N. Leontiev, "The Nature and Formation of Human Psychic Properties," in Simon, ed., *Psychology in the Soviet Union,* p. 228.

53. Kostiuk, in Simon, ed., *Educational Psychology,* p. 45.

54. Chang Chih-kuang, *Tsen yan ch'ü liao-chieh,* p. 34.

55. *KMJP,* July 4, 1956, and October 15, 1956. See also Chien Nan-hsiang, "Lüeh-lun kao-teng hsüeh hsiao ti ch'üan-mien fa-chan ti chiao-yü fang-chen."

56. Doubtless under the influence of such Soviet practices as are described in Simon and Simon, eds., *Educational Psychology,* p. 2.

57. Article by Chang Ling-kuan in *Jen min chiao-yü* [People's education] (Peking), no. 2 (1955). Chang Yeh-ming, *HHPYK,* no. 3 (101) (1957), p. 77; *Jen-min chiao-yü,* no. 2 (1957), especially p. 23, and no. 3 (1957), especially p. 43.

58. *KMJP,* December 2, 1961. *JMJP,* February 3, 1963, reports on special tributes paid to a mathematics teacher who excelled at gearing his teaching to individual differences in mathematical aptitude. Stories in *Chung-kuo ch'ing-nien* [China youth] for the same year make the same point concerning teacher obligations. At

this time psychologists were also being enjoined to focus their studies on the differences between the abilities of students; see *KMJP*, March 13, 1962.

59. Ch'en Yu-sung, "Chien-ch'a Hu Shih tsai chiao-yü fang-mien ti fan-tung ying-hsiang ho Hu Shih szu-hsiang tui-wo ti ying hsiang" ["An examination of Hu Shih's reactionary influence in the education sector and the influence on me of Hu Shih's thought"], in *Tzu-ch'an-chieh-chi chiao-yü p'i-p'an*, pp. 193–97. Also *KMJP*, May 15, 1956.

60. Ch'en Po-ta, p. 7; Wang T'ieh, *Ch'ing nien ying-kai tsen-yang fa-chan ko-hsing?*, pp. 34–42; and Kuo Mo-jo, "T'ien-ts'ai yü ch'in-fen," pp. 2–5 and 8.

61. *Hung-wei pao* (Peking), November 23, 1966.

62. This complaint is by no means unique to China. One of the chief themes of the early stages of the progressive movement in American educational reform is described by Lawrence A. Cremin as the charge that "rural education was unimaginative and irregular, that it dealt too much with books and too little with life, that it educated away from the country and toward the city, and that only a massive infusion of agricultural studies could save it from complete decay." (Cremin, p. 43.)

63. *Kuo Hsing-fu chiao-hsüeh fang-fa*, p. 22.

64. Chang Hao-po, p. 8.

65. *Chiao-shih pao* [Teacher's news], March 7, 1958.

66. *Wen-hui pao*, May 8, 1964, and *KMJP*, May 15, 1964.

67. *Chiao-shih pao*, March 7, 1958.

68. *Kung-jen jih-pao*, July 21, 1960.

69. A. V. Lunacharsky (First Commissar of Education of the Russian Republic) speaking in 1952, quoted in Counts, *The Challenge of Soviet Education*, p. 52. Richard Levy brought this passage to my attention.

70. Whyte, "Inequality," pp. 698–705.

71. "Discussions Held by China's Economists in Recent Years on the Question of Productive Forces and Production Relations," *Ching-chi Yen-chiu* [Economic research], no. 2 (February 17, 1963), in *SCMP*, March 25, 1963, pp. 32–40. This debate was brought to my attention by Andrew Walder.

72. Menninger, pp. 242–43.

73. Rosenthal and Jacobson.

74. Ibid., p. 182.

75. Wen Wei, p. 14.

Chapter 4

1. Quoted in Dai, p. 203.

2. See Plamenatz, vol. 2, pp. 363–67.

3. Bauer, p. 36.

4. Meyer, *Leninism*, pp. 202, 276, and 291.

5. A more generalized human limitation on learning is suggested by the post-1930 Soviet reworking of the Leninist "theory of reflection." This epistemological doctrine claims that men can only achieve relative truth, which they do by testing out theories in practice. The more testing, the more they approximate absolute truth. The doctrine ties into the Marxist morphology of history in that each successive societal stage gets closer to the truth. In the present epoch, the theory that serves the interest of the Bolsheviks (and is known to them) is closest to being an accurate account, because they are the vanguard of the most progressive class.

The following passage echoes the usual Soviet position:

> We have seen, then, that most truth is approximate, partial, and incomplete, and that error is to be found in truth, and truth in error. Hence, on any subject we generally possess a measure of truth, but not absolute truth. (Cornforth, p. 140.)

However, coexisting with doctrines of relative and absolute truth derived from Lenin is the Marxist theory of practice that in its original formulation does not allow a place for absolute truth. As people act on Nature with concrete operations in their production of goods (practice), they continually change Nature and also change themselves. Whatever truths they acquire are a product of these interactions. Nature, of which man is a part, constantly changes. There is no place for fixed and absolute truths.

6. Lenin, *Selected Works,* vol. 1, p. 143.
7. Chiang Lung-ch'i, p. 53.
8. Plamenatz, *Man and Society,* vol. 2, pp. 393 ff.
9. Waley, *The Way and its Power,* 22, p. 171.
10. Mencius said:

> A True King is one who, practicing Humanity, resorts only to virtue. Such a one has no need of a major state. T'ang the Successful had a state of only seventy miles square, and King Wen a state of only a hundred miles square. They were True Kings. Allegiance which is gained by the use of force is not an allegiance of the heart—it is the allegiance which comes from imposing upon weakness. Allegiance which is gained by the exercise of virtue is true allegiance. (Dobson, *Mencius,* 6.7 [2A.3], p. 136)

The other side of the same matter is found in the remark of Hsün Tzu that the quickest way for a powerful state to be transformed into a politically insignificant one is for its ruler to use force to try to conquer others; he will "acquire land but lose the people." In both his own state and those he seeks to conquer the people will turn away from him. The ruler who will prevail is a ruler who knows that "one who understands the nature of force does not use it." (See the discussion in Munro, *Man in Early China,* p. 239, n. 15. The quote is from the *Hsün-tzu,* Wang chih, 5.7a, in Wang Hsien-ch'ien's edition.)

11. Legge, *Li ki,* xvi.1 (*Hsio ki*).
12. Legge, *The Doctrine of the Mean* 22, in vol. 1, p. 416.

13. Ch'eng I, *Erh Ch'eng ch'üan-shu,* I chüan i.51b, quoted in Ts'ai, p. 146.
14. *JMJP,* May 31, 1963, in *SCMP* no. 3000 (June 17, 1963).
15. In this discussion, when we refer to the function of government, we are referring to its desirable role as defined by Confucian principles. Needless to say, cases of varying strength could be made for the claim that the actual purpose of government was to perpetuate the privileges of those who already had them, or that it was to collect taxes, or to preserve order. The most accurate assessment of people's motives is usually to admit that they are mixed.
16. Yü Shu-lin, p. 754.
17. Ch'en Ch'ing-chih, pp. 226, 377. Also, Taga Akigoro.
18. Much of our knowledge of these schools comes from the studies of Taga Akigoro.
19. The researches of Tilemann Grimm have thrown light on these.
20. The researches of Evelyn Rawski have revealed that during the Ch'ing, in Kwangtung, Fukien, Kiangsi, and Chekiang, the term *she-hsüeh* was used to refer to charitable schools. Thus in certain regions *i hsüeh* and *she-hsüeh* were not differentiated.
21. Buddhist monasteries provided two kinds of educational programs that must be considered in an overview of unofficial education in premodern China. One variety was externally oriented, to youths not formally part of the monastic organization. Tun-huang documents speak of monks serving as instructors in this capacity during the T'ang. And Dennis Twitchett has found evidence of exercises, texts, catechisms, rhyming lists, Buddhist terminology, mathematical problems, maps, and the *Thousand Character Classic* that were used by the monks in teaching. During the Northern Sung a monk named Tsung I wrote a book on Ch'an temple regulations, from which evolved a widely used book for the education of children—*Sayings for the Education of Children* (*T'ung hsing chiao-yü lun*), in which the emphasis was on self-perfection (*li-shen*) and diligence. (Yü Shu-lin, pp. 581–85.) At the same time in the T'ang, monasteries also maintained schools for younger monks, headed by a vice-abbot specifically charged with educational affairs.
22. Wen Chün-t'ien, pp. 96–97. Also, Masabuchi Tatsuo, pp. 77ff. and 190ff.
23. Wakeman, pp. 9–10.
24. Taga, p. 233.
25. Sakai, p. 335.
26. Ibid., p. 346.
27. Mao Tse-tung, "Some Questions Concerning Methods of Leadership," in *Selected Works,* vol. 3, p. 119.
28. O. H. Shin, "The Epistemological Foundations of Maoism," Institute for Cross-Cultural Studies, Keimyung University (Korea), 1976.
29. O. H. Shin has traced the mass line theory to the substantive and textual relation between Mao's December, 1936, lecture entitled "Problems of Strategy in China's Revolutionary War," and the 1937 "On Practice." Knowing a war situation involves data collection (perception), data analysis (conceptualization), and execution (practice). On April 2, 1948, Mao wrote that "for over

twenty years our Party has carried on mass work every day, and for the past dozen years it has talked about mass line every day." (*Selected Works,* vol. 4, p. 241.) Liu Shao-ch'i may be given credit for developing operational features of the mass line in the Border Regions in the early 1940s, though denied credit in post-Cultural Revolution hagiographies of Maoists. But important elements of the theory of the mass line do seem original with Mao.

30. "Sharp Weapon for Criticizing Idealism," *Peking Review,* no. 22 (March 28, 1971), p. 4.
31. Mao, "Where do Correct Ideas Come From?", p. 135.
32. Quoted in *The Great Socialist Cultural Revolution in China,* no. 3 (Peking: Foreign Languages Press, 1966), p. 9.
33. An example: "Struggle in Philosophy and Class Struggle," *Peking Review,* no. 4 (January 22, 1971), p. 5.
34. Marx, *A Contribution to the Critique of Political Economy,* pp. 11–12.
35. Ibid., p. 12.
36. Meyer, *Leninism,* pp. 47, 79, and 213.
37. Mao Tse-tung, "Where Do Correct Ideas Come From?" in *Four Essays,* p. 134.
38. Marx, *A Contribution to the Critique of Political Economy,* p. 12.
39. Andrew Walder argues well for this interpretation in his "Marxism, Maoism, and Social Change," in *Modern China* (1977). Such interpretations have the virtue of being consistent with the portrait of the materialist conception of history that Engels tried to paint in his later years (for example, in the famous letter to Joseph Bloch). They have the possible problem of explaining why Mao himself felt obliged to apply a strict "European" periodization to China (primitive communism, slave society, feudalism) prior to the modern era, when he opened the door for variation by calling China after the Opium War "semi-colonial and semi-feudal" (see "The Chinese Revolution and the Chinese Communist Party"). If Marx preached flexibility in the attribution of stages to various societies, why did not Mao himself feel comfortable explaining China's entire history in a manner not involving references to the stages of history that pertain to Europe? The traditional explanation of Marx that emphasizes the determining role of productive forces and social relations is also the one that was accepted by many Russians during the 1920s. Those interpretations are now condemned as "mechanistic Marxism." Did the writings of Marx provide good cause for such interpretations then? Certainly, to claim that at least some ideology is false consciousness or illusion is to suggest that those who entertain the beliefs are passive recipients. A final possible problem lies in assuming that Marx was always internally consistent and never altered his positions once he left his Hegelian youth. But another explanation is that he was for some time something of a strict economic determinist and gradually accepted a greater role for the superstructural elements, as problems in his earlier approach became evident. Like the rest of us, Marx may have changed his views over time.
40. Dai, p. 192.
41. Quoted in Jerome Ch'en, p. 103.

42. Ibid., p. 23.
43. This point is well stated in James Hsiung's *Ideology and Practice*.

Chapter 5

1. Fokkema, p. 68.
2. Wu Chiang, p. 33.
3. Wen Wei, p. 14.
4. In his famous essay on Yen Hui, Ch'eng I used Yen Hui as a model to convey to his readers the purpose of study. He said, "For what reason did Yen Tzu alone love to study? He studied in order to achieve the way of the sage." (*Erh-Ch'eng ch'üan-shu, I ch'uan wen-chi*, 4.1a.) The phrase "to be an ideal person" was used as far back as the Chou-Han period, and remained popular in Neo-Confucian thought.
5. For example, in the following passage from a work of the Ch'ing Neo-Confucian, Ku Yen-wu (1613–87) one can identify in the first part his divergence from others on the matter of the means to sagehood. But at the end of the passage, one encounters a legitimacy criterion applicable to literary activity that would find a broad acceptance among Confucians:

    According to my view, the way to sagehood is to start by studying at a low [empirical, or physical] level, and thence ascend to a high [metaphysical, *tao*] level. The principles of behavior are filial piety, brotherhood, loyalty and sincerity. . . . Duty in daily life is to clean and sweep, to question and answer, and to present one's self and withdraw. For these the literature to read is the *Book of Odes*, the *Book of History*, the three *Books of Rites*, the *Book of Changes*, and the *Spring and Autumn Annals*. . . . The purpose of literary activity is to contribute to the promotion of good order, to prevent misrule, and to improve the people's moral climate for the people should be able to enjoy peace and prosperity. . . . (Quoted in Carson Chang, vol. 2, p. 223.)

6. Waley, *Analects,* xvii.9.
7. Perhaps one historical reason for such forced commentaries was the actual practice of statesmen in the Spring and Autumn Period (770–481 B.C.) of using poetry to issue veiled criticisms; some of these are included in the "Airs" (Kuo-feng) section of the Odes. Watson, *Early Chinese Literature*, p. 211.
8. *Yen Shih chia hsüan-chi* (Yen Chin-t'ui), p. 368.
9. Lu Shih-i, p. 22a. On Chu Hsi, see Liu Po-chi, p. 211.
10. Yu Shü-lin, pp. 572, 776.
11. Shu Hsin-ch'eng, p. 197. See also pp. 88, 90, 199, and 202.
12. Ibid., p. 11. See also pp. 405 and 434.
13. Lu-Shih-i explains this. Brought to my attention by Charles P. Ridley.
14. Yü Shu-lin, p. 960.
15. Ibid., pp. 989–97.
16. Ts'ai Yüan-pei, the first minister of education under the new Republic and later president of Peking University, had been a student for four years at the Univer-

sity of Leipzig. He also had very Chinese solutions to his country's problems. In his own writings he differentiated sharply between the way education was carried out under the empire and the way it should be carried out in the new Republic. In the former case, its content was "subordinate to politics," aiming to engender a respect for authority, loyalty to the dynasty, and acceptance of Confucian principles. In the latter case, it should be only partially subordinate to politics. To this end, he made room for national military education, utilitarian education (technological training) and ethical education (stressing liberty, equality, fraternity) to help strengthen the society. Ts'ai claimed that the other half of the education that all students should receive should cater to the unique needs of the individual and thereby contribute to the greater happiness of society—echoes of Dewey. Yet, when we examine the nonpolitical half of his actual program, we find once again that any advocacy of students' engaging in study for its own sake as intrinsically pleasant or because it satisfies some private interest was intolerable. He simply changed the content of the traditional value infusion, but not its ultimate social, Confucian goal. He gave the name "aesthetics" to that infusion. All people appreciate beauty, according to Ts'ai. By cultivating feelings for beauty in students, educators can enable them to transcend the normal obstacles that divide people into hostile or unsympathetic groupings, develop feelings of affection in them for all living things, and promote the transformation of "the myriad things into one harmonious family." (Duiker, p. 391.) Thus no student will emerge from the educational experience without being conditioned to use his education to work for the social utopia. Unless Ts'ai is permitted to use the phrase "subordinate to politics" (referring to the first half of the curriculum) only in the narrowest sense of "serving the present interest of the present rulers," his entire dichotomy breaks down. *Both* of his educational dimensions involved fosterage aiming at the cultivation of students who would work to transform each other and society as a whole in accordance with some antecedent model.

17. Lenin, *Selected Works,* vol. 3, p. 476.
18. Ibid.
19. Upbringing (*vospitanie*), takes place primarily but not entirely outside the classroom. Special stress began to be placed on it beginning in 1947. The content of *vospitanie* is supposed to include: Communist morality (proper attitude toward national wealth and labor, patriotism, interpersonal propriety such as treating others with dignity, such personal qualities as patience, and atheism); learning and labor; social behavior (good manners); aesthetics; and physical training. (Cary, pp. 67–107.)
20. Counts, *The Challenge of Soviet Education,* p. 93.
21. Medlin, in *Teaching in the Social Sciences and the Humanities in the U.S.S.R.,* p. 1.
22. *Filosofskaia entsiklopediia,* vol. 3, pp. 454–55.
23. Counts, *The Challenge of Soviet Education,* p. 93.
24. Ibid.
25. Kautsky, *The Labour Revolution,* pp. 221–22.

26. De Witt, p. 80.
27. Their positions are recorded in the "Theses of the Central Committee of the C.P.S.U. on Education" and in Khrushchev's memorandum entitled, "On Strengthening the Ties between School and Life and on the Further Development of Public Education." A translation of the "Theses" can be found in George S. Counts, *Khrushchev and the Central Committee Speak on Education* (Pittsburg: University of Pittsburg Press, 1968).
28. Counts, *Khrushchev*, p. 5.
29. Quoted in Grant, p. 99.
30. Counts, *Khrushchev*, p. 2.
31. Because of the need for specialized technical skills in school graduates entering the job market, the idea of polytechnical training even under Khrushchev's reforms rapidly became in fact monotechnism. There were not the time nor the facilities for the broad exposure to a multitude of production experiences that would have produced Marx's Leonardo-like all-round ideal.
32. Most of these slogans were grouped together in "Mao chu-hsi yü-lü [Quotations from Chairman Mao], *Hung-ch'i* [Red flag], no. 8 (July, 1970), pp. 1–4.
33. Ibid. This statement is originally from "On the Correct Handling of Contradictions Among the People," p. 110.
34. "Mao chu-hsi yü-lü," p. 1.
35. The slogan was current in the mid-1950s but achieved final prominence only in 1958.
36. "Strengthen Class Education Among Children" (*Chiang-hsi chiao-yü*) [Kiangsi education], no. 2 (February 25, 1965) in JPRS, no. 33330 (December 15, 1965).
37. Chiang Lung-chi, "Hsing wu mieh tzu," p. 38.
38. Teng Ch'u-min, "Tsen-yang p'ei-yang ch'ing-nien," p. 96.
39. Ch'en, *Mao Papers*, p. 64.
40. Lower primary school: Chinese language, general knowledge of social and natural science, arithmetic, fine arts, music recreation (playing games), and manual skills (plus general production knowledge). Upper primary school: citizenship (general political knowledge), Chinese, arithmetic, social science (including history and geography), natural science, hygiene, fine arts, physical culture, and manual skills (productive labor). The lower schools met twenty hours a week and the upper twenty-six.
41. Factual data for the above and quotations are derived from "Shen-kan-ning Government Reports," given to John Service in Yenan from July to October, 1944, located under University of California, Berkeley, Center for Chinese Studies Library, call no. 4292.24/9475. In some cases translations have been modified slightly.
42. Yen Chien-han, et al., eds. One of the largest repositories of these Yenan textbooks in America is the Hoover Institution, Stanford University.
43. *Suan-shu k'o-pen: ch'u-chi hsiao-hsüeh shih-yung*. Information derived primarily from bk. 2, p. 24; bk. 3, pp. 12, 13, 26, 35, 41; bk. 5, pp. 2, 39.
44. Ibid.

45. Ibid.
46. Yen Chien-han, et al., eds., lesson 7, p. 7.
47. *Kao-hsiao tzu-jan chiao-k'o-shu,* lesson 4, p. 9.
48. Yen Chien-han, et al., eds., lesson 13, p. 14.
49. *Kao-hsiao tzu-jan chiao-k'o-shu,* lesson 13, p. 34.
50. *Suan-shu k'o-pen: ch'u-chi hsiao-hsüeh,* vol. 5, p. 16; vol. 6, p. 30.
51. Mao Tse-tung, "Talks at the Chengtu Conference," in Schram, *Chairman Mao Talks to the People,* p. 98.
52. A host of articles appeared at the same time from principals of rural primary schools indicating how they were applying the policy of introducing moral education in every class: studying about tractors, calculating the number of work hours in a day, singing songs about labor, pretending to milk cows and plough in their dances, inviting the school cook to share a meal with them. (Tung Ch'un-ts'ai, ed., *Wo-men shih tsen-yang chin-hsing lao-tung chiao-yü ti,* pp. 51–54.)

    Needless to say, as in the Soviet Union, the teaching of reading and composition was supposed to be highly politicized. In giving examples of how to use new words, Chinese teachers were enjoined to use political examples. Stories incorporating the new characters learned should be political, reminding students of laborers who furnish their daily physical needs, of patriotic ideals, and of heroic workers and soldiers. Repeating the Russian line, the instructions for teachers insist that the purpose of reading the literature is to develop a proper understanding and outlook on life. (Wen I-chan, p. 2. For an example of the same position in the 1960s, see *KMJP,* June 6, 1962.)
53. *Tzu-jan: kao-chi hsiao-hsüeh k'o-pen.*
54. *Chu-suan: kao-chi hsiao-hsüeh k'o-pen.*
55. Wang Chün-heng, et al., eds.
56. *Wu-li hsüeh: kao-chi chung-hsüeh k'o-pen.* On Yenan middle schools, see *Chiao-hsüeh yü yen-chiu,* no. 10 (1958), pp. 10–13; and Chiang Lung-ch'i, "Shih Ch'e chiao-yü," p. 50.
57. *KMJP,* March 17, 1956, and September 14, 1957.
58. Ibid.
59. *KMJP,* June 13, 1960.
60. As an example of how this message was voiced by those below the ministry level, see Ts'ao Fu, p. 1.
61. Lenin, *Selected Works,* vol. 3, p. 476.
62. Tung Ch'un-ts'ai. For a later, retrospective view of the period and these policies, see *KMJP,* October 22, 1969.
63. "Tsai ko-ming ti ta p'i-p'an chung shen-ju k'ai-chan hsüeh-hsiao tou-cheng p'i-kai."
64. Munro, "Egalitarian Ideal and Educational Fact," in Lindbeck, p. 280.
65. Ibid., p. 282.
66. "Tai hsüeh-sheng tao sheng-ch'an-tui li ch'ü lien-hsi suan-shu pen-ling," p. 16.
67. Unlike the half-and-half schools, the institutions existing after the Cultural

Revolution did not abandon many academic subjects to make room for labor. Middle schools continued to devote at least 70 percent of the in-class time to regular "cultural" subjects. The program in a typical urban middle school consists of (a) mathematics, languages, physics, chemistry, history, geography, and physical education; (b) general political education, farming/factory work, study of revolutionary art and culture; (c) study of Mao's writings. About eight weeks during the year is spent working on a farm or in a factory.

68. For example, as late as 1968 he said in a speech that the school years have been too long, that there was too much repetition of basic courses at various levels, and that the examination system should be abolished. (*Mao Tse-tung wan sui*, vol. 3, p. 643.)

69. Munro, "Egalitarian Ideal and Educational Fact," in Lindbeck, p. 284.

70. From Mao's speech at the Chinese Communist Party's National Conference on Propaganda Work, March 12, 1957. Reprinted in *Quotations from Chairman Mao Tse-tung*, p. 215. An example of the use of the term "contradictions" to stand for "problems" occurs in Li Chang-mao, p. 11.

71. Lenin, *Marx-Engels-Marxism*, p. 333.

72. Meisner, p. 159.

73. In JPRS, no. 49826 (February 12, 1970), p. 66.

Chapter 6

1. *JMJP*, March 7, 1966, and March 7, 1968.

2. See the discussion in Munro, *Man in Early China*, p. 96. Therein reference is made to this and subsequent classical citations.

3. *Analects* viii. 2.2, in Legge, vol. 1, p. 208.

4. *The Great Learning* ix. 8.9. in ibid., p. 372.

5. The major aberrations from the principle over the long course of China's intellectual history take the form of injunctions to people to look more within themselves rather than to models. Thus the late Ming iconoclast Li Chih (1527–1602) said, "Each man Heaven gives birth to has his own individual function and he does not need to learn this from Confucius. If he did need to learn it from Confucius, then in all the ages before Confucius, could no one have achieved real manhood?" (Quoted in de Bary, "Individualism and Humanism," in de Bary, *Self and Society*, p. 199.) However, this was not the dominant theme in Confucian thought.

6. Munro, *Man in Early China*, p. 111.

7. Chi Ping, "Attach Importance to the Role of Teachers by Negative Example," *Peking Reveiw*, no. 13 (March 31, 1972), p. 5.

8. Schram, *Talks to the People*, p. 201.

9. *JMJP*, February 24, 1964.

10. From "Sixty Points on Working Methods," in Jerome Ch'en, pp. 65–66.

11. Hsieh Ch'ien-ch'iu, p. 259.

12. Quoted in JPRS, no. 49826 (February 12, 1970), p. 58.

13. Ibid., p. 60.

14. "Lead the General with the Typical Model," in JPRS, no. 31704 (August 25, 1965), p. 10.

15. *Shensi jih-pao,* August 26, 1956, and *Wen-hui pao* (Shanghai), April 28, 1956.

16. *Kung-jen jih-pao,* July 25, 1963.

17. Moore, Jr., p. 179.

18. Mao Tse-tung, "Pi-hsü hsüeh-hui tso ching-chi kung-tso," pp. 1013–19.

19. *Ta-kung pao* (Tientsin), June 27, 1956.

20. Chang Ch'ang, "Fang jen-min tai-piao," p. 14.

21. *Mao Tse-tung wan sui* vol. 2, pp. 361–62. This section was drawn to my attention by Ms. Jean Oi.

22. "Chien-ch'ih cheng chih kua shuai p'i-p'an wu-chih li-chi-ta-lien chi ch'e ch'e liang ch'ang ti tiao-ch'a pao-kao" [Insist on politics being in command. Criticize material incentives—investigation report of the Ta-lien motor vehicles factory], Hung ch'i 5, 1975, pp. 60–63.

23. Schram, *Chairman Mao Talks to the People,* pp. 43–44.

24. See chapter 7 for a discussion of the pressures for reducing distributive inequalities of a quantitative kind. We argue that such inequalities cause tension because they impede status equality, the kind of equality in which the Maoists are most interested.

25. Moore, Jr., p. 243.

26. *Szu-ch'uan jih-pao,* April 29, 1956, and January 21, 1957.

27. *Kung-jen jih-pao,* October 22, 1956; Wang Sun.

28. *KMJP,* January 11, 1966.

29. "Tsai chi-shu ko-ming chung piao-hsien ko-ming ying-hsiung ch'i-kai ti Su Kuang-ning"; *Hang-chou jih-pao* [Hangchow daily], September 26, 1957; *KMJP,* June 28, 1963; *Yang-ch'eng wan-pao* [Yang-ch'eng evening news], (Canton) March 2, 1963; *JMJP,* January 23, 1963.

30. Based on interviews.

31. *Shen-Kan-Ning Government Reports,* pp. 21, 14.

32. Liu Tzu-chiu; *Kung-jen jih-pao,* February 7, 1963; *Chiao-shih pao* [Teacher's news], February 22, 1957; *Wen-hui pao* (Shanghai), September 20, 1968.

33. Gliksman, et al., pp. 77–93.

34. *JMJP,* March 6, 1964.

35. The "five-good soldier" was (1) good in political thought, (2) good in military technique, (3) good in three-eight style, (4) good in filling responsibilities, and (5) good at molding the body physically. "Three-eight style" refers to three phrases and eight additional characters identifying the ideal virtues of a PLA soldier.

The "five-good worker" is (1) good in political thought, (2) good at fulfilling tasks, (3) good at observing discipline, (4) good in studying in a regular manner, and (5) good in achieving unity and rendering mutual assistance.

36. *JMJP,* March 7, 1966. The "from point to surface" theory that derived from guerrilla warfare strategy was already applied to model emulation even during the period in the 1950s, when the Soviet campaign approach was dominant. See

for example, "Pan hao hsüeh-hsiao, pi-hsü t'uan-chieh, i-k'ao chiao-chih," p. 57.

37. Quoted in *JMJP,* March 7, 1966.

38. Kan Wei-min, pp. 23–24; *JMJP,* November 5, 1969.

39. *JMJP,* October 31, 1969.

40. Gliksman, pp. 86–87.

41. Interviews with industrial workers indicate that from 1956 to 1966, in industrial organizations, the proper procedure entailed the following steps. Each work unit (*hsiao-tsu*), consisting of roughly twenty-five workers, would hold an open discussion under the leadership of the trade union work unit leader, on instructions of the head of the production department of the trade union. Out of this open but guided discussion perhaps five names of potential candidates would be selected and passed on to the work section (*kung-tuan*) for further evaluation and weeding. The names would then be sent to a union meeting in which the union representatives in each work unit participate. The Party committee, consisting typically of the factory manager, vice-manager, Party secretary, vice-Party secretary, and head of the political department, would make the final selection.

42. *KMJP,* June 26, 1965, trans. in *SCMP,* no. 3499 (July 19, 1965), p. 5.

43. Kan Wei-min, p. 26.

44. "Lead the General with the Typical Model," p. 11.

45. *Wen-hui pao* (Shanghai), May 28, 1956.

46. *CKCNP,* October 29, 1959.

47. *KMJP,* January 11, 1966; "Pan-hao hsüeh-hsiao pi-hsü t'uan-chieh i-k'ao chiao-shih," p. 57; *Kung-jen pao* (Peking), February 20, 1963; also "Fa chieh-chi chih-fen," p. 12.

48. "Lead the General with the Typical Model," p. 13.

49. *KMJP,* June 26, 1965, in *SCMP,* no. 3499 (July 19, 1965), p. 5.

50. Liu Tzu-chiu.

51. The Chinese are not the only people to recognize the utility of these devices. In Israel, some Kibbutzim employ remarkably similar techniques. Spiro, pp. 85, 153–67.

52. Albert Bandura, ed., *Psychological Modeling: Conflicting Theories* (Chicago: Aldine-Atherton, 1971).

53. Cheng Chih-kuang, "Tsen-yang p'ei-yang tu-li szu k'ao," p. 10.

54. "Anonymous Performers of Good Deeds in Shanghai," in *SCMP,* no. 3452 (May 7, 1965), p. 18.

55. *Mao Tse-tung szu-hsiang wan-sui,* vol. 2, p. 362.

56. This point was made by Mr. Abisi Sharakiya.

57. *Wen-i pao* [Literature and art news] (Peking), February 11, 1960. In URI, no. 41171-1959-60.

58. This information is derived primarily from interviews. A written source that reveals the problem is the article by Hsing Ch'ien-t'ang in *CKCN,* no. 1 (1963), pp. 20–21.

Chapter 7

1. Marx, *Capital,* vol. 1, p. 396.
2. The Chinese do not use their counterpart of our ethical term "equality" (*kung-p'ing*) as frequently as we use it to describe the same phenomena. The relations between people and treatment of people are more likely to be discussed in class terms in China. Therefore, we are primarily clarifying the applicability of a Western philosophical content to the Chinese situation. Occasionally, however, they do use a phrase that can be translated as "social status equality" (*she-hui ti-wei p'ing teng*), and such a phrase is quite an acceptable counterpart of "status equality" as it will be used in this chapter. "To treat people equally" in the sense of refusing to regard them with attitudes of superiority or inferiority, except when justifiable reasons can be provided, is expressed with the phrase *p'ing-teng tai jen.*
3. This is found in the *Book of Rites (Li Chi),* sec. 9.
4. Bedau, especially p. 180.
5. Quoted in Schram, *The Political Thought of Mao Tse-tung,* p. 199. This position was repeated by Mao in 1957 (Ch'en, *Mao Papers,* p. 56), and is regularly the subject of articles in philosophy and economics.
6. We would claim that the right of freedom of conscience has been the most important right. But we would admit the complexities involved in this claim. In 1960, Leonard W. Levy, dean of the Graduate School at Brandeis, published *Legacy of Suppression,* in which he attempted to document that the late-eighteenth century and subsequent leading Americans did not believe in freedom of belief in the realm of politics. It is important to remember that the doctrine of freedom of conscience referred first to religious belief and only gradually was extended to other matters. Later, it was still possible for the American leaders who gave nominal assent to freedom of expression on political matters to go the route of Calvinists in practice. That is, to demand freedom of belief on political issues for themselves and their society against an outside authority (the Crown) and yet to be relatively intolerant of dissent internally. This hypocrisy does not destroy the long-term cultural impact of the doctrine of the right to freedom of conscience, however.
7. Moore, Jr., pp. 226–28.
8. For example, selfishness would be rendered *wu szu hsin ti* and selfish intentions would be *szu-i.*
9. *Chu-tzu ch'üan shu,* 44.12b.
10. Plamenatz, "Equality of Opportunity," p. 84. In *A Theory of Justice* (1971), John Rawls orders the principles of justice so that there are no rights that conflict with equality of opportunity.
11. Plamenatz, "Equality of Opportunity," p. 93.
12. Marx's notion of "truly human needs" is both descriptive and prescriptive. People should feel the real needs even if they do not, and they would be happier if they did and were able to fulfill them. Thus, on the matter of equality of

opportunity, the Marxist position would be that people should be given the opportunity, for example, to indulge in mental labors, and if necessary strongly induced to take advantage of the opportunities, even if they are not doing so and making no complaints about it.

13. A 1931 decree opened universities to offspring of engineers and other high level professionals, whose children had home lives more conducive to learning than those of manual laborers.

14. Potter, p. 214.

15. Wood, p. 222.

16. Ibid.

17. Quoted by Milovan Djilas in "There'll Be Many Different Communisms in 1984," p. 28.

18. In a Soviet factory, for example, wage grades exist so that remuneration can be geared to skill. Khrushchev took the major steps to minimize stratification barriers in terms of income and occupational status as between mental and manual laborers. He pushed for wage increases for low paid workers and a narrowing of the differences between various branches of industry. But even he did not seek the kind of "harmful egalitarianism" that Stalin had criticized. He did not oppose the high wages of the elite. (Matthews, pp. 75–79.)

19. Ibid.

20. Chi Yen, "Ideological Weapon for Restricting Bourgeois Right," *Peking Review,* no. 22 (May 30, 1975), pp. 8–9.

21. Ibid.

22. Whyte, "Inequality," pp. 684–93.

23. In 1958–59 the basic accounting unit was over one hundred families. This made it possible to even out the income within a wider group of people and provided less opportunity for concentration of earnings within limited parameters than the previous accounting unit. In other words, villages that work good lands were more likely to have to share income with those who work less favorable lands. After 1959, the unit became about thirty families. This caused an increase in differences in income levels as between smaller groups of people in the rural areas. Thus, "distributively" speaking, 1958–59 was the most egalitarian period in rural China.

24. Zuckerman, p. 218.

25. Ibid., p. 219.

26. Lenin, *Selected Works,* vol. 2, pp. 293–94.

27. Matthews, p. 239.

28. The Chinese definition of legitimate occupations would be different from those in Western countries. They would not include such professions as hermit-poet or wandering minstrel, or the life-styles associated with them. To this extent, their vision of social equality and ours would differ, in that they would tolerate a narrow range of occupations potentially subject to egalitarian attitudes.

27. "Study 'Serve the People,' " in *Peking Review,* no. 2 (January 6, 1967), p. 10. Mao's statement is in "The Tasks of 1945."

30. Schram, *Chairman Mao Talks to the People,* p. 99.

31. Quoted in J. Ch'en, p. 68.
32. Malraux, p. 464.
33. See the discussion and references in Munro, "Egalitarian Ideal and Educational Fact," pp. 272–73.
34. Mai Sui, "Treat Others as Equals and Build Close Ties with the Masses," *CKCN*, nos. 9–10 (May 7, 1962); in *SCMP*, no. 316 (June 4, 1962), pp. 9–12.
35. And this is probably a good thing for the Chinese, because their utopian visions of what changes are possible in the school's system have had to be modified frequently. In 1964 and early in the Cultural Revolution there was much talk of modeling all universities on the factory school (Shanghai College of Machine Building was the prototype). One aim was to terminate the status difference between vocationally oriented factory schools and regular institutes of higher learning. This has not materialized. In regular comprehensive universities, workshops normally are found only in natural science or engineering departments, where they are research and teaching service centers. Part-time schools are not included in statistics dealing with ordinary primary and middle schools, indicating differential categorizing of them, probably with status implications.
36. For a treatment of the utilitarian function of the "selflessness" ideal, see Benjamin I. Schwartz, "China and the West in the 'Thought of Mao Tse-tung'," and the "Comment" by Donald J. Munro, in Ping-ti Ho and Tang Tsou, *China in Crisis*, vol. 1, pp. 365–89.

Chapter 8

1. Yü T'ing-ying, p. 7.
2. Mao Tse-tung, "On the Correct Handling of Contradictions," in *Four Essays*, p. 89.
3. Po Yeh, p. 8.
4. Skinner, p. 88.
5. See Nozick, pp. 440–72.
6. John Plamenatz has made this point in his critiques of Soviet Marxism.
7. Mao Tse-tung, "On the Correct Handling of Contradictions Among the People," pp. 81–82. An example of this idea as it related to incentives is in JPRS, no. 61269-2 (February 20, 1974), p. 282.
8. Again, I have benefited from Plamenatz here.
9. Quoted in George R. Geiger, "Dewey's Social and Political Philosophy," in Schilpp, ed., p. 349.
10. John Dewey, "Philosophies of Freedom," in Bernstein, p. 139. See also p. 271.
11. Quoted in George R. Geiger, "Dewey's Social and Political Philosophy," in Schilpp, ed., p. 346.
12. Quoted in *SCMP*, no. 2458 (March 13, 1965).
13. "[The makers of our Constitution] conferred as against the Government, the right to be let alone—the most comprehensive of rights and the right most

valued by civilized men." Dissenting opinion in Olmstead v. United States. *United States Reports* (Washington D.C.: U.S. Government Printing Office, 1928), pp. 277, 438.

14. Mill, p. 97.
15. Wolff, pp. 24–25.
16. Marx, "Private Property and Communism," in Bottomore, p. 165.
17. W. von Humboldt, *The Sphere and Duties of Government* (1791), quoted in Lukes, p. 68.
18. Marx, "Alienated Labour," in Bottomore, trans., *Early Writings,* p. 128.
19. Marx, "Private Property and Communism," in ibid., p. 165.
20. Mill, "On Liberty," p. 72. Lukes has a useful discussion of the Marx-Mill-German-Romantic link.
21. Cf. Plamenatz, *Man and Society,* vol. 1, 352.

Glossary

ch'ang hsin 常心

ch'ang lao-tung mo-fan 廠勞動模範

ch'e chien 車間

che ko tzu yu shen-mo i-szu 這個字有甚麽意思

chen chih hsing 眞知行

chen ya 鎭壓

ch'eng i 誠意

cheng ming 正名

cheng-ch'üeh ti tu-shu tung-chi 正確的讀書動機

chi 幾

ch'iang-p'o 強迫

chiao-hsüeh yü chiao-yang hsiang chieh-ho 教學與教養相結合

chiao-yü 教育

chiao-yü chiu kuo 教育救國

chia-teng lao-tung mo-fan 甲等勞動模範

chia-t'ing ch'eng-fen 家庭成份

chia-t'ing ch'u-shen 家庭出身

ch'i-chih 氣質

chi-chih chih hsing 氣質之性

chieh-chi hsing 階級性

ch'ien 淺

Ch'ien Tzu Wen 千字文

[a]chih 志

[b]chih 智

[c]chih 知

chih chih fa tung shih i 知之發動是意

chih hsing ti pen-t'i 知行的本體

chih shih hsin chih so chih i chih ch'u ti 志是心之所之一直去底

chih-chüeh 知覺

chih-shih 智識

chih-tao 知道

ching 敬

ch'ing 情

ching chi-hsüeh—che-hsüeh shou-kao 經濟學—哲學手稿

ch'ing-kan 情感

ch'ing-kuan 清宮

ching-shen huang-hu 精神恍惚

chiu chang suan-shu 九章算術

chou-hsüeh 州學

chu li 燭理

chü yu chi-chi i-i, yeh k'o-neng chü yu hsiao-chi i-i 具有積極意義也可能具有消極意義

ch'u yü jen-lei pen-hsing ti jen-tao chu-i 出於人類本性的人道主義

ch'uang-tsao hsing 創造性

ch'üan-mien fa-chan 全面發展

chu-kuan fang-mien t'iao-chien 主觀方面條件

chung-ch'eng 忠誠

221

chün-tzu 君子
ch'u-shen 出身

erh ho wei i 二合爲一

[a]fa 發
[b]fa 法
fa pien 發便
fan hsing 反性
fang-chen 方針
fang-fa 方法
fu-fan 浮汎
fu-hsüeh 府學

hao 好
Ho Szu-ching 何思敬
hsiang-hsüeh 鄉學
hsiang-yüeh 鄉約
hsiao-hsüeh 小學
hsiao-jen 小人
hsiao-tzu 小組
hsien-chin chiao-shih 先進教師
hsien-chin chiao-yü kung-tso che 先進教育工作者
hsien-chin kung-tso che 先進工作者
hsien-hsüeh 縣學
hsien-t'ien ti 先天的
hsin yüeh 新月
[a]hsing 刑
[b]hsing 行
[c]hsing 性
hsing chüeh 醒覺
hsing i yeh 性一也
hsing-ko 性格
hsiu shen 修身
hsüeh 學
hua shen 化身
hung-wen-kuan 弘文館

[a]i 義
[b]i 意

[c]i 一
i che hsin chih so fa 意者心之所發
i chih 意志
i fen wei erh 一分爲二
i hsüeh tso jen wei chu 以學做人爲主
i hua 異化
i li fu jen-k'ou, i li fu jen-shin 以力服人口, 以理服人心
i shen tso tse 以身作則
i shih 意識
i-chih 意志
i-hsüeh 義學
i-i 意義
i-shu 義塾
i-szu 意思

jen 仁
jen, i, li, chih 仁, 義, 禮, 知
jen ti hsin-li sheng wu hua liao 人的心理生物化了
jen-che jen yeh 仁者人也
jen-chüeh 人爵
jen-hsin 人心
jen-sheng i fu-wu wei mu-ti 人生以服務爲目的
jen-shih 認識
jen-shih kuo-ch'eng 認識過程
jen-shih lun 認識論
jen-shih shang ti tso-te tung-chi 認識上的道德動機
ju i 儒醫

kai-tsao 改造
kan hsing jen-shih 感性認識
kan-chüeh 感覺
k'ang ta 抗大
k'o su hsing 可塑性
ko-hsing 個性
ko-jen ch'eng-fen 個人成份
ko-jen ch'u-shen 個人出身

ko-jen ming-li szu-hsiang 個人名利思想

ko-jen ming-li tung-chi 個人名利動機

ko-jen ying-hsiung chu-i 個人英雄主義

kuang-wen-kuan 廣文館

kung 公

k'ung hsin 空心

kung tuan 工段

k'ung yen 空言

kung-hsin 公心

kung-min 公民

kung-nung su-ch'eng chung hsiao hsüeh 工農速成中小學

kung-ping 公平

kung-she lao-tung mo-fan 公社勞動模範

kuo 菓

kuo-feng 國風

kuo-tzu-chien 國子監

kuo-tzu-hsüeh 國子學

lao-tung ying hsiung 勞動英雄

[a]li 禮

[b]li 理

[c]li 利

li hsing jen-shih 理性認識

li hsüeh tsung-chih 立學宗旨

liao-chieh 了解

li-hsing 理性

li-lun 理論

ling-ch'u 靈處

lo 樂

meng-ch'iu 蒙求

ming 命

ming-lang ti t'ien 明朗的天

min-pan hsiao-hsüeh 民辦小學

mo-fan kung-tso che 模範工作者

mo-fan min shih 模範民師

mo-fang 模仿

nei-hsin ti tao-te t'i-yen 內心的道德體驗

ni che-yang tso tao-ti yu shen-mo i-szu 儞這樣做到底有甚麼意思

pa jen sheng wu hua 把人生物化

pai chia hsing hsüan 佰家姓選

pai hua 白話

pei hsüeh ch'ao pang 北學超幫

p'ei-yang 培養

pen-chih 本質

pen-shen 本身

pi 蔽

pi hsüeh kan pang 比學趕幫

pi yeh 畢業

piao shuai 表率

piao-ping 標兵

p'ing-teng tai jen 平等待人

pu cheng 不爭

pu k'o i 不可移

pu pi wei chi 不必爲已

San Tzu Ching 三字經

shao erh ching 少而精

she hsüeh 社學

she-hui ti-wei p'ing-teng 社會地位平等

shen 深

shen chiao sheng yü yen chiao 身教勝於言教

shen pu yu chu 身不由主

sheng 升

sheng erh chih chih 生而知之

sheng yüan 生員

sheng-jen 聖人

shih hsüeh 實學

shih-fei chih hsin 是非之心

shih-shih tung yüan ta hui 誓師動員大會

shu-jen 庶人
shuo fu 說服
shu-pen chih-shih 書本知識
shu-yüan 書院
su-tsao 塑造
su-yüan hua 疏遠化
su-yüan hua ti lao-tung 疏遠化的
　勞動
su-yüan ti ts'un-tsai 疏遠的存在
[a]szu 私
[b]szu 思
szu-hsiang 思想
szu-hsiang chiao yü 思想教育
szu-hsiang p'in-chih 思想品質
szu-hsiang wu-ch'i 思想武器
szu-i 私意
szu-lü 思慮
szu-men-hsüeh 四門學
szu-wei 思維

ta-hsüeh 大學
t'ai hsüeh 太學
tang hsing 黨性
tao hsin 道心
ta-t'ung 大同
te 德
te chih t'i chu fang-mien ch'üan-
　mien fa-chan ti jen-ts'ai 德智體
　諸方面全面發展的人材
te ts'ai chien pei 德才兼備
t'e-teng lao-tung mo-fan 特等勞動
　模範
t'i 體
t'i li 體理
t'ien-chüeh 天爵
t'ien-chün 天君
t'ien-hsia wei kung 天下爲公
tien-hsing 典型
t'ien-ti chih hsing 天地之性
t'ien-ts'ai chiao-yü 天才教育
tsai Mao Tse-tung szu-hsiang te

yang-kuang yü-lu p'u-yu hsia 在
　毛澤東思想的陽光雨露哺育下
tso jen 做人
tso jen tao-li 做人道理
ts'ung tien tao mien 從點到面
tsung-chih 宗旨
tsung-wen-kuan 宗文館
tuan lien 鍛鍊
tui t'a ti hun-shih ni ti i-szu ju-ho
　對他的婚事你的意思如何
tui tu-shu mu-ti jen-shih cheng-
　ch'üeh ti yu pai-fen chih chi 對
　讀書目的認識正確的有百分之幾
t'ui-chien ho hsüan-pa hsiang chieh-
　ho 推薦和選拔相結合
tung 動
t'ung hsüeh 同學
tung yüan hui 動員會
t'ung-ch'ing-hsin 同情心
tung-shih 懂事
tun-tien 蹲點
tzu hua 自化
tzu-wo kai-tsao 自我改造
tzu-yu i-chih 自由意志

wai hua 外化
wai tsai hua 外在化
wan wu ko tang ch'i fen 萬物各當
　其分
wei jen 爲人
wei jen-min fu-wu 爲人民服務
wei-hsieh 威脅
wen ming 文明
wen-chiao ying 文教英
wen-yen 文言
wu chih 無知
wu hao chan shih 五好戰士
wu szu 無私
wu szu-hsin ti 無私心的
wu yü 無欲
wu-ch'ang 五常

ya-li 壓力
yang-ch'eng 養成
yang-shih 養士
yen-ko yao-ch'iu ho nai-hsin shuo
   hsiang chieh-ho 嚴格要求和耐
   心說相結合
yin 因
yin jen shih chiao 因人施教
yin ts'ai shih chiao 因材施教
yü 慾

yu i-i te 有意義的
yu k'o i chih li 有可移之理
yu wai chih hsin 有外之心
yu-hsiu chiao-shih 優秀教師
yu-hsiu chiao-shih t'e-teng chiang
   優秀教師特等獎
yung-shih 用世
yün-niang 醞釀
yün-yung 運用

Bibliography

An Tzu-wen. *Ch'ien-ch'ui pai-lien, kai-tsao tzu-chi* [Under numerous tests, reform oneself]. Tientsin: Tien-chin jen-min ch'u-pan-she, 1957.

"Anonymous Performers of Good Deeds in Shanghai," NCNA (Shanghai), English edition, May 4, 1965. In *SCMP*, no. 3452 (May 7, 1965).

Bandura, Albert, ed. *Psychological Modeling: Conflicting Theories*. Chicago: Aldine-Atherton, 1971.

Bauer, Raymond A. *The New Man in Soviet Psychology*. Cambridge: Harvard University Press, 1952.

Bedau, Hugo A. "Radical Egalitarianism." In *Justice and Equality*, edited by Hugo A. Bedau. Englewood Cliffs, N.J.: Prentice-Hall, 1971.

Bernstein, Richard J. *John Dewey*. New York: Washington Square Press, 1966.

Bottomore, T. B., ed. and trans. *Karl Marx: Early Writings*. New York: McGraw-Hill Book Co., 1964.

Bruce J. Percy. *Chu Hsi and His Masters: An Introduction to Chu Hsi and the Sung School of Chinese Philosophy*. London: Probsthain and Co., 1923.

Chan Wing-tsit, trans. *Instructions for Practical Living and Other Neo-Confucian Writings by Wang Yang-Ming*. New York: Columbia University Press, 1963.

―――. *A Source Book in Chinese Philosophy*. Princeton: Princeton University Press, 1963.

Chang, Carson. *The Development of Neo-Confucian Thought*. 2 vols. New York: Bookman Associates, 1957–62.

Chang Ch'ang. "Fang jen-min tai-piao ch'ing-nien lao-mo Lo Shih-fa" [Visiting people's representative, youth labor model Lo Shih-fa], *Chung-kuo hsin-wen* [China news], April 18, 1960, p. 14. In URI, no. 3246616.

Chang Chih-kuang. *Tsen-yang ch'ü liao-chieh hsüeh-sheng ti ko-hsing?* [How can we go about understanding the personality of students?] Shanghai: Hsin chih-shih ch'u-pan-she, 1958.

Chang Hao-po. "Yao shan yü ch'i-fa ch'ing-nien kai-tsao szu-hsiang ti tzu-chüeh-hsing" [One must be skilled at enlightening youth in the rebuilding of thought consciousness], *CKCN*, no. 2 (1962).

Chang Ling-kuan in *Jen-min chiao-yü* [People's education] (Peking), no. 2 (1955).

227

Chang Man-hua. "Pu tang chiu-shih hao hsi-fu: yung-yüan yao tso ko-ming jen" [Don't be a good old-style daughter-in-law: always be a revolutionary], *CKCN*, no. 7 (April 1, 1966).

Chang Yeh-ming. "Ho Chiang Nan-hsiang t'ung-chih shang-ch'üeh chiao-yü fang-chen wen-t'i" [Discussing some questions about educational guidelines with comrade Chiang Nan-hsiang], *HHPYK*, no. 3 (1957).

Chao I-ping. "Communist China's Achievements in Pavlov's Theory During the Past Decade," *Sheng-wu-hsüeh t'ung pao* [Biology bulletin], no. 10 (October 2, 1959). In JPRS, no. 1118-D (January 15, 1960).

Che-hsüeh hsiao tz'u-tien [Small philosophical dictionary]. Hong Kong: Hsiang-kang hu-yang chu-pan she, 1974.

Ch'en Chan-ch'iao. "T'an pi-chiao" [On comparison], *Hung-ch'i* [Red flag], no. 23–24 (1962).

Ch'en Ch'ing-chih. *Chung-kuo chiao-yü shih* [Educational history of China]. Taipei: Shang-wu yin-shu-kuan, 1963.

Ch'en Jerome, ed. *Mao Papers: Anthology and Bibliography*. London: Oxford University Press, 1970.

Ch'en Kuei-mei. "Tui hsin-li-hsüeh ti tui-hsiang, jen-wu ho fang-fa ti chi-tien k'an-fa" [A few points on the object, aim and method of psychology], *Hsin Chien-she* [New construction], June 7, 1959.

Ch'en Po-ta, et al. *Jen-hsing, tang-hsing, ko-hsing* [Human nature, party nature, individual nature (Personality)]. Hong Kong: Ch'ao-hsi she, 1947.

Ch'en Yu-sung. "Chien-ch'a Hu Shih tsai chiao-yü fang-mien ti fan-tung ying-hsiang ho Hu Shih szu-hsiang tui-wo ti ying-hsiang" [An examination of Hu Shih's reactionary influence in the education sector and the influence of Hu Shih's thought on me]. In *Tzu-ch'an-chieh-chi chiao-yü p'i-pan* [A critique of capitalist education]. Peking: Wen-hua chiao-yü ch'u-pan-she, 1955.

Cheng Chih-kuang, ed. *Tsen-yang p'ei-yang tu-li shih-k'ao ho tu-li kung-tso ti neng-li?* [How do we cultivate independent thinking and working ability?]. Shanghai: Jen-min ch'u-pan-she, 1957.

Chiang Lung-ch'i. "Hsing-wu mieh-tzu hung-t'ou chuan-shen, wei chien-she kung-ch'an-chu-i ti hsin Pei-ching ta hsüeh fen-tou" [Raise up the proletariat; annihilate the capitalist; be Red through and through and highly qualified; fight to establish a Communist New Peking University], *Pei-ching ta-hsüeh hsüeh-pao* [Journal of Peking University], no. 3 (1958).

———. "Kuan-ch'e chiao-yü wei cheng-chih fu-wu chiao-yü t'ung sheng-ch'an chieh-ho ti fang-chen" [Thoroughly implement the policy of education in the service of politics and education in combination with production], *Pei-ching ta-hsüeh hsüeh-pao* [Journal of Peking University], no. 3 (1958).

Chien Nan-hsiang. "Lüeh-lun kao-teng hsüeh-hsiao ti ch'üan-mien fa-chan ti chiao-yü fang-chen" [A summary of the education guidelines for "all-round development" in institutions of higher learning], *CKCN*, no. 20 (1956).

"Chien-ch'ih cheng chih kua shuai p'i-p'an wu-chih li-chi-ta-lien chi ch'e ch'e liang ch'ang ti tiao-ch'a pao-kao" [Insist on politics being in command; criticize material incentives—investigation report of the Ta-lien motor vehicles factory], *Hung ch'i*, no. 5 (1975).

Chin, Robert, and Chin, Ai-li S. *Psychological Research in Communist China: 1949–1966.* Cambridge, Mass.: The M.I.T. Press, 1929.

Chou Yang. *The Fighting Task Confronting Workers in Philosophy and the Social Sciences.* Peking: Foreign Languages Press, 1963.

Chung Ching-wen. "Nu-li hsüeh-hsi lao-tung jen-min ti yü-yen" [Strive to learn working people's language], *Yü-wen hsüeh-hsi* [Language learning] 8 (August 1952).

Chu-suan: kao-chi hsiao-hsüeh k'o-pen [Abacus: upper level elementary school text]. 2 vols. Prepared for primary school grades five and six. Peking: Jen-min chiao-yü ch'u-pan-she, 1955.

Chu-tzu ch'üan-shu [The complete works of Chu Hsi] K'ang Hsi 52 (1714) ed.

Connor, Walter D. *Deviance in Soviet Society.* New York: Columbia University Press, 1972.

Cornforth, Maurice. *The Theory of Knowledge.* New York: International Publishers, 1963.

Counts, George S. *The Challenge of Soviet Education.* New York: McGraw Hill, 1957.

————. *Khrushchev and the Central Committee Speak on Education.* Pittsburgh: University of Pittsburgh Press, 1968.

Cremin, Lawrence A. *The Transformation of the School: Progressivism in American Education, 1876–1957.* New York: Vintage Books, 1961.

Dai-shen-yu. "Mao Tse-tung and Confucianism." Ph.D. dissertation, University of Pennsylvania, 1952.

de Bary, William Theodore. "Individualism and Humanitarianism in Late Ming Thought." In *Self and Society in Ming Thought,* edited by William Theodore de Bary. New York: Columbia University Press, 1970.

DeWitt, Nicholas. *Education and Professional Employment in the U.S.S.R.* Washington, D.C.: National Science Foundation, U.S. Government Printing Office, 1961.

Djilas, Milovan. "Djilas Revisits Orwell: There'll Be Many Different Communisms in 1984," *New York Times Magazine,* March 23, 1969, pp. 28, 134–40.

Dobson, W. A. C. H., trans. *Mencius.* Toronto: University of Toronto Press, 1963.

Duiker, William J. "The Aesthetics Philosophy of Ts'ai Yüan-p'ei," *Philosophy East and West* 22, no. 4 (October 1972).

Engels, Friedrich. *Ludwig Feuerbach and the Outcome of Classical German Philosophy.* Edited by C. P. Dutt, New York: International Publishers, 1941.

Erh Ch'eng ch'üan-shu [The complete works of the two Ch'eng brothers] In *Szu-pu pei yao* [Comprehensive collection of the four categories]: *I-shu* [Posthumous works]; *I-ch'uan hsien-sheng wen-chi* [Mr. I-ch'uan's works]; *Chou-i ch'uan* [The book of changes.] Shanghai: Chung-hua Shu-chü, n.d.

"Fa chieh-chi chih fen" [Stir up class enthusiasm], *Chiang-hsi chiao-yü* [Kiangsi education], no. 11 (1965).

Filosofskaia entsiklopediia. 1st ed. Moscow: Sovetskaia entsiklopediia, 1964.

Fokkema, D. W. *Literary Doctrine in China and Soviet Influence: 1956–1960.* London: Mouton and Co., 1965.

Fu Yung. "Lun jen-hsing" [On human nature], *CKCN,* August 16, 1957.

Fundamentals of Marxism-Leninism: Manual. Edited and translated by Clemens Dutt. Moscow: Foreign Languages Publishing House, 1961.

Fung Yu-lan. *A History of Chinese Philosophy*. Vol. 2. Princeton: Princeton University Press, 1958.

Furth, Charlotte. *Ting Wen-chiang: Science and China's New Culture*. Cambridge: Harvard University Press, 1970.

Geiger, George Raymond. "Dewey's Social and Political Philosophy." In *The Philosophy of John Dewey,* edited by Paul Arthur Schilpp. Evanston: Northwestern University, 1939.

Gliksman, Jerry G., et al. *The Control of Industrial Labor in the Soviet Union*. Santa Monica: Rand Corporation, 1960.

Graham, A. C. *Two Chinese Philosophers: Ch'eng Ming-tao and Ch'eng Yi-ch'uan*. London: Lund Humphries, 1958.

Grant, Nigel. *Soviet Education*. Baltimore: Penguin Books, 1964.

Grier, Philip T. *Contemporary Soviet Ethical Theory*. Ph.D. dissertation, The University of Michigan, 1973.

Hamilton, Alexander; Jay, John; and Madison, James. *The Federalist*. New York: Modern Library, 1941.

Hansen, Chad. "Freedom and Moral Responsibility in Confucian Ethics," *Philosophy East and West* 22, no. 2 (April 1972).

Ho Peng-ti and Tang Tsou. *China in Crisis*. Vol. 1. Chicago: University of Chicago Press, 1968.

Hobbes, Thomas. *The Leviathan*. New York: Everyman Edition, E.P. Dutton Co., n.d.

Hoffmann, Charles. *Work Incentive Practices and Policies in the People's Republic of China, 1953–1965*. Albany: State University of New York Press, 1967.

Hsieh Ch'ien-ch'iu. "Ch'ing shao-nien tao-te p'ing-chia neng-li ti i-hsieh yen-chiu" [Studies on the ability of adolescents to make moral judgments], *Hsin-li hsüeh-pao* [Acta psychological sinica], no. 3 (1964), pp. 258–68.

Hsin-li hsüeh: Szu-fan hsüeh-hsiao erh-nien-chi shih-yung [Psychology: for teachers' college second year]. Peking: Jen-min chiao-yü ch'u-pan-she, 1957.

Hsiung, James Chieh. *Ideology and Practice: The Evolution of Chinese Communism*. New York: Praeger, 1970.

Hsü Shu-lien, "Ts'ung hsin-li-hsüeh ti kuan-tien k'an ko-hsing wen-t'i" [Considering personality from the viewpoint of psychology], *CKCN,* no. 15 (August 1, 1956).

Huang Yin-an, et al., eds. *Pien-chen wei-wu chu-i ming-tz'u chieh-shih* [Explanation of terms of dialectical materialism]. Peking: T'ung-chu tu-hu ch'u-pan-she, 1957.

"'Hung-se hsüan-ch'üan-yüan' ti szu-hsiang kuang-hui: Ch'ao-hsien hua-chü 'hung-se hsüan-ch'üan-yüan' tso-t'an chi-lu" [The bright thoughts of *Red Propagandist:* a record of the talk on the Korean play *Red Propagandist*], *CKCN,* no. 2 (January 16, 1963), pp. 5–8.

I Fan. "T'ien-ts'ai ho ch'in-fen" [Ingenuity and perseverance], *CKCN,* no. 17 (June 1, 1954), pp. 16–17.

Kan Wei-min. "Chua-hao tien-hsing" [Grasp well typical models], *Hung ch'i* [Red flag], November 1969.

Kant, Immanuel. *The Fundamental Principal of the Metaphysic of Ethics.* Translated by Otto Manthey-Zorn. New York: Appleton-Century-Crofts, 1938.

Kautsky, Karl. *The Labour Revolution.* Translated by H. J. Stenning. London: L. MacVeagh, The Dial Press, 1925.

Kenyon, Cecelia M. "Conceptions of Human Nature in American Political Thought: 1630–1826." Ph.D. dissertation, Radcliffe College, 1949.

Kuan Feng. "On Human Nature and Class Nature," *Hsüeh Hsi* [Study], no. 17 (September 3, 1957). In *ECMM,* no. 112.

Kuo Hsing-fu pa-t'iao chiao-hsüeh ching-yen" [Kuo Hsing-fu's eight articles of teaching experience]. In *Kuo Hsing-fu chiao-hsüeh fang-fa* [Kuo Hsing-fu's teaching methods]. Shanghai: Jen-men ch'u-pan-she, 1965.

Kuo Mo-jo. "T'ien-ts'ai yü ch'in fen" [Natural ability and diligence], *CKCN,* no. 12 (1962).

Lau, D. C., trans. *Lao Tzu Tao Te Ching.* Baltimore: Penguin, 1963.

"Lead the General with the Typical Model," *CKCNP,* July 31, 1965. In JPRS, no. 31, 703 (August 25, 1965).

Legge, James, ed. *The Chinese Classics.* Vol. 2: *The Works of Mencius.* Vol. 3: *The Shoo King.* Hong Kong: Hong Kong University Press, 1960.

———, trans. *The Li Ki, XI–XLVI.* London: Oxford University Press, 1885.

Lenin, V.I. *Marx-Engels-Marxism.* Moscow. Foreign Languages Publishing House, 1953.

———. *Selected Works.* 3 vols. Moscow: Progress Publishers, 1971.

———. *Materialism and Empirio-Criticism: Critical Comments on a Reactionary Philosophy.* New York: International Publishers, 1947.

Levitov, H. D. *Erh-t'ung chiao-yü hsin-li-hsüeh* [Educational psychology of children]. Peking: Jen-min chiao-yü ch'u-pan-she, 1961.

Li Ch'ing-t'ien, and Chao I-min. "Humanism Is a Product of Capitalist Relationships," *Che-hsüeh yen-chiu* [Philosophical investigations], no. 3 (May 25, 1964). In *SCMP,* no. 247.

Li Pai-shu and Chou Kuan-sheng. "Shao-nien erh-t'ung tao-te hsing-wei tung-chi t'e-cheng ti hsin-li feng-hsi" [A psychological analysis of motivational characteristics of the moral behavior in children], *Hsin-li hsüeh-pao* [Acta psychologica Sinica], no. 1 (1964), pp. 25–32.

Li Pao-heng. "Tzu-jan k'o-hsüeh ho che-hsüeh ti kuan-hsi" [The relationship of natural science and philosophy], *Che-hsüeh yen-chiu* [Philosophical investigations], no. 2 (1962).

Li Shih-sheng. "Tsai lao-tung chung pien ch'eng hsin-jen" [Transform oneself into a new man through labor], *Hung ch'i* [Red flag], no. 18 (1960), pp. 31–35.

Li Yu-ning. *The Introduction of Socialism into China.* New York: Columbia University Press, 1971.

Lin Chung-hsien. "Psychological Disposition Necessary for the Study of Flying," *Hang-kung chih-shih* [Aviation knowledge], no. 3 (March 8, 1960), pp. 24–25. In JPRS, no. 2973 (July 6, 1960), pp, 9–10.

Lindzey, Gardner, and Aronson, Elliot, eds. *The Handbook of Social Psychology.* Vol. 3. Reading, Mass.: Addison-Wesley Publishing Co., 1968.

Liu Po-chi. *Liu-i tung-lun* [Discussions of the six arts]. Taipei: Chung-hua shu-chü, 1956.

Liu Shao-ch'i. "Jen ti chieh-chi-hsing" [Man's class nature]. In *Lun szu-hsiang* [On thought]. Peking: Ch'ün-chung shu-tien, 1949.

Liu Tzu-chiu. "Wo-men kuo-chia wei-shen ma ying-hsiung pei-ch'u" [Why does our country produce heroes in great abundance?], *Chung-kuo kung-jen* (pan-yüeh k'an) [Chinese worker bimonthly], no. 20 (October 27, 1959).

Lodge, Henry Cabot, ed. *The Works of Alexander Hamilton.* Vol. 2. New York: G. P. Putnam's Sons, 1904.

Lu Shih-i. *Szu pien lu chi pao* [A record of miscellaneous expositions]. Vol. 130. Taiwan: Commercial Press, 1973.

Lukes, Steven. *Individualism.* Oxford: Basil Blackwell, 1973.

Ma Wen-ping. "Lun tzu-ch'an chieh-chi jen-tao chu-i" [On the humanitarianism of the bourgeoisie], *Wen-i pao* (Literary and art news), September 26, 1960. In URI, no. 41171/59–60, pp. 62–82.

Malraux, André. *Anti-Memoirs.* Translated by Terrance Kilmartin. New York: Bantam Books, 1968.

Mao Tse-tung. "On Contradiction." In *Four Essays on Philosophy.* Peking: Foreign Languages Press, 1966.

———. "On the Correct Handling of Contradictions Among the People." In *Four Essays on Philosophy.* Peking: Foreign Languages Press, 1966.

———. "On the People's Democratic Dictatorship." Peking: Foreign Languages Press, 1961.

———. "Pi-hsü hsüeh-hui tso ching-chi kung-tso" [It is necessary to learn well how to do economic work]. In *Mao Tse-tung hsüan-chi* [Selected works of Mao Tse-tung]. Shanghai: Jen-min ch'u-pan-she, 1966.

———. "Shih-chien lun" [On practice]. In *Mao Tse-tung hsüan-chi* [Selected works of Mao Tse-tung]. Peking: Jen-min ch'u-pan-she, 1964.

———. "Some Questions Concerning Methods of Leadership." In *Mao Tse-tung hsüan-chi* [Selected works of Mao Tse-tung]. Peking: Jen-min ch'u-pan-she, 1964.

———. "Talks at the Yenan Forum on Art and Literature." Peking: Foreign Languages Press, 1960.

———. "Where Do Correct Ideas Come From?" In *Four Essays on Philosophy.* Peking: Foreign Languages Press, 1966.

Mao Tse-tung hsüan chi [Selected writings of Mao Tse-tung]. Harbin: Tung-pei shu-tien, 1948.

Mao Tse-tung szu-hsiang wan-sui [Long live Chairman Mao's thought]. 1969 edition.

"Mao Tse-tung tui wen-ko chih-shih hui-pien" [Collection of Mao Tse-tung's Directives during the Cultural Revolution], *Tsu-kuo* [China Monthly] (Hong Kong), no. 66 (September 1, 1969), pp. 41–46.

Marx, Karl. *Capital*. 3 vols. Chicago: Charles Kerr and Co., 1915.

————. *A Contribution to the Critique of Political Economy*. Translated from the 2d German ed. by N. I. Stone. With an Appendix Containing Marx's Introduction to the Critique Recently Published among His Posthumous Papers. Chicago: Charles H. Kerr and Co., 1904.

————. *Critique of the Gotha Programme*. Rev. trans. Edited by C. P. Dutt. With Appendices by Marx, Engels, and Lenin. New York: International Publishers, 1938.

————. *Economic and Philosophical Manuscripts*. In *Karl Marx: Early Writings*, edited and translated by T. B. Bottomore, New York: McGraw-Hill Co., 1964.

————. *The Poverty of Philosophy*. Edited by C. P. Dutt and V. Chattopadhyaya. With an Introduction by Friederich Engels. New York: International Publishers, 1936.

————. "Theses on Feuerbach." In *Marx and Engels: Basic Writings on Politics and Philosophy*, edited by Lewis S. Feuer. New York: Anchor Books, 1959.

Masabuchi Tatsuro. *Chūgoku Kogai shakai no kenkyū* [The society and state of ancient China]. Tokyo: Kōbundō, 1960.

Matthews, Mervyn. *Class and Society in Soviet Russia*. New York: Walker and Company, 1972.

Medlin, W. K. "Analyses of Soviet History Textbooks Used in the Ten-Year School." In *Studies in Comparative Education: Teaching in the Social Sciences and the Humanities in the U.S.S.R.* Washington, D.C.: Office of Education, Division of International Education, U.S. Department of Health, Education, and Welfare, December, 1959.

Meisner, Maurice. *Li Ta-chao and the Origins of Chinese Marxism*. Cambridge, Mass.: Harvard University Press, 1967.

Mendel, Arthur, ed. *Essential Works of Marxism*. New York: Bantam Books, 1965.

Menninger, Karl. *The Crime of Punishment*. New York: The Viking Press, 1968.

Menzel, Johanna M., ed. *The Chinese Civil Service: Career Open to Talent?* Boston: D. C. Heath and Co., 1963.

Meyer, Alfred G. *Leninism*. New York: Frederick A. Praeger, 1957.

Mill, John Stuart. *On Liberty*. New York: Library of Liberal Arts, 1956.

Moore, Barrington, Jr. *Soviet Politics—the Dilemma of Power: The Role of Ideas in Social Change*. New York: Harper and Row, 1965.

Munro, Donald J. *The Concept of Man in Early China*. Stanford, Ca.: Stanford University Press, 1969.

————. "Egalitarian Ideal and Educational Fact in Communist China." In *China: Management of a Revolutionary Society*, edited by John M. H. Lindbeck. Seattle: University of Washington Press, 1971.

Nivison, David S. "The Problem of 'Knowledge' and 'Action' in Chinese Thought since Wang Yang-ming." In *Studies in Chinese Thought*, edited by Arthur F. Wright. Chicago: The University of Chicago Press, 1953.

Nozick, Robert. "Coercion." In *Philosophy, Science, and Method*, edited by Sidney

Morgenbesser, Patrick Suppes, and Morton White. New York: St. Martin's Press, 1969.

"Pan-hao hsüeh-hsiao pi-hsü t'uan-chieh i-k'ao chiao-shih" [To manage schools well one must unite with and depend on teachers], *Jen-min chiao-yü* [People's education], July 9, 1956.

Passmore, John. *The Perfectibility of Man,* New York: Scribners, 1970.

Plamenatz, John. *Man and Society: A Critical Examination of Some Important Social and Political Theories from Machiavelli to Marx.* 2 vols. New York: McGraw-Hill Book Co., 1963.

————. *German Marxism and Russian Communism.* London: Longmans, Green and Co., 1954.

————. "Equality of Opportunity." In *The Concept of Equality,* edited by W. T. Blackstone. Minneapolis, Minn.: Burgess Publishing Co., 1969.

Po Yeh. "Shuo li" [Persuading through reason], *CKCN,* no. 6 (1962).

Potter, David M. "The Quest for the National Character." In *The Reconstruction of American History,* edited by John Higham. London: Hutchinson and Co., 1962.

Quotations from Chairman Mao Tse-tung. Peking: Guozi Shudian, 1967.

Redl, Helen B., ed. and trans. *Soviet Educators on Soviet Education.* New York: The Free Press of Glencoe, 1964.

Roazen, Paul. *Freud: Political and Social Thought.* New York: Vintage Books, 1968.

Rosenthal, Robert, and Jacobson, Lenore. *Pygmalion in the Classroom.* New York: Holt, Rinehart and Winston, 1968.

Sakai, Tadao. "Confucianism and Popular Educational Works." In *Self and Society in Ming Thought,* edited by William Theodore de Bary. New York: Columbia University Press, 1970.

Schram, Stuart R. *Chairman Mao Talks to the People.* New York: Pantheon, 1974.

————. *The Political Thought of Mao Tse-tung.* New York: Frederick A. Praeger, 1963.

Schwartz, Benjamin. "China and the West in the 'Thought of Mao Tse-tung'." In *China in Crisis,* vol. 1, edited by Ping-ti Ho and Tang Tsou. Chicago: The University of Chicago Press, 1968.

Shen Chih-yüan. "Lun chih-shih fen tzu szu-hsiang kai-tsao" [On the thought reform of intellectuals], *Chan-wang chou k'an* [Outlook weekly] (Shanghai), August 1952.

Shen Kan Ning Government Reports (given to John Service in Yenan in July–October, 1944). Berkeley: University of California, Center for Chinese Studies. Call No.: 4292.24/9475.

Shu Hsin-ch'eng. *Chin-tai chung-kuo chiao-yü shih tzu-liao* [Materials on modern Chinese educational history]. Peking: Jen-min ch'u-pan-she, 1961.

Simon, Brian, ed. *Psychology in the Soviet Union.* Palo Alto: Stanford University Press, 1957.

Simon, Brian, and Simon, Joan, eds. Translated by Joan Simon. *Educational Psychology in the U.S.S.R.* Stanford, Ca.: Stanford University Press, 1963.

Skinner, B. F. *Beyond Freedom and Dignity.* New York: Alfred A. Knopf, Inc., 1971.

Suan-shu k'o-pen: ch'u-chi hsiao-hsüeh [Arithmetic text book: lower level elementary school]. 8 vols. Approved by Ministry of Education. Chungking: Ta-tung shu-ch'ü, 1946.

Taga Akigoro. *Tō-dai kyōiku-shi no kenkyū* [A study of the history of education in the T'ang Period]. Tokyo: Fumaidō shoten, 1953.

"Tai hsüeh-sheng tao sheng-ch'an-tui li ch'ü lien-hsi suan-shu pen-ling" [Lead students to production teams to practice arithmetic skills], *Chiang-hsi chiao-yü* [Education in Kiangsi], no. 3 (1965).

Teng Ch'u-min. "Tsen-yang p'ei-yang ch'ing-nien ti kung-ch'an chu-i tao-te p'in-chih" [How to cultivate communist moral qualities of the Youth]. Shanghai: Hsin chih-shih ch'u-pan-she, 1956.

Trilling, Lionel. *Freud and the Crisis of Our Culture,* Boston: Beacon Press, 1955.

"Tsai chi-shu ko-ming chung piao-hsien ko-ming ying-hsiung ch'i-kai ti Su Kuang-ning" [Su Kuang-ning who reveals the bearing of a revolutionary hero in the technical revolution], *Chung-kuo hsin-wen* [China News] (Canton), January 13, 1965.

"Tsai ko-ming ti ta p'i-p'an chung shen-ju k'ai-chan hsüeh-hsiao tou-cheng p'i-kai" [In the great decisions of the revolution, wholeheartedly begin the struggle to correct the schools], *Chiao-yü ko-ming* [Educational revolution], no. 4 (May 6, 1967).

Ts'ai Yung-ch'un. "The Philosophy of Ch'eng I: A Selection of Texts from the Complete Works, Edited and Translated with Introduction and Notes." Ph.D. dissertation, Columbia University, 1950.

"Tsen-yang hsüeh ying-hsiung" [How should we learn from heroes?], *CKCN,* no. 1 (1966), pp. 26–27.

Tucker, Robert. *The Soviet Political Mind.* New York: Praeger, 1963.

Tung Ch'un-ts'ai, ed. *Wo-men shih tsen-yang chin-hsing lao-tung chiao-yü ti* [How should we conduct labor education?]. Shanghai: Hsin chih-shih ch'u-pan-she, 1955.

Tzu-jan: kao-chi hsiao-hsüeh k'o-pen [Natural science: upper level elementary school text]. 4 vols. Peking: Jen-min ch'u-pan-she, 1956.

Wakeman, Frederic, Jr. *History and Will: Philosophical Perspectives of Mao Tse-tung's Thought.* Berkeley: University of California Press, 1973.

Waley, Arthur, trans. *The Analects of Confucius.* New York: Random House, 1938.

————. *The Way and Its Power.* New York: Grove Press, n.d.

Wang Chun-heng, et al., eds. *Chung-kuo ti-li: ch'u-chi chung-hsüeh k'o-pen* [Geography of China: junior middle school text]. Hupei: Hupei jen-min ch'u-pan-she, 1956.

Wang Hsien-ch'ien, ed. *Hsün-tzu chi-chieh* [Hsün-tzu with collected annotations]. Taipei: Shih-chih shu-chü, 1957.

Wang-Sun. "Pa ko-ming ying-hsiung-chu-i ti ch'i-chih chü-te keng kao" [Raise even higher the flag of revolutionary heroism], *Chung-kuo kung-jen* (pan-yüeh k'an) [Chinese worker bimonthly], no. 20 (October 27, 1959).

Wang T'ieh. *Ch'ing-nien ying-kai tsen-yang fa-chan ko-hsing?* [How should youths develop their personalities?] Peking: Chung-kuo ch'ing-nien ch'u-pan-she, 1959.

Watson, Burton. *Early Chinese Literature*. New York: Columbia University Press, 1962.

———. *Mo Tzu—Basic Writings*. New York: Columbia University Press, 1963.

Wei Yü-p'ing. *Wo ho-te liao cheng-ch'üeh ti ch'u-fa-tien* [I obtained the correct starting point]. Peking: Jen-min wen-hsüeh ch'u-pan-she, 1952.

Wen Chün-t'ien. *Chung-kuo pao-chia chih-tu* [The pao-chia system in China]. Changsha: Shang-wu yin shu kuan, 1935.

Wen I-chan. *Hsiao-hsüeh yü-wen chiao-hsüeh ching-yen* [Some experience concerning the teaching of primary school language arts]. Peking: Pei-ching ch'u-pan she, 1957.

Wen Wei. "Chiao-yü tzu-nu ch'eng-wei kung-ch'an-chu-i chieh-pan-jen" [Educate children to be successors of communism], *CKCN*, no. 9–10 (May 7, 1962), pp. 13–15, 22.

Whyte, Martin King. "Inequality and Stratification in China," *China Quarterly* 64 (December 1975): p. 684–711.

Wolff, Robert P. *The Poverty of Liberalism*. Boston: Beacon, 1968.

Wood, Gordon S. *The Creation of the American Republic*. Chapel Hill: University of Carolina Press, 1969.

Wu Chiang. *Kung-ch'an chu-yi tao-te wen-t'i* [Questions concerning communist morality]. Peking: Kung-jen ch'u-pan-she, 1955.

Wu I-ling and Li Cho-min. "Shao-nien erh-t'ung hsüeh-hsi mu-ti yü tung-chi ti fen-hsi" [An analysis of the aims and motives of learning of children], *Hsin-li hsüeh-pao* [Acta psychologica Sinica], no. 2 (1966), pp. 137–45.

Wu-li-hsüeh: kao-chi chung-hsüeh k'o-pen [Physics: upper level high school text]. Compiled by Jen-min chiao-yü ch'u-pan-she. Shanghai: Hua-tung jen-min ch'u-pan-she, 1954.

Yao Wen-yüan. "P'i-p'an Pa Jen ti 'jen-hsing lun'" [Criticize Pa Jen's "theory of human nature"], *Wen-i pao* [Literature and art news], January 26, 1960. In URI, no. 41171/59–60.

Yen Chien-han, et al., eds. *Shih-yung tzu-jan: kao-chi hsiao-hsüeh k'o-pen* [Applied natural sciences: upper level elementary school text]. 4 vols. Compiled by Department of Education, Su-Wan Border Region Government. N.p., 1946.

Yen-shih chia-hsün chu [Commentaries on "the family teachings of the Yen clan"] Original edition 1790. Taipei: Chung-hua shu kuan, n.d.

Yü Shu-lin. *Chung-kuo chiao-yü shih* [History of Chinese education]. Taiwan: Tai-wan sheng-li shih-fan ta-hsüeh ch'u-pan-tsu, 1966.

Yü Ting-ying. "Chia-ch'iang tui ch'ing shao-nien ti cheng-chih szu-hsiang chiao-yü" [Strengthen political thought education toward adolescents], *Hung ch'i* [Red flag], no. 9 (1963).

Zuckerman, Michael. *Peaceable Kingdoms*. New York: Alfred A. Knopf, Inc., 1972.

Index